Astrology

DO THE HEAVENS RULE OUR DESTINY?

JOHN ANKERBERG
AND
JOHN WELDON

HARVEST HOUSE PUBLISHERS
Eugene, Oregon 97402

P9-DBL-054

ASTROLOGY
Do the Heavens Rule Our Destiny?
Copyright © 1989 by Harvest House Publishers
Eugene, Oregon 97402

Library of Congress Cataloging-in-Publication Data

Ankerberg, John, 1945-
    Astrology : do the heavens rule our destiny? / John Ankerberg and John Weldon.
    Bibliography: p.
    Includes index.
    ISBN 0-89081-717-0
    1. Astrology—Controversial literature.   I. Weldon, John.
II. Title.
BF1713.A65 1989
133.5—dc19   88-24591
                                        CIP

Printed in the United States of America.

Acknowledgements

We wish to acknowledge Dr. Clifford A. Wilson, President and Professor of Apologetics at Pacific College of Graduate Studies, Melbourne, Victoria, Australia, and Dr. Sherman P. Kanagy II (Ph.D. Astronomy), Assistant Professor of Physics at Purdue University, for their kind assistance in the production of this volume.

We would especially like to acknowledge and thank three dear ladies who are a special blessing from the Lord. First, Mrs. Louise Ebner, M.A., who has diligently sat with us through the evolution of each of our books. She has faithfully assisted us, page by page, in refining and correcting our manuscripts, including this one. Her spirit and good cheer are a source of constant blessing. Finally, we thank two excellent and patient typists, Lynda Lane and Rhonda Spence.

Contents

Preface

Some 30 to 40 million Americans believe in astrology, and a Gallup poll estimates, surprisingly, that at least ten percent of evangelicals do as well.

Perhaps some people you know are into astrology. So what should *you* know about astrology?

If you look for information, you will discover only a handful of critical treatments on astrology and no definitive treatment covering most of the important aspects of this topic. Yet, a thorough analysis of this important subject is badly needed. That is why this book addresses the vital issues of astrology authoritatively and in some depth.

This book, therefore, is unique for the following reasons:

1. The authors have conducted numerous discussions and interviews with professional astrologers. For example, we attended the July 4, 1988, 50th Anniversary of the American Federation of Astrologers (AFA) Convention in Las Vegas, Nevada. The AFA is the largest and most influential of American astrology organizations. We attended seminars, had numerous discussions (some with leading astrologers), distributed questionnaires, and conducted interviews.

In addition, both of us were involved in a debate with two professional astrologers: Psychic Maxine Taylor, the first vice president of the AFA, and Terry Warneke, an astrologer with an M.S. degree in astronomy.

2. The authors are academically qualified to examine the evidence for *and* against astrology and its relation to

Christian faith. John Weldon holds six earned degrees, including an M.A. degree in Christian Evidences from the Simon Greenleaf School of Law, a Master of Divinity degree in Biblical Studies, and a Doctorate in Comparative Religion with an emphasis in Eastern Religion. He has authored or coauthored 15 books as well as a multivolume encyclopedia on the cults.

John Ankerberg holds masters degrees in Church History and the History of Christian Thought, and a Master of Divinity degree from Trinity Evangelical Divinity School. For ten years he has hosted the award-winning "John Ankerberg Show" which presents dialogue and debate between Christian and non-Christian scholars on critical subjects. Preparation for each show demands intensive study of the evidences for the true claims concerning each topic.

3. This book is based upon thorough acquaintance with the authoritative literature of astrology—over 300 sources relevant to astrology were read or consulted, including over 200 serious astrology texts.

4. This book concentrates on thorough analysis. Most critical astrology texts have dealt largely with single issues (e.g., the scientific, historic, sociological, or biblical aspect of astrology) to the exclusion of other important areas. This text, however, examines most of the important issues raised concerning astrology.

We have treated many issues that have never before been discussed. For example, we have documented the spiritistic nature of astrology. To our knowledge, no other text has explored this connection between astrology and spiritism.

Very few Christian writers have written on astrology. Yet, even though some chapters of this book are written from a strictly Christian point of view, other chapters are written to answer questions that everyone has about astrology. Therefore, many of the issues, evidences, and arguments we present are entirely unrelated to our personal religious convictions. As a result, this book is both for Christians and those with no religious point of view.

So, whether you are a professional astrologer, a "Christian" astrologer, or just a "dabbler" in astrology, we challenge you to try and answer the issues raised in this book. We think that you will be unable to deal effectively with the arguments raised. If you are going to test your beliefs, this is one book you cannot ignore.

John Ankerberg
and
Dr. John Weldon

1

*The Power
and Influence
of Astrology*

*"No one has ever been known to make a
serious study of astrology and then reject
it"* (42:VIII).

— Nicholas DeVore
The Encyclopedia of Astrology

More than one billion people worldwide believe in
astrology in some fashion, claims science writer, engineer, and astrology critic Lawrence Jerome (102:1). In
fact, the number of those who believe in astrology may
be far greater than anyone suspects. One must include most of the one billion Chinese who believe in it
and virtually all the 700 million Indians (mostly Hindus).
Its popularity in many European countries is growing,

(Note: References are correlated to the bibliography and cited by text
number and page. For example, 150:13 will be found in reference
150, page 13; citations that include more than one book are noted in
the following manner with e.g., 181; 343 or 17–18.)

11

evidenced by the fact that most papers carry astrology columns. In the United States, astrology boasts tens of millions of followers, including ten percent of Christian evangelicals (323a:1). ABC Moscow correspondent, Walt Rogers, was quoted in well-known astrologer Sydney Omarr's column (Aug. 16, 1988) as saying, "There is plenty of interest in astrology" in Russia.

Many find it surprising that some government leaders in the world believe in and follow astrology. These leaders include the current president of India and the recent United States president, Ronald Reagan. The acceptance of astrology by such important men is frequently cited by American astrologers as proof of its validity. For example, noted astronomers Culver and Ianna, in their text *Astrology: True or False—A Scientific Evaluation,* have remarked: "Astrologers...have hailed the acceptance of astrology at the highest levels of government in one of the most powerful nations on earth as a confirmation of its legitimacy" (206:IX). The huge numbers of those who believe in astrology and the influential people who are turning to astrology for guidance reveal that astrology is not just a passing fad; it is a widely accepted practice.

What Is Astrology?

Astrology is a practice based on the assumption that the stars and planets mysteriously influence the lives of men. It teaches that the influence of the heavens begins at birth and continues throughout a person's life. Thus the *Shorter Oxford English Dictionary* defines astrology as "the art of judging the occult influence of the stars upon human affairs." But there is no one authoritative definition of astrology among astrologers themselves, as demonstrated by the following:

> 1) "Astrology is a study of the heavens [stars and planets]... and the influence they exert

upon the lives and affairs of humanity" (23:22).

2) "Astrology is the system of interpreting *symbols* [here, heavenly bodies are assumed to stand for certain influences that allegedly exist in the universe] correlated to human behavior and activities" (3:2).

3) "Astrology is the science of life's reactions to planetary vibrations" (32:4). ("Vibrations" here are mysterious forces that supposedly influence as the moon's gravity influences the ocean tides on earth.)

4) "[Astrology is] the science which treats the influence upon human character of cosmic forces emanating from celestial bodies" (42:28).

5) "Astrology is the science of certain cryptic [hidden or mysterious] relations between the celestial [heavenly] bodies and terrestrial [earthly] life" (28:13).

6) "...astrology is the science of synchronicity [a meaningful coincidence]" (95:V).

7) "Astrology is a ritual...an intuitive science ...a connection with higher intelligence which involves identifying with symbols" (137:28).

Note how often the term "science" is included in these various definitions. Notice also that the term "occult" is completely excluded, even in the seventh definition. Yet when astrologers claim that "astrology is a candid, as well as a profound and noble science..." (199:74), are they telling the truth? We will examine this question in the coming chapters.

But to further answer the question, "What is astrology?" we must also realize there are many different kinds of astrology. For example, when someone refers to *ancient* astrology, he is referring to a belief that the heavenly bodies were gods or related to the gods, and as such they ruled and influenced life on earth. The ancient Babylonians believed this. Today, some occult groups still believe and practice similar principles of astrology.

Others hold to *material* astrology, believing that "emanations" or "influences" come from actual planets in our solar system and thus rule or affect life on earth.

Still others believe in *symbolic* astrology and teach that the stars and planets are merely symbols for energies that exist and influence the human personality. Symbolic astrology is also called *humanistic* astrology.

Actually, there are dozens of other kinds of astrology, each with different assumptions. Nevertheless, the kinds of astrology we have just mentioned already reveal three diverse sets of assumptions. For them, the planets are either 1) gods, 2) impersonal heavenly objects, or 3) mere symbols.

Obviously, there is a vast difference between a living god, an inanimate object, and a mysterious symbol. So how can people claim the planets influence life on earth when they disagree with each other as to what the planets are?

Bertrand Russell once observed that if two or more views claim to be true, but all contradict each other, one or the other may be true, but they all cannot be true at the same time. They may also all be wrong. The same can be said about astrology. Logically, the different kinds of astrology can't all be true when they contradict each other. It remains to be seen if any one of them is true.

The Influence of Astrology

Historically, very few religions can claim to have exerted the influence that astrology has. The *Encyclopedia Britannica* observes that astrology has "a sometimes extensive ... influence in many civilizations both ancient and modern" (186:219). Professor Franz Cumont, a leading authority on ancient astrology and curator of the Royal Museum of Antiquities at Brussels (47:IX) has stated that "up to modern times [astrology] has exercised over Asia and Europe a wider dominion than any religion has ever achieved... [and has] exercised an endless influence on the creeds and ideas of the most diverse peoples..." (47:XI,XIII).

Historian Keith Thomas has documented that, "During the Renaissance... astrology pervaded all aspects of scientific thought. It was... an essential aspect of the intellectual framework in which men were educated" (46:285).

In our own country, as far back as 1933, there has been a revival of interest in astrology. At that time well-known occultist and philosopher Manly P. Hall bragged, "Astrology today has probably a greater number of advocates than ever before in its long and illustrious history.... Astrology and all its branches is sweeping over America in a wave of enthusiasm" (31:9).

The statistics seem to support Manly Hall. In 1941, nearly two-thirds of the adult population glanced at or read some astrological feature quite regularly. It is also known that the interest and belief in astrology steadily increased after World War II (98:13-14).

In 1946, the astrological manual, *The "Moon-sign" Book,* had an astonishing circulation of one million copies (Ibid.). Over 25,000 astrologers were registered and practicing astrology in America (Ibid.). Both in America and in the British Empire, most women's journals, mainly monthly periodicals, promoted astrology.*

Thousands of private astrologers did an extensive business through the mail. Specialized astrological

---

*Today, journals such as *Cosmopolitan, Red Book, New Woman,* and others carry astrology columns and supplements (327).

booklets and magazines sold hundreds of thousands of copies (Ibid.).

In our own day, astrologers West and Toonder have concluded that astrology currently "enjoys a popularity unmatched since the decline of Rome" (12:1). Astronomers Culver and Ianna refer to this modern interest as "the greatest resurgence in astrology" since the Renaissance (96:IX).

In 1988, astrology even made headlines in America because of the influence it achieved at the highest level of national government—the White House. According to Donald Regan, in *For the Record: From Wall Street to Washington,* "virtually every major move and decision the Reagans made" was based upon the astrological advice of Joan Quigley, Mrs. Reagan's astrologer (198: 3; 295–298). The implications of this are anything but insignificant.

The White House revelations caused a flood of new interest in astrology. Astrologers and psychics appeared before the nation with every major talk show host (Phil Donahue, Oprah Winfrey, Geraldo Rivera, Johnny Carson, Larry King, etc.) and in local radio and television interviews throughout the country. Major astrology organizations, such as the AFA,* were swamped with requests for speakers and information. Singlehandedly, the White House had produced a revival of interest in astrology, the effects of which we are still feeling.

Astrology enjoys a following at all levels of society including those of high IQ and those in academia. For example, up to ten percent of the nonscience faculty at UCLA believe in astrology (319:8). And in a survey of over 200 professors at a Canadian university, about one in four answered "yes" or "I think yes, but I am not

---

*The American Federation of Astrologers

sure" to the question, "Do you believe in astrological signs?" A smaller sampling of Mensa members and their escorts indicated an even greater degree of belief in astrology (316:216). (Mensa members must score higher on accepted intelligence tests than 98 percent of the population.)

Bernard Gittelson, a former public relations consultant for the West German government, the European Common Market, and the U.S. Department of Commerce, is now a New Age human behavior researcher. Gittelson has calculated the circulation of newspapers and magazines carrying astrological columns in the United States, Europe, Japan, and South America to be over 700 million (22:338). Concerning France and Germany he states, "In both ... it is common for companies to have an astrologer and graphologist on staff, to be consulted in matters of hiring, firing and promotions. I learned this firsthand ... " (22:63-64).

According to astrologer Dr. John Manolesco, there are an estimated 30,000 practicing astrologers in France. An official opinion poll taken in France revealed that, in 1963, 58 percent of the French knew their Zodiac sign and what it meant. In addition, over 40 percent of the people believed that an astrologer was a scientist who made no mistakes. Over half the people who believed in astrology were men. Seventy-one percent of all believers in astrology were between the ages of 18 and 25 (6:91-92).

In Germany some 30 percent of all Germans over 18 believe in astrology, and another 20 percent declare astrology is possible (Ibid.). In Japan, over eight million horoscopes are sold every year (6:91-92).

In the West, astrology is the subject of over 100 magazines, including such titles as: *The Journal of Astrological Studies; Correlation; American Astrology; Dell Horoscope; Today's Astrologer; Astrology Guide;* and *Astrology and Psychic News*. In addition, there are at least a thousand different astrology books *in print,* with collective sales in the tens of millions. Since 1960 the annual production of new astrological titles has doubled every ten years (172:167).

Astrological societies abound, including: The Astrologers Guild of America in Mt. Pocono, Pennsylvania; The International Society for Astrological Research in Los Angeles; The National Astrological Society (NASO) in New York; The American Federation of Astrologers (AFA) in Tempe, Arizona; The National Council for Geocosmic Research (NCGR); Professional Astrologers, Incorporated; the Western States Astrological Association; the London Faculty of Astrological Studies; and many others.

In the West, astrology has influenced even consumer products. For example, today we have "Zodiac Malt Liquor," astrology games (e.g., the "Inner Wheel"), Jeane Dixon's horoscope-by-phone service, and stock investing through astrology. At least one magazine has reported that some businessmen consult astrologers when they hire people, when they introduce new products, and when they determine business deals and investments (324:48). The Cable News Network (CNN) cited astrologers who claim "at least 300 of the Fortune 500 [companies] use astrologers in one way or another" (325:5).

Astrology has also influenced the legal profession. At a kidnapping trial in Cincinnati, Ohio, reported in the Cleveland Press, attorneys for the defense first consulted astrologers to help in jury selection (206:214).

Even our days of the week are reminders of the influence of astrology:

Monday—Moon day.

Tuesday—Mars' day (Day of Tiw, the Norse "Tyr," the Martian god of war).

Wednesday—Mercury's day (Woden's day, the Norse Odin, god of the runes).

Thursday—Jupiter's day (Thor's day, the Nordic god of thunder).

Friday—Venus' day (Frigg's day, wife of Odin and goddess of marriage).

Saturday—Saturn's day.

Sunday—Sun day.

No wonder astrologers confidently assert "there is no area of human experience to which astrology cannot be applied" (39:60). Even occult practices (e.g., numerology and Tarot cards) have logical connections to astrology; many world religions and religious cults (e.g., Hinduism and Theosophy) have their own brands of astrology; and astrologers have even attempted to integrate many of the sciences, such as medicine and psychology (109–127; 205:209).

Proof for the astrologer's assertion that there is no area of human experience to which astrology cannot be applied may also be seen by checking a local bookstore. Here is a small sampling of astrological titles which indicates its wide application:

Your Dog's Astrological Horoscope
Your Baby's First Horoscope
Astro-power at the Racetrack
The Teenager's Horoscope Book
Cat Horoscope Book
Pluto: Planet of Magic and Power
Chinese Astrology
Cooking With Astrology
Diet and Health Horoscope
Earthquake Prediction
Medical Astrology
The Astrologer's Guide to Counseling
Horoscope of Murder
Find Your Mate Through Astrology

Astrology and Biochemistry
Astrological Themes for Meditation
Sex Signs
An Introduction to Political Astrology
Astro Numerology
Stock Market Predictions
Homosexuality in the Horoscope
The Astrology of I Ching
Sex and the Outer Planets
From Humanistic to Transpersonal
   Astrology
Financial Astrology
Astrology and the Edgar Cayce Readings
Aztec Astrology
Astrology and Psychology
Woman's Astrology
Esoteric Astrology
Hindu Astrology
Astrology and Past Lives
Astrology: Key to Holistic Health
Astrology, Alchemy and the Tarot
Asteroid Goddesses
Astrology of Theosophy
Astrology in the Bible
Horoscope of Canada
A Guide to Cabalistic Astrology

Astrology's influence today can be seen by its impressive list of "who's who" believers, including the British royal family (Prince Andrew and Fergie, and Princess Diana), and Hollywood stars (Robert Wagner, Phyllis Diller, Jill St. John, Angie Dickinson, Lauren Bacall, Goldie Hawn, Olivia Hussey, Rona Barrett, Olivia Newton-John, Debbie Reynolds, Joan Collins, Liza Minnelli, Arlene Francis, Jane and Peter Fonda, and many others [296:111; 22:352-53]).

In the field of education, astrology is offered for credit on some high school and college campuses (138:130). In

1972 spiritist, Rosicrucian, and astrologer Mae Wilson-Ludlam taught the first accredited high school astrology course (161:198). Now astrology's influence extends to classes taught at Emory University in Atlanta (161:175), Stanford University (138:133), the University of California Extension (138:125), and to the granting of Ph.D.'s in astrology from universities such as the University of Pittsburgh (205).

Research scientist Geoffrey Dean estimates there are as many astrologers in the Western world as there are psychologists (172:167). And over 80 percent of all U.S. newspapers now carry horoscope columns.

Over all, astrology is estimated to be from a 200-million to a one-billion-dollar industry (96:2; 6:91).

What is clear from all of this is that astrology is not a minor issue. It has had and continues to have a powerful impact in the lives and thinking of millions of people.

But Why Is Astrology So Popular?

Astrology is popular because it claims to provide important information that people want to know. For example, it claims to protect, bring success, provide guidance, reveal the future, and help people understand themselves. But this is not all astrology offers. Below are eight reasons why people say they seek help from astrologers.

Reasons Why People Consult Astrologers

1. *People seek help from astrologers because of emotional pain or turmoil in their lives.* A person can gain some relief by simply consulting a person—any person—who cares about him. And to receive sympathetic advice, a person usually can consult an astrologer for less money than if he sought help from a psychoanalyst, (although astrologers' rates are steadily increasing and soon this may not be true. In 1988, astrologers charged

from $45 to $125 a reading. Famous astrologers charged up to $500 [22:383]).

In addition, people seek help from an astrologer to avoid the social stigma they feel may be attached to seeing a psychiatrist. Interestingly, a 12-year survey of American astrologers and other diviners—palmists, numerologists, Tarot readers, etc.—indicated that almost 100 percent of the diviners were "utterly untrained," and that worse, "many were unscrupulous and dishonest" (172:174). Yet people still seem to prefer help from an astrologer over a trained counselor.

One psychologist who has appraised this situation has written, "The astrological consultant has, willing or not, been usurping what was once the role of the priest, the physician, and the psychiatrist" (124:XII).

2. *People seek help from astrologers because, in addition to giving commonsense advice, empathy, compliments, and insight, an astrologer usually supports a client's self-esteem and stresses possibilities for future success.* In other words, because an astrologer can read anything he wants to out of a chart, he will emphasize what he believes the client wants to hear. The astrologer can also advise a person to look out for his self-interests—again, exactly what he wants to hear. The client leaves feeling reinforced, positive, self-assured, and satisfied. This feeling proves to the client that astrology "works."

3. *People seek help from astrologers because astrologers do not offer moral advice.* Astrology is amoral—it requires no moral response. A person who goes to a Christian minister knows the counseling session will be based upon the premise that there are absolutes of right and wrong. A person who wishes to justify personal behavior finds it much easier to see an astrologer who does not believe in absolutes and will not moralize.

4. *People seek out astrologers to gain meaning for the events in their life.* They feel astrology furnishes an

answer to the spiritual needs and concerns they have, such as, "Am I significant?" Astrology offers an "explanation" for personal failure or even senseless tragedies (such as, "It was ordained in the stars"). In addition, since most astrologers teach reincarnation, they offer their clients the "hope" of a spiritual future life.

Astrologers also provide clients with a sense that there is more to life than meets the eye. They generate excitement and awe over their ability to "read" the stars. As one attorney noted after his first session with an astrologer, "That was an amazing experience. I feel like I had four years of therapy in two hours. How can she describe my relationship with my father and be so on target, knowing nothing about me except when and where I was born?" (22:352). Astrology sometimes provides amazing and profound self-disclosures about a person that seem to confirm the truth of astrology. In later chapters we shall examine why astrology seems to work.

5. *Astrology is personally satisfying to many people* because: a) It is a substitute religion for those who dislike traditional religion; b) it offers simple solutions to complex problems; c) it offers a flattering experience (you occupy center stage); d) it is entertaining and fascinating in its complexity; e) it claims to offer answers to specific questions people consider important in relationships, finances, career, etc. (173:271).

6. *People turn to astrology because it is gaining in social acceptance and credibility.* More and more psychologists and psychotherapists are integrating astrology into their practices (116–127; 164; 205; 209).

7. *People turn to astrology because they are promised control over their future and are told how to develop their "inner potential."* As astrology begins to control the client's life, he acquires a feeling of power over his life and starts to believe he is living in actual harmony with the "cosmic forces." One astrologer has remarked, "The use

of astrology in a person's life should be as that of a road map in traveling...to show us what preparations we must make and what detours we must take" (30:3).

8. *Finally, for the astrologer, the art offers a lifetime of challenge.* Astrology is extremely complex, requiring a lifetime of learning and application. Even a basic working knowledge of astrology may require a year of study (172:167). As one astrologer has remarked, "[Astrology] requires many years of study and will be a lifetime pursuit which will be all-consuming from the standpoint of sharpening your perceptions and relating astrological principles to all phases of your affairs" (30:3).

In summary, people seek help from astrology because it supposedly offers them "control" of their own destinies. It also provides a ready-made justification for failure or guilt. It offers hope that through the "knowledge" of the stars, one can understand the forces that will influence people or events and use this knowledge for his own welfare or personal desires. It provides quick answers concerning relationships, finances, personal health, and happiness.

Above all, astrology claims to provide hope—and today people need hope desperately! In every age of social breakdown, the masses have turned to astrology for solace and counsel. Today is no exception.

Why do people believe astrology has such power over their lives? Because the claims made by astrologers encourage such belief.

The Claims of Astrology

The claims made by astrology are incredible. Astrologers think their charts are "the greatest tools in the universe" (144:3) and consider themselves to be the enlightened messengers of a coming new age. Famous English astrologer Richard James Morrison ["Zadkiel"] went so far as to declare that astrology was capable of infallibility in its predictions (48:VI, cf. 160:211)—a belief shared by many other astrologers today.

But the most amazing claim astrology makes centers on the godlike power and control the planets supposedly exert on human life and affairs. Consider a few examples:

> Pluto is the god of the underworld and of death: hence the planet is the planet of destruction responsible, above all, for the discovery of the atomic bomb (27:149).

> On January 22, 1979, Neptune and Pluto switched orbits. Neptune's veil had been lifted, allowing further [occult] illumination and transformation of humanity (151:X).

> ...just before and after the discovery of Uranus, planet of equality and freedom, in 1781, humanity witnessed the American and French revolutions. When Neptune, planet of mysticism and illusion, was discovered in 1846, idealist movements such as transcendentalism and spiritualism [spiritism] emerged. ...The first four feminine named asteroids were discovered in the nineteenth century as the women's movement, led by Susan B. Anthony and Elizabeth Cady Stanton [began]. ...Consequently, society [soon] saw the widespread entrance of women into the fields of politics, arts, education, sports, and other professional careers. It [the discovery of the asteroids] also marked a time of the rediscovery of women's history and the revival of the Goddess in women's spirituality (128:1-2).

Each individual planet is said to deeply influence our lives and decisions. One astrologer advised her clients, "An analysis confined to the influences of the planets in the signs is in some respects indispensable, since it gives insight into the [human] wants and wishes likely to be generated by the planets..." (121:VII).

The astrological idea that the planets should exercise such powers over us is one reason the ancients worshiped the planets as literal gods. Through the years not much has changed. Today, astrologers believe the planets exercise powers over our lives just as the pagan gods of old did. The only difference is that modern man does not believe the planets are gods.

2

How Astrology Claims to Work

Astrology supposedly works by the planets or stars affecting our lives. The main tool astrologers use for interpreting this alleged influence on human lives is the astrological chart, called a *natal* [birth] *horoscope*. (Strictly, the term "horoscope" also involves the interpretation [*delineations*] of the chart, although the terms "chart" and "horoscope" are used interchangeably.)

The horoscope calculates the exact position of the heavenly bodies at the moment of birth, usually from the baby's first breath. The baby's first breath is crucial with most astrologers. They accept a premise of magic called "correspondences," that everything in the heavens is supposedly correlated with everything on the earth; thus, events in heaven parallel events on earth. Astrologers believe that the child's first breath permanently "stamps" him with the corresponding heavenly stamp or pattern existing in the sky at that moment. This unique pattern impressed upon the child shapes his character and ultimately his destiny. "As above, so below" is the ancient (Hermetic) formula expressing this magical principle. ("Hermetic" is a term derived from Hermes Trismegistus, the Greek name for the Egyptian god Thoth, the inventor of the occult sciences, here referring to a universal occult principle of correspondences said to exist between the heavens and the earth.)

For most astrologers, the "permanent stamp" is the influence sent out by the heavenly bodies absorbed by each of us as we drew our first breath at birth. Some astrologers go as far as to say these heavenly bodies send out influences which forever determine up to 80 percent of our potential personality and destiny (15:15).

Other astrologers claim the heavenly stamp is not supposed to correspond to the actual planets. Rather, it is assumed to correspond to the mysterious influences that astrologers interpret by their symbols. One way or the other, for our entire lives, astrologers claim the heavenly planets continue to influence in predictable ways (to them) our original pattern at birth.

In addition to the birth horoscope, astrologers use other charts. For example, they will use a *mundane* chart, supposedly to examine the fortunes of cities, states, or countries. An *electional* chart is drawn up to decide the best time to undertake some activity. The *horary* chart is composed to answer questions on any given topic.

Astrologers say these charts are important because the heavens are in constant motion. Since the planets change their positions in the heavens, new charts must be made to determine their current influence on us. These charts (called *progressed horoscopes* and *directed horoscopes*) supposedly give more specific information to relate to our birth chart and help reveal how we are likely to act and choose at any given time. This is why astrologers will draw a chart for any particular moment of time to determine particular heavenly influences.

Whether or not the stars or their magic symbolism really do influence us, one fact should be clear: Once we accept the premises of astrology, astrology does indeed exert a powerful influence on us. But this is because of our belief in astrology itself or other factors, not any influence of the stars. In reality, when we grant power to the astrologer to accurately interpret the alleged heavenly influences acting upon us, this is a dramatic yielding of our lives. Once we yield our lives, in many cases no other major decision will ever be made without first consulting an astrologer.

What are the basic terms and concepts necessary to a basic understanding of astrology?

Astrology usually confuses the average person because of its complexity and the many unfamiliar words astrologers use. For example: "Ascendant," "Aspect," "House," "Sextile," "Cusp," "Sesquiquadrate," "Imum Coeli," "Opposition," "Quadruplicity," "Quincunx," "Trine," and "Descending Node." The following definitions and concepts are basic to understanding astrology.

The *Zodiac* is an imaginary "belt" of sky containing the 12 astrological signs or constellations around which the ancients drew human and animal figures. (The Zodiac and the constellations are both imaginary geometric configurations.) They are imaginary because the Zodiac is the path described by the earth's revolution around the sun, divided into 12 segments referred to as "signs," *irrespective* of the actual positions of the constellations which form the backdrop to the Zodiac.

The *signs* are the "signs of the Zodiac," also known as "Sun-signs." Everyone is born under one of these 12 signs or constellations (Pisces the fish, Leo the lion, Gemini the twins, Taurus the bull, etc.).

The *houses* are the 12 sections of the Zodiac which together symbolize every aspect of life. The planets move through the houses, so when a planet falls into the sphere of a given house, it comes under its respective influence. The astrologer plots all of these factors and more on a chart. This chart is called a horoscope.

The *horoscope* is a "map" of the heavens at the moment of the birth of a person, or any specific time thereafter. On the horoscope, an astrologer plots the positions of the planets, signs, and houses for a given moment. The chart is then interpreted by numerous complex rules, many of which vary greatly from one astrologer to another. Technically, a *delineation* is the art of defining a single astrological factor or unit in the horoscope. *Interpretation* is the result of combining two or more delineated factors. Analysis or *synthesis* is the "complete" interpretation of the chart as a whole.

A mental picture might be helpful in understanding the basic ideas of astrology just defined, but we should first understand that the "world" of astrology is based upon an ancient view of the universe, not a modern scientific one. The ancients constructed their view of the universe based entirely on how things *appeared*. Thus, observing the sky at night, they concluded the stars and planets were moving along the inner surface of a great hollow globe, a celestial sphere. The sun, moon, and planets appeared to revolve around the earth.

Imagine a huge glass ball with a thin white belt encircling it. According to astrology, the glass ball is the *celestial sphere*. The *white belt* encircling the *glass ball* is the *Zodiac*. Divide the *white belt* into 12 sections, giving each section a name. The name is of a symbolic animal or person representing the imaginary *constellations* (Aries the ram, Virgo the bull, Leo the lion, Gemini the twins, etc.). These symbols of animals and men are the *signs of the Zodiac* or the "*Sun-signs*." This is what is meant when people say, "My sign is 'Libra,' 'Pisces,' 'Aries,' 'Gemini,' etc."

At the center of this glass ball is a tiny green marble, symbolic of the earth. Divide all the space inside the glass ball into 12 sections, representing what the astrologers call "houses." These houses would start at a point in the middle of the glass ball (the earth) and extend out to the Zodiac or the encircling white belt. However, these 12 house sections are spaced differently from the 12 Zodiac sections along the white belt. Inside the glass ball, the astrologers place the sun, moon, and eight other planets. As these planets move, they move through the 12 sections on the white belt, the Zodiac, and also enter and pass through the 12 different houses.

In addition to all of this, astrologers believe that each planet "rules" (especially influences) different signs of the Zodiac. For example, Mercury rules or influences Gemini and Virgo, whereas Venus is said to rule Taurus and Libra. In addition, the signs and their ruling planets are considered proper (specifically related) to certain houses.

One more important term used by astrologers, "aspect," must be defined. *Aspect* refers to the angles between the planets as seen or plotted on a horoscope chart. Certain aspects are interpreted as good and others as bad.

For example, two planets angled at 90 degrees to each other (called a "square") are considered to exert a bad influence. However, two planets angled at 120 degrees to each other (called a "trine") are considered to exert a very good influence.

But it is more complicated than this. In addition to good or bad angles, astrologers also must take into consideration whether or not the planets are good or bad. The words "good" or "bad," which can refer to either angles or planets, have been defined by the astrologers themselves. But what is the basis for these angles and planets being defined as good or bad? The astrologers don't know; they simply accept these definitions.

To be fair, some astrologers would say these definitions are the result of thousands of years of observing human experience, while others no longer use the good/bad designations and have substituted milder descriptions—externalization vs. internalization; active vs. passive; hard vs. soft. They usually interpret these to mean a person is accepting challenges to growth or remaining stagnant, but there are various other interpretations. Still, no astrologer has accurately recorded 4,000 years of human experience. And there is no one, final, authoritative tradition that has come down through history that all astrologers follow today. The many conflicting astrological theories prove this.

Just as there are good and evil planets and angles, there are good and bad days for undertaking certain activities. When a planet crosses or "transits" a specific point on the horoscope chart, the astrologer feels he can advise a client as to favorable, unfavorable, or cautious times concerning a given activity. This was why Hitler shaped his war strategy by the stars and why even some American presidents have sought the advice of the stars as to the planning of their activities.

Unfortunately, all of this astrological interpretation is highly subjective. Who can explain, for example, why the different houses represent what they do? Why is it that the first house represents personality, the second house money, the third house communication, the eighth house death, the tenth house occupation, etc.? Many different aspects of life have been assigned to each of the different houses, but who said so, and on what factual basis do astrologers make these assertions?

Astrologers claim their information comes from 4,000 years of human observation. But such observation has not led to one final tradition. Astrologers still do not agree on any foundational definitions, for they have no factual basis for what they say.

Some astrologers claim their definitions are derived from numerology, i.e., from the meanings allegedly inherent in numbers, which are then related to astrological theory. But if these meanings are derived from numerology, who gave the correct interpretation? And why then don't all astrologers agree? Again, they can give no logical reason why their system should be believed.

There is even further disagreement among astrologers concerning how to divide the houses. A given house for one astrologer may be a different house for another, and, therefore, entirely different influences would be suggested (96:62-64).

Actually, astrological interpretations rest on a very inconsistent foundation. An astrologer may choose from up to 30 different Zodiacs (sidereal, tropical, draconic, etc. [18:25]); from 6 to 28 different "signs" (96:87); and from at least 10 different house systems (e.g., the quadrant house systems—Alcabitius, Campanus, Koch, Placidus, Porphry, Regiomontanus, etc.; the nonquadrant systems—Equal, Zariel, Morinus, etc. [84:64]). Astrologers do not agree on the meaning of any of these Zodiacs and signs, thus different house systems conflict and lead to diverse interpretations (96:63,87).

But the astrologer's job of interpretation is still not finished. He must also choose whether or not to use the concept of the various *nodes*. The moon's nodes refer to the intersection of the moon's orbit and the ecliptic and are believed to exert certain influences. But, in addition, there are also the influences from the nodes of the planets, the points at which the orbits of the planets intersect the ecliptic.

Then, too, astrologers must consider the four elements known as the *triplicities* (the elements fire, earth, air, and water) that also are supposed to exert influences. They are called triplicities because each of the four elements embraces three zodiacal signs. For example, the water signs are Cancer, Scorpio, and Pisces; the earth signs are Capricorn, Taurus, and Virgo. The four elements group the signs by various basic characteristics: For example, the water signs are called the Emotional Group; the earth signs are called the Practical Group. Astrologers group the signs according to these psychological aspects or types.

In addition, the astrologer must consider the *modes* or *quadruplicities,* named thus because each one embraces four Zodiac signs. These determine whether or not the signs are cardinal, mutable, or fixed (e.g., the "fixed" signs are Leo, Scorpio, Aquarius, and Taurus). Depending on whether a sign is cardinal, fixed, or mutable, each means something different.

Further, key words or key phrases are associated with each of the signs. Pisces supposedly means "appreciation" or "I believe."

The astrologer must also distinguish between the angles and the aspects. We referred to the aspects earlier as denoting the angular relationships between the planets. Aspects may either be applying (or forming) when the space between the planets is decreasing or they may be separating when the space between them is increasing. But again, although the term *aspects* deals with angular relationships, the astrological term *angles* is something different. This term refers to the cardinal points on the horoscope called 1) the Ascendant, 2) the Mid-Heaven or Medium Coeli, 3) the Descendant, and 4) the Imum Coeli.

If this is not enough to confuse someone, the astrologer must consider the *dignities* or *debilities*—how the influence of a planet is increased (dignity) or decreased (debility) by its placement on the chart. There are dozens of such conditions (96:8). He must also determine whether the signs are positive (active) or negative (passive), and pay special attention to the rising or *ascending sign,* the sign which was rising on the eastern horizon at the moment of birth (42:17,338).

In addition to the nine basic aspects (conjunction, trine, quincunx, etc.), astrologers must keep track of at least eight *orbs,* the space within each aspect believed to be effective. These are ranges, from 5 to 17 degrees, and are given different values by different astrologers. Thus, "As to exact orbs, there are few points on which authorities differ so radically" (42:273).

An astrologer also must determine the *nature* of the planet, how it is *influenced* by the properties of its sign and house, its *location* within the sign or house, its *relation* to other planets, etc. (96:7-8).

And after all of this, the astrologer is still not finished. He must choose which method of prediction he will use. Three common methods are: 1) the previously mentioned transits, 2) primary directions, and 3) secondary progressions (42:315). (The last two methods foretell events by analogy.) But, "No phase of astrology is subject to such differences of opinion" as these and other means of predictions (42:121).

In *primary directions*, for example, if Mars is 25 degrees from Venus in the birth chart and Mars is "directed" to the position of Venus, then supposedly an event of some relevance may be expected in the person's twenty-fifth year. Primary directions may be applied to the planets, angles, and other chart factors, producing a great number of possible predictions (42:121,315).

With *secondary progressions,* astrologers believe that every one day of motion for a planet equals a year for a person's life. Thus, if the moon is in conjunction with Venus 35 days after the moment of birth, when the person becomes 35 years old, something significant may be expected (42:121,315; 96:9-10).

Unfortunately, even after all of this detail, we have hardly scratched the surface of astrological complexity. For example, Noel Tyl wrote a 12-volume series, *The*

Principles and Practices of Astrology, which is considered introductory material!

It is no wonder that astrologers do not follow one final astrological tradition. After all, there are so many conflicting astrological theories. Yet, people still commit their lives to following the unproven assumptions of their astrologer.

3

The World View of Astrology

A world view consists of those particular, fundamental assumptions by which a person approaches life. This world view is formed by various aspects of life, including: upbringing, education, reflection, and experiences. Especially powerful experiences may affect and change a person's world view.

Our world view is extremely important, for it is the "grid" through which we interpret and respond to the world. But our world view can bring us unforeseen consequences if it is wrong.

Consider the Marxist world view, based in part upon a philosophy of state control and dialectical materialism. In other words, authoritarianism and atheism are two of the "grids" through which the world is viewed (326:17-36). This world view has weakened the economy of every country it has dominated, and has also placed literally hundreds of millions of people in economic and physical bondage. According to Alexander Solzhenitsyn, in his *Warning to the West* (314:128-29), it has also resulted in the deaths of up to 110 million people. Had Marxism never existed, the world would have been a far different place (326).

No one can say world views are unimportant. Every aspect of a world view has implications, including those of the astrological world view. Here are some of its characteristics:

1. *Most astrologers have a prescientific world view.* Astrology is still prescientific, accepting the mistaken astronomical views of the ancients and rejecting the factual discoveries of modern astronomers. When the ancients viewed the night sky they based their conclusions on how things appeared, not knowing that appearances were deceptive. To them the earth stood still and the sun and planets moved about the earth. They also connected the visible stars together with imaginary lines to form fanciful constellations of animals, men, and objects. They observed the planets moving slowly "through" the "fixed" constellations so that at one point Jupiter was in Aries and later in Pisces. Actually, the constellations are at great distances beyond our solar system.

Although the stars exist and their imaginary groupings are useful for navigation on earth because they are easy to identify, the constellations of astrology do not exist at all. The ancients seemed to have connected the constellations together because of the brightness or positions of the stars. However, a very dim star may appear a hundred times brighter on earth than a very bright star, simply because it is much closer to this planet. One needs only to look through a telescope to totally dispel the imaginary lines. By using the ancient and prescientific view of the universe in constructing their charts, astrologers have failed to include some very important stars, just because they could not be seen without a telescope. Clearly, astrology has failed to keep up with scientific advances (97; 102–103). The constellations have now shifted one full position relative to the earth, yet astrologers still accept the constellations as they appeared 2,000 years ago. That means the Aries of 2,000 years ago is now actually Pisces. Thus, a person's astrological sign, if it were based on the way that the heavens appear today, would be completely different. By not considering this precession of the equinoxes (the shifting of the equinoxes caused by planetary action that alters the plane of the earth's orbit), much of modern astrology reveals how unscientific it is.

In addition, much of contemporary astrology accepts only seven planets, completely ignoring the implications (the influences) of newly discovered planets.* Astrologers debate whether or not to accept the influences of Uranus, Neptune, and Pluto. (If they exist, obviously they must exert an influence.) Incredibly, astrologers accept only 12 constellations and ignore the other 76 that are known to exist. Even more confusing, much of astrology today doesn't bother to consider the "influence" of the planets' moons, the major asteroids, or comets. Yet, while ignoring *known* physical objects, some astrologers calculate the alleged influence of over 100 *unknown,* invisible "planets" (54:4; 151:6).

Astrologers sensitive to scientific criticism explain that their art is not concerned with the literal physical constellations or planets, but only with the *symbols* of the constellations and planets. But as soon as astrologers switch the foundation of astrology from observable

---

*In astrology the sun and moon are considered planets, but the influence of the earth as a planet is not considered at all. Thus, out of 11 major bodies in our solar system, ancient astrology accepted 7 and modern astrology accepts either 7 or 10, depending on whether it accepts Uranus (discovered in 1781), Neptune (1846), and Pluto (1930).

data to such nonobservable data, they no longer may claim astrology is scientific.

2. *Most astrologers have a nonscientific (magical) world view.* Astrology claims to deal with the influence exerted by the planets, but in composing a horoscope, an astrologer is not at all concerned with a planet's size, density, weight, rate of rotation, etc. The physical characteristics of a planet are entirely irrelevant to the astrological influences it emits.

On the other hand, science tells us it is impossible that the planets could affect us physically in any manner whatsoever, because of their enormous distances from us. Astrologers respond that the influences exerted by the planets are not physical, but acausal—because the influences exist without any physical cause.

Astrologers claim the influence of the planets is real, but every effect must be produced by a cause. Since astrology allegedly produces effects without cause, then no causal relationship can exist: The astrologer is forced to hold a magical world view of supposedly known effects occuring without a cause.*

Astrologers believe in the principle "as above, so below." This principle plays an important part in magic. To illustrate, consider the practice of black magic or voodoo. A doll symbolically represents a person and what is done to the doll occurs to the intended victim. This is the kind of effect astrologers refer to when they

---

*Causal relationships exist (at the macrocosmic level) in everything science investigates—whether or not the process as a whole is understood. Because this is not true in astrology, its alleged influence must be considered magical. At the subatomic level causality may be denied. For astronomers to claim that *planets* may exert causal effects by appealing to subatomic *particles* is an invalid argument. Even physicists who accept acausality at the microscopic level would deny that it can be applied to the macrocosmic (planet) level.

claim whatever happens in the heavens also happens to people upon the earth. Thus a bad day, a financial disaster, a romance—anything and everything—are related to corresponding events in the heavens.

Astrologers illustrate this principle when they assert, for example, that the sun and Mars in the eighth house in opposition to Neptune could symbolically indicate a person may mysteriously be lost and die (140:112). And a weak Mars could indicate "a weak, colorless person" while "Neptune always figures in alcoholism and drugs" (140:101,111).

Here the astrologers' belief of how the world works is clear. The "microcosm" (man) and the "macrocosm" (the universe) are magically and symbolically connected. When a man is born on the earth below, he is at that same moment somehow connected to and imprinted by the heavenly pattern above.

This magical (occult) connection rules and affects him the rest of his life. What happens inside of him is but a symbolic reflection of the entire cosmic pattern existing at any given moment. By determining the cosmic pattern at the time of birth or any subsequent point in life, the astrologer claims he can determine the heavenly influences present within a person and his environment, and the probable or actual consequences of those influences.

We believe this is a form of fantasy for it does not correspond to reality. Astrologers are constructing a fantasy environment (from the horoscope chart) and telling their clients that this astrological information can reveal their true inner nature and that which controls their destiny.

3. *Most astrologers have a pragmatic world view.* Astrology is goal-oriented, open to using whatever works to attain its goals. Astrology sees its primary goal as helping a person achieve harmony with himself and the

universe. But an approach to life that is entirely pragmatic, and disregards the reason *why* something works, is dangerous. Astrologers say they are not primarily concerned with why their art works. After all, if something is "working," why question it? This uncritical, practical philosophy opens them to the possibility of psychological and spiritual deception. Consider these typical views expressed by astrologers:

> I don't attempt to prove anything about the validity of astrology.... I simply see that it exists, and has existed for thousands of years. ...There's no need to prove it, or disprove it. It's a tool, a tool to use as you wish (137:26).

> Despite its scoffers the science of astrology has lived on through the centuries and is constantly gaining fresh legions of followers largely because "it works" (42:VII).

> I "believe in" astrology for the same reasons that you "believe in" the multiplication table or the intoxicating effect of alcohol. It works (30:2).

But astrologers should consider that just because something works does not establish it as true or worthy to be followed. Truth may be completely unrelated to results. For example, an experienced thief can regularly gain unlawful entry by picking a lock, but that result does not demonstrate that it was a right way to enter the building, or that entry was the right result. But it did work (315:113)!

4. *Most astrologers have an amoral world view.* Astrology does not perceive any moral absolutes from its observation of the chart or the heavens. In astrology, man is a god unto himself and decides for himself what is right or wrong. Because the heavens are impersonal, moral considerations are subjective and totally optional. The result is an easy justification for one's own ways.

5. *Most astrologers have a pantheistic world view.* Astrology is comfortable with the idea that everything in the universe is divine and somehow connected. This idea is called "pantheism." Pantheism (*pan*—all; *theism*—God) teaches God is all and all is God. This leads astrologers to accept the idea that in themselves they are also divine—a part of God. Obviously, if someone believes in his own divinity, he will see no reason to repent of wrong action and place his allegiance in Christ.

But philosophically, no man can affirm a strictly pantheistic world view. According to pantheism, no finite, individual reality exists apart from God or the absolute; therefore, a strict pantheist must affirm, "God is, but I am not." But this is self-defeating, since one must exist in order to affirm he does not exist.

Some astrologers attempt to avoid the philosophical problems of strict pantheism by giving man a "manifestational" or "emanational" status, as a self (at least temporarily). Philosopher Dr. Norman Geisler has commented:

> Their attempt, however, is unsuccessful because when all is said and done, there is no reality in the finite individual that is his own. His selfhood is real only at the point at which it is one with the absolute. Logically this means that *as finite* and *as individual* it is not real, despite all attempts to say that it has some kind of lesser reality. They wrongly assume that whatever is not really ultimate is not ultimately or actually real (315:188).

Astrologers who embrace pantheism, in other words, cannot logically defend their world view.

6. *Most astrologers believe in reincarnation and an evolving universe.* Many astrologers believe that the entire universe is really an impersonal God who is evolving. Men can partake of this impersonal God's divine

evolution through the process of cyclic (continually recurring) reincarnation (the soul living many life-times). They believe that all men are slowly evolving back into a realization of their own godhood. (Either they merge with the impersonal God as a single drop of water merges and becomes one with the ocean, or they perceive in themselves a feeling and realization of complete harmony with all that exists.) But in this scheme of things, history is going nowhere, directed by no one but vague, impersonal cosmic forces. To most astrologers God is not personal and there is no assurance that in the future good will win out over evil.

7. *Most astrology has stemmed from a polytheistic world view.* The ancients believed the planets were either the living gods themselves or somehow related to them. For example, some believed the planets were the homes of the gods, or the bodies of the gods. Since the stars and planets were thought to be gods, people believed they were to be worshiped and given sacrifices. Roman rhetorician Seneca (55 B.C.–39 A.D.) said, "The stars are divine and worthy of worship" (97:130). In the Bible, the nation of Israel repeatedly fell into this form of idolatrous star worship, even to the point of murdering children in sacrifice to the star gods (2 Kings 17:16; 21:3-6; Zephaniah 1:46, cf. Leviticus 18:21; 20:1-6).

The ancients believed that the gods (or stars) ruled the affairs of men and had personality (emotion, disposition, etc.). They thought this was true for both the stars and the planets. For example, they believed the god of Mars could be angry and cause wars and violence. When the ancients saw a lunar eclipse, they believed the moon god was being attacked by powerful demons, giving it great pain and causing its energy to fade. They believed that rituals of worship, human sacrifice, even madness, could "restore" the moon to its original state.

Even though most Western astrologers are not polytheistic (believing the planets are literal gods), nevertheless, the influence of the "gods" remains to this day. What many people do not know is that modern astrology derived its view of the planets' "natures" and "personalities" from those ancients who believed the stars and planets possessed the natures and personalities of the ancient gods. While worship of these ancient gods is rarely present today (in the Western world), the personalities of the gods still remain via the planets' influences on the lives of men (81:1-17).

Surprisingly, in spite of all of this, astrology still claims to be a precise science.*

---

* Besides the above characteristics, astrology is also *eclectic*. In addition to astrology itself, the astrologer may add any number of other beliefs or practices, whether secular, scientific, occult, religious, psychological, etc. Thus, in any astrologer's practice, one may find not only astrology, but Eastern or occult philosophies and practices (Tantra, Theosophy, yoga, meditation, etc.); humanistic, transpersonal, or New Age psychological practices (especially Jungian views, as well as Reichian and Neo-Reichian approaches, Robert Assagoli's psychosynthesis, Fritz Perl's Gestalt psychology, etc.); many occult arts of divination (Tarot cards, I Ching, runes, etc.); Western magical practices (alchemy, Cabalism); endless numbers of holistic health practices, etc.

4

The Truth About Chart Interpretation

"It is true of course that most astrologers who call themselves such are not really competent to offer guidance or even interpret a chart. Much of what they say is made up on the spur of the moment" (6:136).

—Dr. John Manolesco
Astrologer

The astrological chart or horoscope allegedly enables the astrologer to accurately advise a client about his problems or to predict his future. As the astrologer examines the many symbols on his client's chart, he determines how these symbols reveal secret information of great importance to that individual.

No issue is more vital to the claims of astrology than whether or not an accurate interpretation of the astrological chart is possible. If the chart cannot be accurately interpreted, then it will provide inaccurate information that will not help the client. In fact, wrong information for a client could be devastating. Yet the average client will still act upon the astrologer's advice, regardless of the consequences, simply because the client trusts him.*

The legitimacy of astrology depends entirely upon the astrologer's claim of ability to accurately interpret the celestial influences that act upon a client (past, present, and future), as found in the horoscope. But can astrologers defend their claim? If it can be proved that all astrologers, in essence, *guess* at what the interacting symbols on a chart mean, then all chart interpretation is subjective and can provide no objective assessment of a person's needs, condition, or the solution to his problems.

On the following pages are examples of two astrological charts. The crucial question is, can an astrologer plot the position of the planets and stars and reveal crucial information about the individual?

Interpreting the horoscope is something like interpreting inkblots in the Rorschach Inkblot Test. Not only are there all manner of inkblots (as there are astrological factors and theories), but different people will interpret the same inkblot in an endless number of ways. In the same way an endless number of factors or variables are used to interpret a chart, and no astrologer interprets these different factors in the same manner.

So why do different astrologers interpret the same "data" in the chart in widely diverse ways? Joanne Sanders, an astrologer and coordinator of the Washington, D.C., Astrology Forum, explains, "Their readings vary with the differences in their philosophical outlooks" (209:14). In other words, astrologers' interpretations depend upon their particular astrological schooling, their personality, goals or purposes, their assumptions, or many other factors.

---

*We assume the astrologer has the ability to first erect the chart correctly—even though most astrologers apparently have a problem with this (see discussion later in this chapter).

	Campanus			Koch	
27♋19	28♏0	13♓44	27♋19	4♏75	18♓2
22♌18	0♑42	12♈39	24♌42	21♐55	12♈39
27♍19	27♑19	28♉0	16♏1	21♑3	13♉43
12♎39	22♒18	0♒42	12♎39	24♒42	21♊55

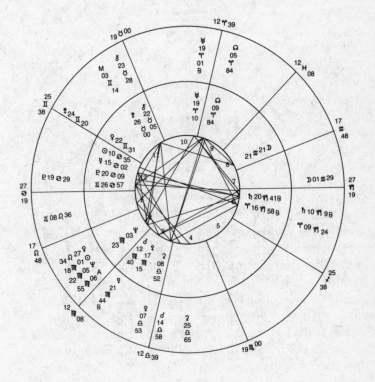

OUTER WHEEL Sidereal Placidus

Progressed date is June 23, 1982 — Third Marriage

Eastpoint 30♌14 • South Node 2♎85 • Anti-Vertex 3♌60

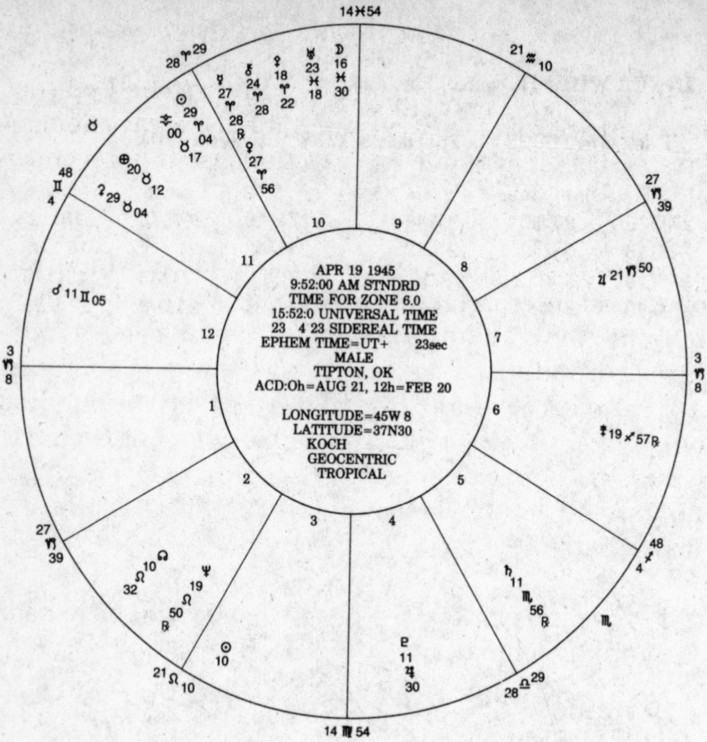

MIDPOINTS ARRANGED IN PLANET SEQUENCE

☉	29♈04	A	03♋08	☉/♅	11♈18	☽/♃	19♒10	☿/♂	22♉11	♀/♂	22♉14
☽	16♓30	M	14♓54	/♆	24♊27	/♄	14♑13	/♃	09♓39	/♃	09♓53
☿	27♈28	☊	10♌32	/♇	05♊10	/♅	20♓01	/♄	04♒42	/♄	04♒56
♀	27♈56	♅]	24♈28	/A	01♊06	/♆	03♊10	/♅	10♈30	/♅	10♈44
♂	17♊05	☉/☽	07♈47	/M	06♈59	/♇	14♉01	/♆	23♊39	/♆	23♊53
♃	21♑50	/☿	28♈16	/☊	19♊48	/A	09♉49	/♇	04♊30	/♇	04♊44
♄	11♏56	/♀	28♈22	/⚷	26♈46	/M	15♓42	/A	00♊18	/A	00♊32
♅	23♓32	/♂	23♉04	☽/☿	06♈59	/☊	28♉31	/M	06♈11	/M	06♈25
♆	19♌50	/♃	10♓27	/♀	07♈13	/⚷	05♈29	/☊	19♊00	/☊	19♊14
♇	11♋14	/♄	05♒30	/♂	01♉47	☿/♀	27♈42	/⚷	25♈58	/⚷	26♈16

♂/♃	04♈27	♃/♅	22♒41	♄/A	07♍32	♆/♇	00♌41	A/☊	21♋52
/♄	29♌30	/♆	05♏50	/M	13♑25	/A	26♋29	/⚷	28♉48
/♅	05♉18	/♇	16♈41	/☊	26♍14	/M	02♊22	M/☊	27♉28
/♆	18♋27	/A	12♈29	/⚷	03♒12	/☊	15♌11	/⚷	04♈41
/♇	29♊18	/M	18♒22	♅/♆	06♊41	/⚷	22♊09	☊/⚷	17♊11
/A	25♊06	/☊	01♏11	/♇	17♉32	♇/A	07♋20		
/M	00♉59	/⚷	08♓09	/A	13♉20	/M	13♉10		
/☊	13♋48	♄/♅	17♑44	/M	19♓13	/☊	26♋02		
/⚷	20♉46	/♆	00♎51	/☊	02♊02	/⚷	03♊00		
♃/♄	16♐53	/♇	11♍44	/⚷	09♈00	A/M	09♉01		

PLANET	SIGN	LONG	HSE	DECL	LAT	GEOCENTRIC N-NODE	S-NODE
SUN E	Ari 29	3 55	11	11N 9	0 00		
MOON	Pic 16	29 42	10	8S 3	2S57	09Le53	09Aq53
MERC	Ari 27	28.2R	10	11N58	1N30	03Ta25	15Ar10
VENU D	Ari 27	55.7	10	9N44	1S 5	18Ta27	12Pi53
MARS	Gem 17	4.6	12	23N59	1N10	10Ta56	18Sa29
JUPI F	Cpr 21	50.2	7	21S42	0S 2	00Ca21	21Cp14
SATU	Scp 11	55.6R	5	12S55	2N38	17Ca27	29Cp27
URAN	Pic 23	32.0	10	3S14	0S44	11Ge25	15Sa38
NEPT	Leo 19	49.6R	2	15N11	0N20	09Le07	12Aq52
PLUT	Can 11	31.6	1	20N59	1S59	17Ca31	20Cp12

To answer this question more fully, we shall present four basic reasons why evidence and logic have demonstrated it is impossible for an astrologer to interpret a chart accurately:

1. *The vastness and complexity of astrology.* The average horoscope contains 30 to 40 major factors an astrologer must interpret, and another 60 to 70 minor indicators that have an infinite number of possible combinations, permutations, and meanings. Jungian therapist and astrologer Alice O. Howell refers to "all the hundred or so factors which interrelate in any birth chart" (120:VIII). For an astrologer to make an accurate chart, he must at least take into account and interpret the importance of:

- the ten planets, the moon's north and south node and fortuna.

- the 12 signs of the Zodiac—Aries, Taurus, Gemini, etc.

- the nine or ten major aspects—conjunction, sextile, trine, sesquiquadrate, etc.

- the four elements—earth, fire, air, water (the *triplicities*).

- the three qualities or "crosses"—cardinal, fixed, immutable (the *quadruplicities*).

- the 12 houses and whether they are angular, succedent or cadent.

- the rulerships (day or night) of the ten planets (or the 36 "deacons").

Doris Chase Doane, president of the American Federation of Astrologers, has admitted that the major cause of an aspiring astrologer's failure on the AFA entrance examination is the inability to properly erect a chart.

(To erect a chart is to remember and accurately list and plot all of the factors.)*

Keep in mind that a good astrological dictionary or encyclopedia will list hundreds of additional factors and concerns that should be taken into account. Also, as we mentioned earlier, different interpretations are given to transits, directions, progressions, midpoints, dynamic contacts, minor aspects, etc. The problem for the astrologer: remember, analyze, sort out, and properly interpret *all* of these factors in a person's chart.

Doris Chase Doane has calculated the *least* possible number of combinations resulting from the most basic or simple chart. Given 12 signs, 10 planets, 12 houses, and 10 aspects, she arrives at the figure of 5.4 times 10^{68}. This number is roughly equivalent to the estimated number of *atoms* in the known universe (159:1)!

One astrologer has admitted that in merely calculating the sun, moon, and rising signs, "there are 1,728 combinations" (138:121). But this does not even begin to cover the many other factors and their varied interrelationships an astrologer should or may take into account. There is also the minimum number of considerations for the position of just a *single* planet in the chart which would include the sign and house in which the planet falls, the sign and house the planet rules, and all the aspects made to the planet by other planets (35:36).

Astrologers must sometimes deal with multiple charts, comparing two or more charts for a single individual. In addition, the chart(s) of other persons (such as other family members) who influence the individual may be compared and related to his chart(s).

That is why, for just a single chart, professional astrologer Eric Russell discloses, "In theory, a full horoscope

---

*But most astrologers are self-taught and are never required to pass a competency exam.

contains what is virtually an infinite number of factors—the total has been calculated at 539,370,750 plus 30 noughts [zeros]" (27:124).

Romanian astrologer Sir John Manolesco, illustrating the complexity an astrologer faces, has concluded that of the tens of thousands of astrologers in the Western world, *fewer than 100* can claim to have mastered the subject. In fact,

> There are at least 43 factors—planets, houses, aspects, strengths and weaknesses, ascendent, critical degrees, sun and moon polarities, constellations, etc.—which combine and influence one another in a thousand different ways. In this labyrinth of complexities, the average (still worse, the untrained) astrologer is as puzzled as his client (6:130).

Astrologer Richard Nolle, who has written over 500 articles and columns on astrology, and is a director of the American Federation of Astrologers' research arm, affirms that astrology "is truly infinite in scope" (85:22).

Astrology critic and research scientist Geoffrey Dean theorizes that, potentially, there are hundreds or thousands of factors the astrologer must consider (172:169).

In addition to the complexity of factors, each astrologer must also obey the cardinal rule of chart interpretation: No factor can be judged in isolation from any other factor. But science has revealed and proven that the average person possesses only limited "immediate" and "short-term" memory. No astrologer has the mental capability to assimilate accurately even 50, let alone the hundreds of factors that should make up a chart. The human mind is capable of juggling only about ten bits of information at any one time (172:169). (To see if this is true, try remembering a ten-digit number.)

Because astrologers have limited memory, just as the rest of us, many have turned to computers. But if the computer could calculate all the factors, astrologers would not be needed. But astrologers do not agree on any final authoritative astrological information to program into their computers—and a computer will put out only what is put into it.

The astrologer's solution to this dilemma is "chart synthesis"—the totally subjective art whereby the factors are "balanced" against each other, usually by intuitive or psychic means, so they "will finally reveal the true purpose of every horoscope" (40:190). In *How to Prove Astrology,* Jeannette Glenn suggests, "The entire chart must be synthesized. One cannot take things out of context; they become disjointed and may even appear to contradict each other" (29:16).

But the problem is not so easily solved, for it is virtually impossible for any astrologer to synthesize the chart "in context" when the context he is synthesizing is a mere fraction of the astrological reality before him. And how does "synthesis" arrive at an answer when one is faced with contradictory interpretations of the data? For example, hear two astrologers pinpoint their dilemma:

> One of the biggest difficulties in traditional chart interpretation is integrating and synthesizing the different astrological influences. Many students in beginning astrology classes ask questions like, "I have five planets in Aries, which means I am impulsive and energetic. Neptune in the sixth house shows that I have little energy. Which one is true?" Answering this question is not easy (83:3).

Interpreting an astrological chart is similar to reading a huge, detailed map of the United States. The facts on the map for one to remember would include at least 50 states, 3,000 counties, and at least 6,000 cities and towns in the United States. Then there are highways, rivers, mountains, lakes, parks, points of interest. In addition, the map's key contains 50 major symbols that allow the map reader to interpret the map properly (e.g., the symbols tell how to determine boundaries, distances, city size, type of road, etc.).

Now, assume the map is an astrologer's chart. How would a person interpret this map if he discovered that every other map he could find contradicted this map? What if he discovered no agreement as to the number of states, counties, and cities, as well as their boundaries? Worse yet, what if he discovered each map defined the 50 symbols differently. What could he conclude about using any of the maps? Wouldn't he conclude this to be a hopeless situation?

On top of all this, what if another person came along and told the reader he knew all the maps contained the secret of safe travel, and unless the reader interpreted them, he would never get to his destination? Just because someone told him this, would that mean he could immediately read the maps correctly? Even if he were desperate, would he risk his life to a psychic "synthesis" of the many factors on the maps? If someone wouldn't follow such maps when they travel, why would anyone trust his life to astrology which faces the same problems?

Many astrologers today recognize the problems just mentioned and turn to another source revealed in these words:

> Before interpreting a chart, it is very good to do one thing: either silently, or aloud, ask for clear guidance *from the powers that you choose* to create... *from your higher self,* from the divine... ask, and you shall receive... (137:104, emphasis added).

Here it is clear that the astrologer's only option is either to guess or to trust in some kind of "higher" power or psychic revelations to sort things out. Even astrologers admit there are "endless combinations of astrological symbols" (137:128), but they insist they have the ability to supply the correct interpretation of those symbols! Unfortunately, no objective method of chart synthesis exists and astrologers themselves disagree as to how such synthesis should be accomplished. Out of the infinite multitude of factors, no astrologer knows he has selected the true or correct cosmic factors pertaining specifically to a given individual. He cannot.

To further complicate matters, we have been discussing only one kind of chart. Astrologers have many different kinds of charts to choose from, not just one, each with varying factors and rules. One authority lists 14 different charts, such as the "solar return," "lunar return," "solar equilibrium," "ingress," "johndro," etc. (151:118). Theoretically, there are as many different charts as individual schools or systems of astrology, and since each system or school can develop its own chart, the number of different charts must number in the hundreds.

Clearly, no astrologer can accurately interpret a chart because there is no accepted interpretation astrologers can turn to for each symbol, and because there are too many symbols to remember.

2. *The existence of contradictory indicators in the chart.* It also is impossible to interpret an astrology chart because of the *nature* of the information, not just the amount of information. The amount of information may be sufficient to frighten a computer, but more importantly, the information is contradictory. Yet the astrologer declares the ability to objectively sort the information out. But Dr. Karen Hamaker-Zondag, an influential Jungian astrologer and parapsychologist in

Holland, disagrees. In her books she acknowledges the problem of the "often conflicting influences and patterns in a horoscope" (121:IX). How, then, does the astrologer know, when information "X" contradicts information "Y," that he has not made an error in a potentially important area?

Astrologers use standard "chart blanks" (primary forms) for their calculations, but astrologer Richard Nolle has shown that even a standard astrological chart blank can be in error. Nolle has reported that because of its layout, the "true ascendant-mid-heaven arc has been concealed..." (84:51). Therefore any astrologer who uses this particular chart blank gives an inaccurate interpretation (84:50-51).

Or consider the astrologer's dilemma when sorting out even the relatively easy factor of interpreting the significance if Jupiter and Saturn are in the same sign. One leading astrologer has listed the different options:

a) Saturn inhibits Jupiter from fully expressing its possibilities;

b) Jupiter is able to lift Saturn out of its low point;

c) when both factors are activated simultaneously, overcaution can mean missed chances;

d) Jupiter can confirm Saturn's overcompensations; but

e) Jupiter can also give the native [client] an insight into the way in which Saturn is making him overcompensate and can weaken his tendency to do so;

f) both factors can strengthen or weaken each other;

g) the native's character can go to extremes due to these strengthening or weakening influences (121:165-66).

This astrologer also notes:

> The problems arising here are completely different from those involved in the partition of the elements. It should be obvious that when Saturn and Jupiter are shedding their influence from the same sign, the result will be entirely different when we are dealing with the superior element from what it is when we are dealing with the inferior element. These may appear to be small points but, nevertheless, they are extremely important (121:166).

Given these choices, how can any astrologer confidently assert he has arrived at the correct astrological interpretation?

To summarize, no astrologer can explain why he knows that a given influence will reveal its good or bad side, whether a given planet and a given sign will manifest themselves in a "primitive or a highly developed form." If endless possibilities are latent in any combination of factors, we heartily agree, "it is extremely difficult to predict" the outcome (121:18-21). In fact, it is impossible!

3. *The dilemma of contradictory schools and methods in astrology.* Another problem relating to proper chart interpretation involves the rules and factors that enter into a given chart. Not only does the astrologer have a potentially infinite number of variables to consider, but there also are hundreds of different astrological schools and methods from which he must choose, each presenting conflicting beliefs and rules.

Scores of contradictory theories correspond to the following: 1) the astrologies of ancient cultures and religions; 2) the astrologies of modern religions and cults; 3) the many eclectic approaches to astrology (combining astrology and something else); and 4) the various schools of modern astrology.

Can a hundred conflicting schools *all* be correct? If not, how does the astrologer pick the right school that will supply him with the right information? Unless he picks the right school, he will not arrive at the correct interpretation.

The following statement made by the authors of a new approach to astrology applies to virtually every approach or school of astrology: "Interpreting a birth chart with the new approach gives a whole different perspective and very often eventuates in different conclusions than a traditional interpretation" (83:3). So what happened to the "traditional interpretation"? Wasn't it the correct interpretation? Apparently "traditional" and "new" mean nothing if both are grounded in totally subjective guesswork.

Consider this brief listing of some of the schools of astrology. How would any expectant astrology student know that one particular school could provide him with truly accurate astrological information?

Hamburg or Uranian (Alfred Witte, 54:1-8)

Sabian (Marc Edmund Jones, 58:5-25; 59:52-65)

Hindu (with scores of sub-schools; 62:IX-X, 41-57; 52:9-79)

Chinese (with scores of sub-schools; 57:11-326)

Aztec (53:16-43,72-88)

Draconic (63:11-34,39-191)

Edgar Caycean (51:1-73)

Theosophical (H. P. Blavatsky, 56:1-62; 140:1-50,128-195)

Wiccan (witchcraft, 149:11-20,137-159; 149; 147:21-23)

Rosicrucian (e.g., Max Heindel's school; 44)

Ptolemic (Greek, Roman)

Jungian/Transpersonal/Humanistic
(e.g., Dane Rudhyar's approach
(117:9-77; 125:11-121)
"Soul Ray" Astrology (151:5-112)
Ebertian (54:1)
Past Life Astrology (92:1-275; 94:5-137)
Transformative/Esoteric/Cosmic, etc.
(23:9-140; 55:3-692; 126:7-121; 44:1-250)
Hermetic (141–143; 151; 159)
New England School of Astrology (35:XV)
Harmonic Astrology (John Addey, 85:59-66)
"Energy schools" (Steven Arroyo, etc.,
116:71-167; 83:3-37)
Galactic Astrology (includes the "effects" of
quasars, black holes, etc., 144:164-90)
Integrationist schools with dozens of
academic and occultic fields added to
astrology (medical astrology,
psychological astrology, cabalistic
astrology, sociological astrology [Noel
Tyl], Tarot astrology, etc.)
Astrologies having influence from various
other cultural astrologies (Burmese,
Tibetan, Arabian, etc., 31:59-106)

The seventy-five percent of astrologers who believe in reincarnation face a further dilemma. They must consider not only one life, but also the influences of many past lives. The factors they must account for include: 1) Current personality makeup and tendencies, 2) past life (lives) influence, 3) the influence of the reincarnating soul on the current personality (the chart is erected for the soul, not the personality), 4) the influence of the soul's afterlife existence while in other spiritual planes or on other planets (visible or invisible), which would require the charting of entirely new (non-earth-centered) planetary configurations and influences.

Amazingly, some astrologers still confidently claim these factors can be accurately determined. Yet where did they get accurate information on the possibly millions of past lives of a client, all from different times, places, and cultures? And why is a client's chart still drawn from the moment of birth rather than from the exact moment of the soul's (the real person) entering the body? One reason might be that occultists tell us the time this occurs varies from any time after conception to four or five months later.

So who has the final answer to these matters? How can astrologers prove they have any basis for using the word "accuracy"? One astrologer has truthfully admitted:

> It is my belief that at the present level of knowledge, there is no way astrologers, *unless they are also psychic,* can determine who and what a person was in the past [life] by studying that person's horoscope. If an astrologer gives you a karmic reading and says, "In your past life you were a Polish peasant farmer..." or anything of the like, without admitting to being psychic, I would pronounce both that astrologer and the methods used suspect (92:8).

But who has proved that psychic interpretations are reliable?

One thing is sure. Whether it is horary, natal, mundane, electional, or any other kind of astrology, the astrologers do not agree on anything. This is why leading astrological authorities give advice such as the following when discussing specific astrological theories and contradictions:

> As authorities vary in approach to, and rules for delineating the horary chart, you can

best prepare yourself by studying one authority in depth (20:49).

This can be very confusing to the student
and there is little that can be done to clarify
the situation except to suggest that the student test in his own experience which house
rules which parent (30:43).

If it works for you, use it (144:121).

Viewing astrological theory worldwide, the contradictions are even more apparent. James Braha observes
that in India "a seemingly infinite number of rules and
astrological techniques have been developed by the
Indians" (62:X). Repeatedly he states that they *contradict Western methods*. The Zodiac, goals, measurements,
signs, houses, horoscope format, ascendant, planets,
etc., are all interpreted differently. (For example, Mercury is exalted in Virgo, not in Aquarius [62:IX-48]).

In ancient Babylon, the practice of "draconic astrology" presented entirely different beliefs, practices, and
sets of rules (63:1-58,95-123,143-189). In China, we discover entirely different astrologies (57; 61; 62).

In Mexico, Aztec astrology is again different from the
above, and so it goes on and on (53:1-90). Within each
school or system, subsystems also contradict each
other.

In addition, the invention of even a single new factor
in a chart can change everything and produce an entirely new astrology. One astrologer demonstrated this
by discovering the "planet" Chiron:

Once I had defined Chiron rulership in my
practice in 1983 and began to apply it to readings, a deeper understanding of all the outer
planets emerged, particularly Uranus and
Neptune, and a whole new form of horary
astrology manifested . . . (130:XX).

To further confuse things, every chart factor, potentially, has not only an exoteric (outer) reality but also an esoteric (inner) reality which supposedly really unveils "the hidden meaning" (151:34). Astrologers inform us that "each planet in a sign holds a multitude of implications. Besides each sign having an exoteric ruler, considered to be the pure outer expression of the sign's characteristics, a sign has an esoteric ruler" (151:34).

But this is not the end of complications. Endless astrologers have their own unique goals or pet theories that they integrate with and thus change their astrological interpretations. Carl Payne Tobey invented a new system involving a "shadow chart" based on Arabic point calculations, a new ascendant, new Zodiac, heliocentric planetary nodes and new house cusps (144:9, 109-21). On the other hand, astrologer Jeff Green refers to four major evolutionary conditions of a person that must be determined first in order to carry out "accurate" astrology (131:25).

In brief, it is impossible for any astrologer to authoritatively say he has correctly interpreted someone's chart.

4. *Conflicting views exist for the meaning of many specific chart factors.* Astrologer Joan McEvers remarks, "There are as many views of aspects and how they are used in the chart, as there are astrologers" (144:5). In its description of the meanings of transits, directions, and progressions, the *Encyclopedia of Astrology* asserts, "No phase of astrology is subject to such differences of opinion and practice..." (42:121).

But this is also true for many other astrological factors and theories. How did such a hopeless situation originate? Astrologer Richard Nolle describes the "evolution" of an astrologer which is summarized and expanded upon below.

a) Begin by learning the "traditional" meanings as they are given (but these are contradictory and the student soon realizes this).

b) The solution is to assimilate the meanings into "our own frame of reference" to "develop our own particular and unique astrological perspective." (There are no objective standards, so add a large dose of subjectivism).

In other words, begin by using standard text interpretations (which vary) and then reject the standard text interpretations and finally discover "the answer is within yourself," which will enable a person to "make your own [new] discoveries" (84:1-2).

This is why Nolle himself acknowledged there are as many different astrologies as there are astrologers (85:22), and that chart interpretation does not utilize "objective laws" but "intuitive selections" (84:84).

Someone has satirically said that the process of becoming an astrologer is one of beginning with a state of initial confusion, leading to a state of greater confusion, that finally is rationalized by "intuitive insight."

Seasoned astrologer Jeff Green's standard work on the planet Pluto tells us that Pluto represents the soul in evolution; that Saturn "defines the boundaries of our subjective consciousness"; that Uranus represents "the individualized unconscious"; and that Neptune represents "the collective unconscious"(131:1)! But how can this be? Until their recent discovery, Uranus, Neptune, and Pluto represented absolutely *nothing* to astrologers. If Jeff Green is right, then astrological interpretation before his book must have been completely wrong. Further, who can say what astronomy will find in the future that astrology doesn't know now?

Astrology's theories, symbols, factors, etc., carry no ultimate definitive meaning. They are merely vehicles to stimulate the thinking of the astrologer. From that point on it is a cosmic grab bag.

Proof of this can be seen in certain statements astrologers make about Jesus Christ. Some say Jesus' teachings were based on astrological forces—claiming this is true because of Jesus Christ's chart! They then conclude Jesus must have been an avatar in the Eastern sense; or a highly evolved soul who will never again reincarnate; or an enlightened master in an occultic sense, etc. (137:2,26,37,170).

Yet the astrologers' descriptions of Jesus are all utterly false, for the historical records clearly show that Jesus Christ was none of those things. The astrological "indicators" are therefore totally wrong. After all, the eyewitnesses who lived with Jesus and heard Him speak are better sources of information than an impersonal astrological chart.

If the astrology charts are wrong concerning Jesus, they must be wrong concerning other people. Therefore, it is clear that the astrologer's world view and presuppositions determine the meaning of the astrological indicators and symbols and influences. The symbols themselves carry no authoritative meaning. As one astrologer admitted, the symbols "can mean whatever I . . . want them to mean" (219). Chart interpretation based on the principles of astrology is not only incorrect, but worse, it is meaningless. So then, who would dare label chart interpretation a true science? Only astrologers.

5

Astrology and Science

Astrologers adamantly proclaim that astrology is a science. They further claim astrology is rationally consistent. Some, such as Carroll Righter, even refer to themselves as scientists (255:1). Astrologer June Wakefield emphasizes, "Astrology is a science. It is not a pseudo-science..." (23:11). Almost every one of the 50 astrologers we interviewed at the July, 1988 American Federation of Astrologers Convention in Las Vegas, Nevada, said astrology was a genuine science.

A poll by the magazine *Horoscope* indicated that 64.1 percent of 305 responding readers agreed with the statement, "Astrology is a science." Only 2.6 percent said "Astrology is a psychic phenomenon," while 10.2 percent said it was both. In addition, 22.7 percent said it was an art/science or none of the above. Only .3 percent said astrology was a superstition (85:56-57).

Astrologer Gray Keen provides the typical response: "Astrology is a system of scientific calculation. The interpretations that derive from this are based on traditional empirical references that have established their validity through centuries of time" (144:17).

Astronomers Culver and Ianna point out there is "nothing more infuriating to the scientist, particularly the astronomer, than the continuing claim...of astrologers that astrology is a science..." (206:ix-xi). Astrologers cannot dispute the fact that not one legitimate scientific body in the world accepts astrology as a science. The reason for this is simple. Astrology rejects the scientific method, and thus does not qualify as being scientific.

Today, few astrologers attempt true scientific research on astrology, because past legitimate scientific testing continually overturned astrological beliefs. Astrologer Richard Nolle complains, "...the astrological community as a whole has shown little interest in serious research to date.... Are we to believe without knowing why?" (85:6).

True science is based upon a number of important factors, one being that true knowledge always builds on past scientific knowledge that has been carefully tested and gathered. True science also involves a commitment to clear, rational thinking, careful observation, and critical reappraisal.

Whenever a scientific hypothesis or theory is proposed, it is subjected to careful testing to see if the results of the testing fit the theory. If the results can be successfully replicated, the theory then undergoes the scrutiny of peer review to see if similar results can be obtained by other experimental researchers. In the end, for a theory to be legitimate, the results must *have explanatory relevance* (the theory must explain something), and *be falsifiable* (i.e., be capable of being disproven). A theory that explains nothing and can never be disproven cannot be considered a scientific theory.

The idea of causality (that given the same set of conditions, the same results will follow) is also an important component of science. Every effect has a cause. But astrology prides itself on being outside the realm of known cause and effect.

Modern astrology denies or rejects virtually every tenet of the scientific method: careful observation (observable cause and effect); critical appraisal; experimental testing; peer review (it can be demonstrated successfully to outsiders); explanatory relevance; falsifiability; causality; etc.

The scientific method is not perfect, of course, because people are not perfect, but every modern technological and scientific advance would have been impossible without it. It is a method that clearly works. Whatever biases modern science has, the role of the scientist is that of skeptic and adversary, not an accepting conformist with personal wishes about how the world operates. "To believe without evidence is imagination; to believe in spite of the evidence is delusion" (96:37). Science has to be concerned with the evidence: data based on tested, observable facts. Concerning astrology, the indisputable conclusion is that the scientific evidence indicates that astrology fails at *everything* it claims to do.

Why then do astrologers call it a science? Maybe because of the prestige and personal importance this label generates. Other astrologers may call it a science because they are ignorant of how true science operates.

Still others redefine science so they may incorporate it into their self-styled beliefs. For example, some astrologers claim to be using a "spiritual" science. But what does that mean? "Spiritual" doesn't change the meaning of science any more than placing the word "spiritual" in front of "bricklayer" changes the meaning of bricklayer. In the end, "spiritual" science is a smokescreen that denies true science and opens the door to pseudoscience and the occult.

Consider the following illustrations of how astrologers misuse and redefine the term "science":

> Yet so spiritually oriented are scorpios, you will often find them interested in areas of *scientific investigation: parapsychology, astrology, the Tarot, palmistry, and witchcraft* (82:5, emphasis added).

> As a *new* science, karmic astrology should be practiced with great care.... we caution all researchers to avoid generalizations whenever possible and to back up their theories with regression material and/or past-life birth charts (92:275, emphasis added).

But to claim that witchcraft, and other occult practices are now a science is absurd! Yet this is what many astrologers teach.

Why do astrologers refuse to accept the factual conclusions of modern science as they relate to astrology? Typically, astrologers respond that scientists are biased and have never honestly investigated astrology. Dr. John Manolesco, for example, asserts, "I have never heard of a single person who attacked astrology on real scientific grounds" (6:12). They claim that, had scientists honestly investigated astrology, scientists would have accepted it. Occultist Manly Hall writes, in *The Story of Astrology*, that "Science does not make a case against astrology, but merely unconditionally condemns without consideration, examination, or research" (31:9).

Another astrologer criticizes astronomy and exalts astrology when he says, "Astronomy is the external lifeless glove; correspondences [astrology] is the living hand within" (141:199). In other words, astrology is the reality behind astronomy! Another astrologer expresses his hope that astronomers will "purge themselves of the poison of academic prejudice" against astrology so that they will not be "laughed off the face of the earth" (106:213).

However, most scientists reject astrology for one principal reason: Given everything they know about how the world and the universe work, astrology cannot be true. They have concluded that the basic claims and methods of astrology are so contrary to all normal human learning and experience that astrology is simply not even worth considering.

Purdue University astronomer Dr. Sherman Kanagy, after three years of investigating astrology, concluded:

> Generally what is being said is that the basic claims of astrologers as they [the scientists] understand them are completely inconsistent with what they believe they already know from their own fields of expertise (97:22).

This is why they do not believe astrology merits examination. If a subject is completely inconsistent with all scientific knowledge, can it logically command the attention of scientists?

No scientist gives serious thought to the claim that man-made communications satellites in space influence or determine human behavior, character, or destiny. Similarly, for scientists to give serious consideration to the idea that the planets and stars influence human behavior would constitute a denial and refutation of all the fundamental processes they have ever learned.

Yet astrologers do not seem to understand why scientists are so "biased," so "close-minded" against astrology. They refuse to understand that scientists perceive the person who claims "the planets influence our destiny" to be on par with the person who claims "lemon water cures cancer." Enough scientific data has been gathered about water, lemons, and cancer for scientists to know, beyond the slightest doubt, that lemon water cannot cure cancer.

Scientists consider astrology in the same way. Too much scientific data already exists against the basic idea of astrology for it to be true or worthy of consideration.

Scientific data from astronomy, meteorology, psychology, biology, physics, chemistry, medicine, physiology, etc., have all disproven astrological theories.

Scientists, of course, cannot understand why astrologers ignore evidence. As astronomers Culver and Ianna have said:

> Are we being close-minded? Quite the contrary. Believing in astrology in the face of the overwhelming evidence against it is being close-minded. To deny the world as it is (astrology is false), because you would like it to be different (astrology is true) is close-minded. True, we haven't practiced astrology, but on the other hand, practitioners have almost never done science, have almost never learned to depend on verification to make observations to confirm ideas. Consequently most astrologers have little idea of the difficulties and hard work required empirically in ferreting out the truth and finding out what the cosmos are really like. Most people prefer pat answers, unchanging certainty, and support for their own personal beliefs. Most astrologers are quite satisfied with the illusion that astrology works. The heavens have a different story to tell. It is a far more beautiful and majestic and exciting story than the astrological fable. And it is fact not fiction (206:220-21).

Some astrologers weakly claim astrology should be considered a science because of the mathematical calculations they use in preparing an astrological chart. The problem with this conclusion is that the mere knowledge of astronomy or math does not automatically make one a scientist. All students in grade school and high school use math tables in doing their homework, yet most parents have never considered their children to be scientists as a result!

Whenever an astrologer prepares a birth chart, he has merely plotted heavenly objects on a graph. How has the scientific method affected this chart? If the astrologer is truthful, it has not entered it at all. Obviously, the mere use of math and astronomy is quite different from engaging in experimental scientific work.

Astrology deals with the alleged influences of heavenly objects, and the interpretation of those objects on a chart that supposedly reveals their influence on us. Astrology could be subject to experimental test at this point (e.g., "Is Libra rising connected with art as a profession, as astrologers say?"), but it has always failed when tested, as we shall see.

And astrology is not just the setting up of an astrological chart; it is the interpreting of that chart. Here astrology enters the world of subjectivism, occultism, and hopeless contradiction that is as far removed from science as the heavens are from the earth. The following chart illustrates this point.

Astrology	**Science**
• Subjective	• Objective
• No preexisting body of scientific data	• Preexisting body of scientific data
• Acausal (e.g., synchronicity)	• Causal
• Based on magical correspondences, not on empirical observation	• Based on empirical observation

Astrology	Science
• No peer review or controlled critical experimental testing	• Peer review and controlled critical experimental testing
• Explains nothing	• Considerable explanatory value
• Loose, subjective definitions of relevant factors	• Strict, meaningful definitions of relevant factors
• Rejects current body of scientific knowledge	• Accepts current body of scientific knowledge
• Many aspects incapable of scientific verification (unfalsifiability)	• A theory must be falsifiable to have value

In spite of all this, astrologers still claim scientific evidence supports their craft.

6

The Alleged Evidence for Astrology

The evidence astrologers set forth to prove their case may be divided into three basic categories: 1) general arguments, 2) statistical studies, and 3) practical results. This third issue, the most important, is the one most often cited by astrologers. Because of its importance, we have devoted several chapters to its examination.

The General Arguments

Approximately a dozen arguments are routinely set forth by astrologers as evidence that astrology is true. However, none of these arguments cites valid reasons to believe in astrology. Below we present their major arguments with a brief response (modified from 172:175).

1. *Astrology is true because it is found in many cultures.* (But so are racism and totalitarianism.)

2. *Many great scholars have believed in astrology.* (But scholars can be biased or wrong; it is also a fact that

far more scholars have not believed in astrology than have believed in it.)

3. *Astrology is true because it has great antiquity and durability.* (But so have bigotry and murder.)

4. *Extraterrestrial or "cosmo-biological" influences exist.* (Scientists do agree that extraterrestrial influences exist, such as the moon's influence on the tides, but the same scientists also agree that this has nothing to do with astrology [102:115-65; 99:158-70]).

5. *Astrology is true because it is based on observation.* (But if it has been observed to be true, then why don't all astrologers agree on the same interpretation?)

6. *Non-astrologers are unqualified to judge astrology.* (But even unqualified laymen are able to make a conclusion on the evidence in a murder trial. In other words, facts presented to unqualified laymen can lead to truthful conclusions. Actually, astrologers typically are the ones unqualified to judge the merits of astrology because they refuse to accept *any* criticism—evidence—as legitimate.)

7. *Astrology is true because it has been proven by scientific research.* (But as we shall see, astrology has been proven false by all scientific research.)

8. *Astrology is true because it is an art or philosophy rather than a science.* (But art does not make truth claims, and even such disciplines as art and philosophy have factual reasons that judge and support their disciplines. Astrology does not. The argument that astrology is a "scientific art" seems an attempt to place astrology in the realm of the unfalsifiable [97:100].)

9. *Elements of modern science and psychology have proven astrology to be true (e.g., quantum physics, synchronicity, etc.).* (But nowhere can quantum physics be applied to proving the theories of astrology [96:36-37]. Further, synchronicity—meaningful coincidences—is

scientifically a meaningless concept. Further, in relation to astrology the supposed correspondences do not in fact exist [97:116-18].)

10. *Astrology is true because it works.* (Much of the time it does not work. When astrology does work, we shall see that it works for reasons unrelated to the theories of astrology.)

11. *Astrology is true.* Critics have never really studied or tested astrology to prove it is true. (Even if true, affirmation without proof leaves one with an untested truth claim. In fact, scientists have tested almost all of the claims of astrology and concluded they are false.)

The real problem here is not that astrology is never investigated, but that when it is investigated, it is found wanting. Astrologers simply do not want to acknowledge this fact. Robert Eisler has remarked:

> They [astrologers] will not acknowledge honestly the decisive fact that their futile practices have been investigated with the greatest care and impartiality by the foremost scholars of the leading Western nations for almost three centuries, and that not one of these has failed to condemn them . . . (98:28).

Even today, the critical scientific literature on astrology is more than sufficient to prove astrology false, although it is scant in comparison to the nonscientific favorable literature published by astrologers. The scientific literature that has been released so damages the claims of astrology that virtually anyone familiar with it, who continues to practice or promote astrology, is guilty of perpetrating fraud on the public (96–106; 172–173; 211–215).

12. *Most people believe astrology is true because they are impressed by their astrologer's ability to sometimes accurately assess their character and personality.* (But

this evidence of astrology is better explained by recourse to non-astrological information. The prime example in this area must be Michel Gauquelin, a researcher at the Sorbonne, the University of Paris. He has investigated astrology for some 30 years and states, "There is a feeling of near reverence for astrological knowledge..." (106:140).

Gauquelin conducted the classic "Marcel Petiot" experiment. A French physician during the Nazi occupation of France in World War II, Petiot lured people to his Paris residence by claiming he would help them escape from the Nazis. But when they arrived, he murdered them, took their money and possessions, and dissolved their bodies in a tub of lime. He was arrested in 1944, and convicted of at least 27 murders (he claimed he had killed 63 people), and was executed on May 26, 1946. Petiot was labeled as "satanic" and as "one of the greatest criminals in the annals of penal law" (104:105-06).

As an experiment Gauquelin determined the "astrological profile" of Dr. Petiot. He found that Petiot was a man of "instinctive warmth" and that he was "endowed with a moral sense which was comforting—that of a worthy, right-thinking, middle class citizen." Gauquelin also found he was "bathed in an ocean of sensitivity" and had great "love for mankind." Petiot's sentimental feelings found "their expression in total devotion to others, redeeming love, or altruistic sacrifices." He enjoyed "having a charming home" (104:106-07). It seemed apparent to Gauquelin that astrological analysis and historical fact were far apart.

For the next step in his experiment, Gauquelin placed an ad in a newspaper offering the public a free personal horoscope. To the first 150 persons that responded, Gauquelin sent the horoscope of Dr. Petiot, prepared by a professional astrologer. Of those who received Petiot's horoscope and responded, 90 percent thought the portrait was "very true" *of them.* Further, 80 percent said this favorable judgment was also shared by their friends and family. Gauquelin concluded:

> Psychologists have taught that we all tend to see a mirror of ourselves in the horoscope; but it is still disquieting that these people should find a resemblance in a profile drawn to fit only one individual—a murderer . . . the satisfaction which people feel in reading their horoscopes does not prove the validity of astrology. "Know yourself," said Socrates, . . . but who can boast of having managed it? Certainly not the clients of astrologers (106:140-41).

In summary, Gauquelin's experiment demonstrated that people can be impressed by false information given to them by their astrologer.

Can Astrology Be Scientifically Tested?

Much of astrology simply cannot be scientifically tested because of the very nature of astrology. For example, it claims to be a practice based upon mystical influences and private, subjective interpretations by individual astrologers reading the horoscope. That is why (at these points) astrology can never by *scientifically* proven or disproven. Its phenomena ("intuition," mystical planetary influences, symbolic correspondences, etc.) lie outside the boundaries of science. Nevertheless, both astrologers and scientific investigators of astrology agree that certain astrological principles do merit scientific testing.

The importance of this should not be underestimated. When examining astrology scientifically, scientists are doing only what astrologers themselves have said they must do. If the results are wholly negative, however, then the astrologer who knows this and continues his practice is a fraud. Research scientist and critic Geoffrey Dean agrees: "... astrology has a solid core of testable ideas" (172:167). Yet, after his 15 years of testing astrology scientifically, he has failed to find any evidence for it, but has accumulated conclusive evidence against it (172:166-84; 173:257-73).

In his book *Astrology as Science: A Statistical Approach*, astrologer Mark Urban-Lurain confidently asserts:

> There is no reason that astrology may not be subjected to scientific scrutiny. Astrologers claim to be capable of predicting behavior and personality characteristics based upon various astronomical configurations at the time of a person's birth. These configurations are easily measured and objectively quantified (37:1).

Leading astrologer Cyril Fagan agrees that astrology must first be scientifically confirmed for it to be claimed as scientifically valid. He explains:

> Since astrology is, or ought to be, an empirical science, the truth or otherwise of its doctrines can only be ascertained when they have been submitted to a rigorous scientific test, otherwise they can have no scientific appeal whatsoever (18:24).

Finally, Richard Nolle, one of the few astrologers who is critical of astrology, acknowledges:

> Any astrological proposition that lays claim to objective validity should be subjected to empirical testing. For example, if you want to make the claim that Libra rising is somehow

connected with art as a profession, then you
should not object to having your claim tested.
And you should be ready to take your lumps
when the test results come in (84:82, cf. 85:23).

Statistical Tests Offered as Proof of Astrology

As mentioned earlier, the second area of evidence
astrologers set forth to prove the validity of astrology
comes from certain statistical studies. We are unable to
cite all major studies here, but we can briefly cite the
results of five major studies.*

1. *The Mayo-White-Eysenck Study* attempted to determine if astrology could predict whether the personality of
an adult would be introverted or extroverted. Over 2,300
adults had their extroversion/introversion scores tabulated on the Eysenck Personality Inventory (EPI), then
these scores were correlated with astrological predictions.

The conclusion: *Marginal* (astrologers read favorable)
results were obtained that could not be accounted for
by chance alone. Five additional studies were performed
in the same area; three of these studies did not support

---

*Every other study of which we are aware encounters the same or
similar problems as these, so it is fair to say that the studies
astrologers cite as proof of astrology have been discredited or are
subject to debate.

Purely statistical research has its own inherent problems due to
its propensity for latitude of interpretation. Thus, great care must
be exercised so that invalid conclusions are not drawn. For example,
Dr. John Warwick Montgomery observes:

Statistical correlation is not equivalent to cause and
effect relationship, and the history of statistics is littered with odd and facetious cases of correlation (the
rise of the tides in Baja, California and the productivity
of the coconut crop in Madagascar . . .). There is also the
sad tale of the statistician who drowned wading across a

the Mayo-White-Eysenck findings, and two did.

It was discovered, however, that the positive results could be adequately explained in a number of different ways, *without* recourse to astrological theories. Eysenck himself, in later research (confirmed by other researchers), concluded that "the entire astrological effect [of the original study] was due to the subjects' expectation and familiarity with the characteristics associated with their Zodiac signs" (179:35). The Mayo-White-Eysenck study, therefore, may not be used as evidence for validating astrology.

Educational psychologists Ivan Kelly and Don Saklofske have reviewed the initial study (published in the *Journal of Social Psychology*) and all relevant subsequent studies. They conclude:

> The Mayo-White-Eysenck "astrological effect" is an instructive example that underscores the need to eliminate all "normal" alternative hypotheses before embracing a paranormal one. In this case, what at first appeared

---

river with an average depth of three feet! Statistical results, in other words, must be *interpreted* (72:112).

Concerning these studies, Lawrence Jerome, an engineer and science writer who has done a great amount of research regarding astrology, has observed:

> If the powerful planetary "effects" that the astrologers postulate actually existed, we would be able to measure them.... All properly conducted statistical tests of traditional astrology have come up blank. The observed data have always fit well within normally expected distributions. The important phrase here is "properly conducted." The number of *im*properly conducted statistical studies into astrology is legend. All too many budding astrological statisticians have poorly understood the real world

to be supportive of a paranormal [astrological] hypothesis was, with subsequent research, destined to have a non-astrological explanation after all and, indeed, to count *against* the astrological hypothesis (179:36).

2. *The Guardian-Smithers Study.* This massive study used official census records to test 2.3 million people, comparing their occupations with their Sun-signs. To do this, education professional Alan Smithers used and compared the predictions of 15 of the "most expert and well-qualified astrologers" in Britain. The results were reported in the prestigious British newspaper, *The Guardian.* Although a mild correlation was noted, Smithers himself remained unconvinced. He decided that most of the data "can be explained in other ways" (e.g., seasonal factors, social habits, belief in astrology, etc.).

Later, a reevaluation of Smithers' research claimed design flaws. It was also noted, as Smithers himself thought, that effects could be explained by additional non-astrological factors. The group of research scientists

----

and have devised statistical tests that underestimate the complexity of the physical problem.... *All statistical studies of traditional astrology—whether conducted by opponents or believers—have found absolutely no evidence of the alleged cosmic influences* (102:137,141, emphasis added).

For those who think Jerome's conclusion is debatable merely because he is a critic of astrology, we may note that astrologers themselves have agreed with him. Consider Richard Nolle, a full-time professional astrologer since 1973, and editor of the AFA's *Journal of Research:*

I'll leave you to your own devices when it comes to applying statistical methods for the purpose of exposing and eventually eradicating falsely objectified

and psychologists who reexamined the study concluded:

> Professor Smithers has produced an interesting study that allows the most detailed look yet at the relationship between Sun sign and occupation. We agree with him that there is "something in the data," but we disagree that it reflects a genuine astrological effect. Our re-analysis of Smithers' results show that they can be explained by statistical fluctuations and self-attribution effects. As pointed out by Charles Harvey, the study had limitations as a test of Sun-sign astrology; nevertheless, we suggest that if there were underlying truths [to astrology] they would shine through despite these limitations. They certainly do not support Sun-sign astrology (178: 336).

The Guardian-Smithers study therefore shows scientific research cannot be used to validate astrology. In fact, it discredits astrology.

---

astrological propositions. There are thousands of such poorly conceived positions running around in the astrological community, and they all need to be probed and punctured (84:84).

In another book, Nolle cites five research studies by astrologers, including himself, examining correlations between airplane crashes and the position of Mars. Four studies gave positive correlations. The largest study, however, which examined 973 air disasters gave only chance correlations. But Nolle admits "not one of us has used a proper control to put our findings into a realistic perspective" (85:76). In other words, the only reason for the positive correlations is because the studies were not properly controlled. Elsewhere in his book he states that astrology should be proven in specific areas where it is testable. If sun in Cancer is supposed to indicate a

3. *A National Enquirer Test.* This study examined 240 people and correlated the astrological sign and personality of each. The paper claimed to show that 91 percent of the people tested had their personality determined by their Zodiac sign. Subsequent testing, however, failed to substantiate the *Enquirer's* claims (180: 34-39).

4. *The Nelson Radio Research.* Electrical engineer John H. Nelson is the author of *Cosmic Patterns: Their Influence on Man and His Communication* (AFA: 1974). Nelson allegedly demonstrated that certain planetary configurations were responsible for improved shortwave radio transmission or the lack thereof. As usual these results were widely disseminated in and by the astrological community as proof of astrology, and especially as confirmation of the use of the astrological aspects—the angular relationships between planets in the birth chart.

Nelson's studies were heralded as evidence of a *physical* influence exerted by the planets. For example, in *My World of Astrology*, famed astrologer Sydney Omarr devotes an entire chapter to Nelson's proof of "ancient astrology." Another professional astrologer writes:

> Mr. Nelson of RCA Communications in New York City, has been able to predict weather and atmospheric conditions for radio transmission by observing the interplanetary positions with a better than 90% accuracy on the long-range basis. This is far superior to the results obtained by meteorologists.... These

---

musical nature, for instance, then most musicians will be Cancers. He says if this "cannot be demonstrated to be upheld by the facts, then the theory is worthless" (85:15). He further says, "Why accept something that can be demonstrated [to be] patently false?" (85:63).

"scientific" observers are proving the basic concepts of Astrology (30:1-2).

In *The Case for Astrology*, astrologers West and Toonder went so far as to say that, based on the positions of the planets, Nelson could predict radio disturbances "with up to 93% accuracy" (12:188).

Nelson claimed most magnetic storms causing radio disruption occurred when two or more planets were in conjunction—either in 90 degree aspect (the astrological "square") or 180 degree aspect to the sun (the astrological "opposition"). Since astrology traditionally held the square and opposition aspects to be evil or disharmonious, the correlation seemed relevant from the astrological viewpoint. In addition, West and Toonder also reported:

> Nelson found that predictably good, *disturbance-free* fields were formed when a number of planets lined up in 60 degree and 120 degree angles to the sun—the "sextile" and "trine" of traditional astrology, from time immemorial the "good," "beneficent," and "harmonious" aspects. Nelson also found that the more planets involved in the various aspects, the more pronounced the disturbance, or lack of it.... This both corroborates and amplifies the usual view of astrological aspects (12:189).

But "several recent studies quite conclusively showed Nelson to have been wrong" (206:216). For example, one study found that Nelson's results could be fully explained as the product of his statistical method, rather than planetary positions. A critical analysis of his methodology proved that his radio correlations could be reproduced on the basis of simple randomicity tests and were therefore not at all related to planetary positions.

Accordingly, his results were invalidated as pertaining to any astrological connection and "cannot be construed as evidence for planetary influence, or as empirical results for astrological aspects" (182:39).

Further studies have also found Nelson's claims cannot be substantiated. One study examined 25 years of Nelson's daily forecasts and failed to find any evidence of a correlation between planetary positions and radio broadcast quality (207:48). This study concluded that "for 30 years Nelson was convinced he saw a correlation that in fact did *not* exist" (172:170, emphasis added).

Even if Nelson's 90-percent accuracy were true, U.S. government forecasts based on scientific methods are 97 to 98 percent accurate, and achieve a far better result without using the planets (207:48).

5. *Gauquelin's "Neo-Astrology."* When it comes to scientific research, astrologers have one and only one "big gun." Perhaps no one has done as much research into astrology and allegedly related astral or cosmic effects as French scientist Michel Gauquelin. Yet astrologers who cite this research as support for astrology typically shoot down their own theories in doing so. Although Gauquelin's "neo-astrology" is subject to debate, Gauquelin has fully discredited traditional astrology. In essence, as we shall see, citing Gauquelin as a defender of astrology is like citing Karl Marx as a defender of capitalism.

The research involving Gauquelin's "Mars Effect" was a scientific study to test whether or not the birth dates of 2,088 sports champions were "statistically significant" according to astrological predictions. In this first study, researchers concluded that a statistically significant number of sports champions were born when Mars was situated between the eastern horizon and the celestial meridian. They figured that a correlation of 21.65 percent (of those sports champions born at the above time) existed against an expected chance correlation of 17.17 percent (the number of sports champions expected to be born).

But the problem for astrology is that the Mars Effect has never been absolutely confirmed in 20 years of subsequent studies. The most that can be concluded to date is "the success of replication [could these same statistics be confirmed?] is a matter of some debate" (96:216; the controversy may be traced in 177; 179; 185; 188).

Even though the Mars Effect has never been confirmed in 20 years, and even though the results are debated, still Gauquelin's research is often noted by astrologers as confirmation of astrology. But astrologers who claim Gauquelin's study as proof of astrology conveniently forget to say that Gauquelin himself since that time has completed perhaps more definitive research to disprove astrology than anyone else.

In one study Gauquelin used 15,560 subjects to test the alleged influence of the Zodiac in relationship to professional success. Gauquelin discovered, "The results were entirely negative" (170:57).

When astrologers objected that "professional success" was "far too crude a criterion to reveal the astral subtlety of zodiacal influences," Gauquelin established further elaborate testing to satisfy their complaints. In these tests he reported the same negative conclusions as before. (Note: Astrologers do claim the heavens influence the likelihood of professional success.)

At that point, astrologers said Gauquelin should have tested not professional success but *personality*, claiming if he did so, that he would have found a real influence.

Ironically, when Gauquelin's data seemed to confirm astrology, the astrologers accepted the criteria of professional success for the sports champions, but when the same criteria disproved astrology, they rejected the data.

In spite of this, Gauquelin obliged the astrologers and tested their claims concerning personality traits and zodiacal predictions. For this test, 52,188 personality traits were systematically collected from 2,000 subjects. What did Gauquelin find? Only that astrological predictions received "a fatal blow" (170:64).

Regardless, today you may read almost any book by a scientific-sounding astrologer and find him citing Gauquelin's works as evidence *for* astrology. Yet just the opposite is the case.

Gauquelin himself never claimed to prove astrology. This can easily be demonstrated from the books he has authored, including *The Scientific Basis of Astrology: Myth or Reality* (1973) and *Dreams and Illusions of Astrology* (1979).

In *Birth Times*, Gauquelin concludes about astrology:

> Over the years, I have tested astrologers (whose anonymity they have asked me to preserve), generally at their own request. The basic model is to present them with 20 horoscopes, 10 belonging to people who have some striking characteristic in common, the other 10 to people with the opposite characteristic. The astrologer has to match the horoscopes with the characteristics in question as correctly as possible.... I have to admit that astrologers regularly fail these tests and are sometimes so disillusioned that they accuse me of rigging the cases (106:139).

Moreover, Gauquelin himself has cogently argued against the scientific validity of astrology:

> Every attempt, whether of astrologers or scientists, to produce evidence of the validity of astrological laws has been in vain. It is now

quite certain that the signs in the sky which presided over our births have *no power whatever* to decide our fates, to affect our hereditary characteristics, or play any part however humble in the totality of affects, random and otherwise, which form the fabric of our lives and mold our impulses to action. *Confronted with science,* modern and traditional astrology are seen to be imaginary doctrines (103:145, emphasis added).

The results of Gauquelin's work are so thoroughly destructive of traditional astrology, such as the essential zodiacal signs, that even some professional astrologers have given up belief in the signs. This is admitted by astrologer Richard Nolle who writes:

There are some people who are experienced in the ways of astrology, who do not accept the validity of the zodiacal signs. They point to the Gauquelin findings, which have failed to uncover any evidence for a connection between zodiacal signs and any definable psychological trait or characteristic (84:79-80, cf. 170:64).

But now we must discuss the area of Gauquelin's research which is so controversial, his research into what he calls "neo-astrology." Gauquelin originally thought he had found an unorthodox astral or cosmic influence related in some way to astrology. But it is too simplistic to say Gauquelin proved conclusively there was an astrological connection. To assess Gauquelin's research, we must note five things:

1) Gauquelin has vacillated between excitement over possible findings, and discouragement and uncertainty over the results and problems of interpretation.

2) His results in this area have never been subjected to conclusive testing and proof or disproof by others. His results are largely *his* results.
3) Gauquelin knows and has clearly stated that, as a whole, astrology is certainly a false belief.
4) Gauquelin is still uncertain as to the relationship that may exist between certain aspects of astrology and possible astral or cosmological influences.
5) Gauquelin's findings on "neo-astrology": a) are subject to debate; b) may have statistical problems (102:141); c) lie beyond anything that science can presently explain; and d) are inconclusive concerning the validity of the implications.

But one thing is certain. The clearest conclusion regarding Gauquelin's research should be known by Gauquelin himself. In his most recent text he has written about his earlier research concerning "neo-astrology," allowing the words of skeptic Anthony Standen to reflect his own thoughts.

But (assuming that his claims are true) has Gauquelin really "proved" astrology? It depends on what you mean—"astrology." If you mean ordinary conventional astrology, which is current in this country (the USA) and in many others, and is so prevalent now days that no one can possibly escape it, then Gauquelin has utterly and completely disproved it. But if you are going to call by the name "astrology" *any* effect that is found that depends on the planets and is unexplained by science, never mind whether it agrees with conventional astrology or is entirely different, then Gauquelin makes a very strong claim to have found such a thing (106:141-42).

Gauquelin sketches a theory for trying to determine if there are planetary "effects" on human traits and heredity, if there is a sort of "chromosomal-cosmic" linkage. In essence, Gauquelin appears to say that babies in the womb will be born when the planetary conditions conform to their hereditary makeup. That is, certain planetary positions affect geomagnetic or electromagnetic fields at the earth's surface which then tend to initiate labor in fetuses which have a particular genetic structure.

But even here, Gauquelin admits his theory and the results of testing his theory do not support astrology. He writes:

> Obviously, there are important differences between my results and the modern practice of astrology: planets are *not* "prominent" in the sky where they should be; only some of them display positive results; zodiacal influences still continue to be *not* vindicated (107:XV, emphasis added).

Elsewhere he discusses his continued skepticism of the link between births, human traits, and astrological theory:

> Even if it becomes solidly established, the planet-geomagnetism link at birth is not the ultimate solution and, in one sense, it simply adds another question to all the other unanswered ones. Paul Couderc expresses the almost unanimous opinion of the scientific community:
>
> > The new statistical interpretations (put out by Gauquelin) seem to me less unacceptable than the old

> ones [but unconvincing nonethe-
> less].... I do not know whether I will
> live long enough to witness the dis-
> covery of an interpretation which
> will seem likely to me (106:158-59).

Dr. Kanagy of Purdue University notes several problems with Gauquelin's assumptions. First, the precise
moment of birth is often a fiction—labor may last from a
few minutes to more than a day, and recorded times of
birth are often inaccurate due to various factors.

Second, Kanagy notes, how could a planetary "heredity" that supposedly influences profession or personality
override the endless number of other infinitely more
powerful forces? For example, what about forces such as
intelligence, aptitude, and social factors? What about
such influences as a mother's use of drugs or alcohol
during pregnancy, naturally induced spontaneous abortion, seasonal variation in birth times, the effects of diet,
and prenatal care or abuse? These and many other influences would all have to be carefully considered (97:
152-57).

In *Forget Your Sun-Sign,* Anthony Standen says scientists who have examined Gauquelin's assumptions
concerning birth, hereditary factors, and planetary influence have rejected those assumptions because they
"cannot bring themselves to believe anything so prepos-
terous" (212:107 in 97:153).

Gauquelin himself betrays his own ideas concerning
astral influence, admitting, "This is the only thing I
am pretty sure of. My ideas on astral influence have
changed continually, swinging back and forth like a
pendulum (106:180-81).

In his latest writing, he confesses:

> Though I am so full of my subject, so deter-
> mined to defend it, so proud of my discoveries, I

am still tormented by two feuding demons. The first is the fear of having been mistaken in asserting that astral influence is real; the second is the agonizing thought of all I have been unable to discover or explain.... *But today I would not allow myself to draw drastic conclusions as I have sometimes done in the past. I will be content simply to have thrown a little light on this vast mystery* which has occupied so many minds over the centuries (106:180-81, emphasis added).

Though Gauquelin's research concerning astral influence is interesting, it cannot be cited as evidence for astrology. Remember, Gauquelin's overall findings convincingly disproved astrology (as commonly practiced). Gauquelin not only disproved Sun-sign validity, but most other aspects of astrology as well. That astrologers continue to cite the work of Gauquelin as proof of astrology only underscores their fundamental bias or ignorance. Far from proving astrology is true, as often is claimed, Gauquelin and science have totally exploded astrological beliefs and shown them to be false (96:64, cf. 106:117-19; 108:7-10).

7

The Scientific Evidence Against Astrology

Sun-Sign Research

A person's "Sun-sign" is the Zodiac sign (Pisces, Libra, Aries, Cancer, etc.) the sun was passing through at the moment of a person's birth. Astrology teaches that a person's Sun-sign has the greatest importance of all in determining overall character. This is why astrologers' columns in the newspapers have singled out this aspect of astrology for mention.*

---

*The *rising sign* (i.e., the sign rising on the eastern horizon at the moment of birth is said to represent the outer self, the personality and how a person expresses himself in the world) and the *Moon-sign* (the sign of the Zodiac that the moon was in at the time of birth is said to represent the inner self, the emotional nature) are also important to astrologers. Astrologers themselves often criticize Sun-sign columns in newspapers (although they continue to write them), because one "rule" of horoscopy (the art of interpreting the horoscope) is that no single factor in the chart is to be interpreted apart from all the other relevant factors. Nevertheless, in the total astrological world view, astrologers agree on the importance and power of the Sun-sign.

In particular, astrologers claim "the Sun is the determining factor in shaping character and inclining one towards a certain type of destiny" because "the position of the Sun in the Zodiac at the time of your birth determines the vital energy released by that planet and affects the cells of your brain and body" (8:2-3, cf. 22:355). Though Sun-signs are the critical foundation pillar supporting astrology, this pillar has been disproven by the extensive research of Gauquelin.

Other studies have also crumbled astrology's main pillar. In "An Empirical Test of Popular Astrology," researcher Ralph Bastedo carefully analyzed the content of astrological literature. He found that it revealed 2,375 specific adjectives for the 12 zodiacal Sun-signs, each sign being described by about 200 adjectives. (For example, a person who is a "Leo" is strong, domineering, tough—a born leader; a person who is a "Taurus" is indecisive, timid, insecure—not a leader.)

In Bastedo's test, 1,000 people were examined for 33 variables, including physical attractiveness, leadership ability, personality traits, social and religious belief, etc. Bastedo concluded that this test failed to prove any astrological prediction. He said, "All of our results can be attributed to random chance" (175:34).

Another test, conducted to find if the planets influenced compatibility in marriage, involved 2,978 couples who married and 478 couples who divorced in 1967 and 1968. The results of this test proved their astrological signs did not significantly alter the outcome of either group. Those born under "compatible" signs married and divorced as often as those born under "incompatible" signs (181:211).

Astrologers also claim that scientists and politicians are favored by one Sun-sign or another. But John McGervy, in researching this claim, compared birth dates of 16,634 scientists and 6,475 politicians and found no correlation to substantiate the astrologers' claims. He concluded the distribution of signs among these two professions was as random as for the general public (187:53).

Finally, researchers have examined over a thousand books, hundreds of journals, written to hundreds of astrologers throughout the world "but were unable to find anybody anywhere who could provide a demonstration that the traditional signs actually work the way they are supposed to work" (206:217).

Current scientific evidence shows there is no validity to the astrologers' assertion that a Sun-sign influences a person's life. But what about the influence of the Moon-sign?

Moon-Sign Research

Second in importance to the sun, the influence of the moon is one of the most vital considerations in astrology. Astrologers often speak of the "extensive research" proving the moon influences human behavior in a variety of ways. But such secondhand reports and studies must be taken with a grain of salt because, all publicity aside, nothing has yet been proven.

For example, in "The Moon Was Full and Nothing Happened," three researchers discuss the results of their 1985 meta-analysis of 37 specific studies examining the relationship between the four phases of the moon and abnormal, criminal, or deviant behavior. They concluded there was no causal relationship. (This analysis was first reported in the *Psychological Bulletin*, Volume 97.)

The researchers comment:

> It is important to note that there are two hurdles to overcome before any findings on lunar variables and human behavior are deserving of public attention. The first hurdle is

that *reliable* (i.e., replicable) findings need to be reported by independent investigators. The second hurdle is that the relationship should not be a trivial one. The lunar hypothesis fails on both counts (180a:139).

The above conclusions are supported by the eminent astrologer George O. Abell, who confirms in his *Exploration of the Universe* (1982, p. 138), that the more careful studies using much larger samples and far better controls "fail to confirm evidence for such lunar effects" (97:157).

In response, astrologers often complain that the scientific tests of *individual* astrological factors are invalid because astrology only works when *all* the relevant factors in a chart are observed and properly correlated. But even apart from the problems of interpretation, this argument of the astrologers is invalid. The astrologers are confusing *measurement* and *interpretation*.

If chart factors cannot be *measured* individually, how does the astrologer know they exert an influence? Do they mean to say that the chart factors, considered individually, have no influence? Not at all, because the individual influences are tabulated in conjunction with many other individual chart factors to produce an interpretation.

Even so, the argument concerning "all the relevant factors in a chart" is invalid because astrologers cannot agree on the number and interpretation of what are the "relevant" chart factors. And when any individual chart factors are considered, astrology still fails careful testing.

For further evidence, consider the results of a test first reported in the *Journal of Clinical Psychology*, Volume 33 (1977):

Astrologers have criticized the personality studies based only on Sun-sign relationships.

Adding additional chart factors did not lead to any more positive results in the study conducted by Hume and Goldstein ... with charts for 196 subjects and their scores from the Minnesota Multiphasic Personality Inventory and the Leary Interpersonal Check List, they compared 13 personality dimensions against the 12 signs, the Moon, and eight planets in the signs and houses, and five planetary aspects. *There was no support* for any relationship between personality and astrological parameters in 632 comparative tests (206:215, emphasis added).

Horoscope Research

Astrology is valuable only if it can reveal useful or true things about a person or his future. If the average astrologer cannot properly interpret a chart, or if its symbols will just as easily (in fact, more easily) lead him to give *wrong* information, then astrology is useless at best, and dangerous at worst.

Chart interpretation is to astrology what the resurrection of Christ is to Christianity. In Christianity everything depends upon the literal physical resurrection of Christ from the dead. Without it, Christianity is a fraud (328, cf. 1 Corinthians 15:13-20). Likewise, without the ability to give a proper chart interpretation, the entire belief system of astrology is proven false.

This inability to provide an accurate chart interpretation is the Achilles' heel of astrology. And, as seen in chapter 4, the very nature of the astrological chart makes an accurate interpretation impossible. Of course, some astrologers might be giving good psychological counsel rather than astrological advice or commonsense information, but such counsel would not come from the astrological truths in the chart.

Perhaps the uselessness of the horoscope is why a few astrologers have abandoned charts! Finding them so unreliable, confusing, and contradictory, they prefer to counsel entirely by psychic means which they believe give them more accuracy!

How do we know that astrologers cannot interpret their own charts? Because sufficiently rigorous testing, conducted repeatedly, has proven it.

At least seven independent studies have each concluded that even when consulting the world's best astrologers, there is little agreement among them as to the meaning of a chart. Geoffrey Dean, who has investigated astrology for over 15 years, has surveyed the research of Clark (1961); Marcharg (1975); Ross (1975); Vidmar (1979); Fourie et al. (1980); Steffert (1983); and Dean (1985). Dean concludes, "... in none of these studies was the agreement between astrologers better than useless. If astrologers cannot even agree on what a chart indicates, then what price [i.e., what value is] astrology?" (173:267).*

If the astrologers are in the dark concerning the meaning of their charts, even more are their clients in the dark. Seven independent studies of the clients of astrologers revealed that people who have horoscopes interpreted for them cannot tell the difference between a right chart

---

* The following are the mean (average) correlations for these studies: Vernon Clark (1961), in a famous blind trial involving some of the world's best astrologers (for example, Charles Carter and Marc Edmund Jones), obtained results that on inspection reveal 0.13 for 20 astrologers matching ten pairs of charts to case histories, and 0.12 for 30 astrologers judging ten pairs of charts for intelligence. Marcharg (1975) found 0.17 for ten astrologers judging 30 charts for alcoholism. Ross (1975) found only 0.23 for two astrologers rating 102 charts on five-point scales of the Psychological Screening Inventory, even though both had received a similar training,

and a wrong chart. In other words, an astrologer's client is likely to identify someone else's horoscope rather than his own as the one that best describes him. (These results could not be explained away by astrologers blaming poor chart interpretation, or by astrologers claiming the people lacked knowledge of themselves (182:30; 172:179-80).

In a survey of several other scientific studies concerning chart interpretation and people's acceptance of them, Dean discusses the research not only of Cummings et al. (1978), but also of Neher (1980), Lackey (1981), Dwyer and Grange (1983), Tyson (1984), Carlson (1985), and Dwyer (1986). In these studies, the researcher asked each subject to decide which of two or more chart interpretations fitted him best. One interpretation was from the subject's own chart; the other chart interpretations had been randomly chosen. (Charts were interpreted by recourse to three standard methods—either by professional astrologers, computers [widely used by astrologers], or by astrology texts.)

In answer to the question, "Can subjects tell right charts from wrong charts?" Dean reported the studies' answers were, "Unanimously no. The overall trend is not even in the right direction" (172:180).

For example, Douglas P. Lackey, whose test used 38 college students (each of whose horoscope contained an

---

both taught astrology at the same college in Miami, and both followed Rudhyar's person-centered approach. Vidmar (1979) obtained results that on inspection reveal 0.10 for 28 astrologers matching five pairs of charts to case histories. Fourie et al. (1980) found 0.16 for two astrologers rating 48 charts on 18 nine-point scales of the 16 PF Inventory. Steffert (1983) obtained results that on inspection reveal 0.03 for 27 astrologers judging the charts of 20 married couples for marital happiness. In other words, *in none of these studies was the agreement between astrologers better than useless* (173:267 emphasis added).

average of 20 paragraphs of information), summarized:

> Nineteen subjects rated the placebo horo-
> scope accurate; 19 rated the placebo horoscope
> as inaccurate.... Nineteen subjects rated their
> own horoscopes as more accurate than the pla-
> cebo horoscopes; 18 subjects rated the placebo
> horoscopes as more accurate than their own
> horoscopes; one subject had the two dead even.
> In short, a person presented with two horo-
> scopes and asked to identify which is his own
> is as likely to pick someone else's as the one
> that "describes me truly" as he is to pick his
> own (182:30).

Dean concluded from all of the evidence,

> According to astrology the subjects should
> certainly tend to pick their own charts. But
> ... in every study the subjects perform no bet-
> ter than chance. In other words, they were just
> as happy with wrong charts as with right ones.
> This suggests that the perceived validity of
> astrology is an illusion (172:179).

It is not uncommon to discover that a given astrological interpretation fits a subject perfectly, even though
the chart is later discovered to be the wrong chart. Nor is
it uncommon to find that a chart of one person, for
example George Bush, is interpreted to accurately fit
him, but is later revealed to be the chart of an entirely
different person, such as Michael Dukakis (172:180).

To illustrate this point, consider a true story about Dr.
Marc Edmund Jones, an ordained Presbyterian clergyman and a leading astrologer in America. Jones relates
that while among a group of astrologers on July 14,

1970, his host, who was also an astrologer, decided to demonstrate the "more troublesome confusions prevailing" in horoscope interpretation (59:172). He noted most astrological interpretations could "fit anybody, most of the time!"

To prove his statement, he asked that the chart of a famous person be chosen at random, but that the name of that person be revealed to no one. He next interpreted the chart as if it were the chart of Richard Nixon, who was at that time the president. (All of the astrologers in that meeting knew Nixon's astrological profile since the president is too important an individual for astrologers not to have already done his chart.)

As each symbol or piece of information was interpreted (Saturn rising, elevated Mars, a tenth house planet buttressed by a trine with Uranus, Uranus and the sun in the sixth house, a preponderance of fixed signs, etc.), the astrologers all agreed: "This has been an undeniable analysis of our president"—in spite of the fact that they knew in advance it could not be Nixon's chart (59:177). They were surprised, though, to find that this chart was really that of the famous psychoanalyst, Carl Gustav Jung (59:171-79).

This incident shows that the chart's own complexity makes it *appear* authoritative and precise to a client, even though any chart can be interpreted a thousand different ways by astrologers. Astrologers, however, are aware of this elasticity in their interpretations. They know that sooner or later they will make enough correct "hits" (something that the person will agree is relevant to him) to fit any person.

Even worse, many tests have revealed people cannot tell authentic charts from charts that have been *deliberately* reversed; people rated reversed charts just as highly as authentic charts. A reverse chart is diametrically the opposite of an authentic chart and should not work. Obviously these people were completely deceived.

Following such a carefully controlled test, Dean concluded:

> These results are most easily understood as indicating that (1) persons are not affected in any way whatsoever by astrological influences, and (2) the symbols in the chart bear no relationship to the personality traits of the individual they are supposed to represent (206:219).

This evidence seems to show astrology is a powerful deception, so why should we be surprised that some astrologers actually use reversed charts and find them just as useful as regular charts? Clinical psychologist, parapsychologist, and astrologer Ford Hunter, founder of the Chthonian Society, "uses a reversed-horoscope method in reading a person's natal chart." He says, "I . . . reverse the chart to find where the energy flow is going" (138:118).

Ultimately, these tests show that people tend to accept *any* chart as valid for a variety of reasons wholly unrelated to astrological theory. These reasons include gullibility, expectation, insecurity, attraction to the astrologer, selective memory (remembering only the hits), positive thinking, payment of a fee, body language, manipulation by the astrologer, emotional need, etc. Dean lists 20 different ways by which astrologers can make their craft *seem* to work and make their clients satisfied—and yet none of the methods require that astrology be true (173:263). Nonetheless, every astrologer claims it is really astrological effects that work.

To further confuse matters, researchers found that astrologers who used charts were no better in their judgments than those astrologers who did *not* use charts—who were just guessing. Incredibly, research shows that astrologers who used charts actually made worse judgments (173:267).

In 1985, Dean conducted another study, reported in *Correlation,* the astrological community's statistical journal. He tested the assumption that astrologers who use charts must perform better than astrologers who do not use charts, but are merely guessing. Astrological charts miserably failed the test.

In his study, 90 astrologers (ranging from beginners to experts) were tested on their ability to determine the introversion or extroversion and stability or instability of 240 subjects. (Forty-five of the astrologers used charts while 45 made their best guesses without charts.) Out of 1,200 initial subjects who had taken the Eysenck Personality Inventory, Dean selected 60 each of the most extroverted, most introverted, most stable, and most unstable. These groups of extreme subjects were equivalent to the top and bottom 1/15th of the general population. Extroversion and stability factors were chosen because they are "perhaps the most major and enduring of known personality factors" and "are supposed to be readily discernible in a birth chart" (173:266).

Most of the astrologers "agreed that the test was a fair one," but the study clearly showed no difference between the astrologers who used charts and the astrologers who did not. One particular statement recorded by Dean in his study stands out: "If anything, the astrologers' judgments were made worse by looking at birth charts" (173:266).

Testing Astrological Predictions

There is still another way to test astrology: Examining the success rate for specific (or even general) predictions of future events. Astrologers often say that the proof of astrology is in their high rate of successful predictions. After ever major event, whether social (the marriage of a movie star), political (an assassination), scientific (medical breakthrough), geophysical (earthquake, flood), or whatever, articles invariably appear in the astrological literature showing the event had been clearly predicted to occur "in the stars." Objective testing by outside researchers, however, has conclusively shown that astrological predictions have an extremely high failure rate. Overall, their record is terrible.

From January 1974 to March 1979, astronomers Culver and Ianna examined 462 predictions of *American Astrology Magazine*, 544 predictions of *Astrology Magazine*, 134 predictions of astrologer/psychic Jeane Dixon, 509 predictions of *Horoscope Magazine*, 532 predictions of *Horoscope Guide*, 128 predictions of astrologer/witch Sybil Leek, 118 predictions of *Sydney Omarr's Astrological Guide*, 123 predictions of the politically influential Carroll Righter, and 461 predictions of miscellaneous astrologers (at least ten predictions each).

The total number of predictions was over 3,000 and the total number of failures was 2,653, almost a 90 percent failure rate. But the failure rate was probably closer to 100 percent because astrologers were given the benefit of the doubt. (Any prediction that could have been attributed to shrewd guessing, vague wording, or inside information was placed in the astrologers' "successful" column.) No astrologer was listed unless the research team could document 100 or more predictions by that person. Culver and Ianna succinctly concluded, "The results ... paint a dismal picture indeed for the traditional astrological claim that 'astrology works'" (96:169-70).

Culver and Ianna exposed the methodology of astrologers: When wrong, astrologers engage in cover-up, equivocation, and doing whatever necessary to hide or rationalize their failures. For instance, leading astrologers predicted in 1968 that Jacqueline Kennedy would not marry that year. Unfortunately for astrologers, Jackie married Aristotle Onassis on October 20, 1968.

Significantly, Jeane Dixon's newspaper column, written to appear the day Jackie was married, reiterated her earlier prediction: "I still stand on my new year's predictions and see no marriage for Jackie Kennedy in the near future" (96:174). She was able to have the column withdrawn before publication and replaced with a corrected version.

Astrologer Zolton Mason defended his prediction about Jackie Kennedy, rationalizing that marriage to a 69-year-old-man "is not a marriage." And Sydney Omarr defended his prediction on the basis he had predicted a *divorce* would make international headlines (96:174).

Is it any wonder Culver and Ianna concluded:

> This is hardly the stuff of which searches for truth are made. In fact, as we journey through the marvelously psychedelic world of astrological prediction we find that the most clever, intelligent, and successful of the astrologers have adopted instead a variety of ploys designed *specifically for reducing or eliminating the impact of their mispredictions* (96:174, emphasis added).

In 1971, Reverchon examined the astrological predictions made in a French astrological journal from 1958-1961 by the renowned André Barbault, a specialist in predictive astrology. Centering on the French-Algerian War, each of his first 11 predictions failed. But for each of them Barbault claimed to find "further indications," thus prolonging the process. Finally, after 11 failed predictions, he made the inevitable hit.

Similarly, on other subjects, Barbault wrongly predicted Kennedy would be reelected in 1964 (he was assassinated in 1963), that de Gaulle would resign in 1965 (he was reelected), that Khrushchev would remain in power until 1966 (he was removed from power in 1964), etc.

Reverchon then compared the predictions of Barbault (concerning world crises) with 105 major world events for 1965, and reported "what was announced did not happen, what happened was not announced" (172:170).

False predictions abound in astrological literature. Western Hindu astrologer James Braha predicted that John Glenn would run for president in 1988, and succeed (62:306). Glenn did neither. Leading astrologers, claiming to know when the much heralded "Age of Aquarius" began or would begin, published predictions between 1969 and 1978. To their embarrassment, they set the Age of Aquarius at dates ranging from A.D. 1781 to A.D. 2740, encompassing a thousand years of variation (96:81-82).

Not only have astrologers repeatedly failed in specific, or even general prediction, but they have failed in predicting major disasters. The following data listed by Playfair and Hill is typical:

> Roger Hunter, a geophysicist with the U.S. National Ocean Survey...found that although seventeen major earthquakes took place between January and August 1970, the forecasters in *American Astrology* missed every single one. Of the sixteen quakes they did predict, naming only the month and the country, they were right for only three minor events. They also missed the 31 May disaster in Peru, one of the worst in this century in which 30,000 people died (216:168).

U.S. Geological Survey scientists, Derr and Hunter, analyzed 240 earthquake predictions made by 27 different astrologers and found their accuracy was worse than guessing (172:169). And no astrologer anywhere predicted the December 7, 1988, Soviet Armenian earthquake that killed at least 30,000.

Most financiers can well remember the Black Monday of October 19, 1987, when the stock market fell more than 500 points. But few people know that a major astrological publication, *Llewellyn's 1987 Moon-sign Book and Gardening Guide* (1986) predicted this optimistic bit of information for the very week that the market crashed (October 18-24): "Look for a *strong rally* that could take us into December..." (206:213, emphasis added). What do you think happened to all the investors who trusted this advice?

The evidence shows that astrologers consistently miss predicting major disasters or events, not only in weather and economics, but in politics, science, medicine and every other field. If these extremely large and significant events cannot be "seen" in the chart, how then can astrologers promise to accurately foretell from the same charts the "little" events in people's lives?

Trusting in astrological predictions can, in fact, be harmful. Astrologer Sydney Bennett, for example, deliberately took a business trip to California to take advantage of "a marvelous combination of [astrological] progressions." Not only did the business venture fail, but Bennett was "struck by a hit and run driver and almost killed." His clients had been complaining of his false astrological predictions, but only when he had experienced disaster for himself did he abandon his faith in astrological progressions. Unfortunately, Bennett replaced these with another system of astrological divination—the Solar Return/Key Cycle (160:14).

The wife of astrologer Robert DeLuse, a past director of the AFA, noted her husband had "predicted the time of his death for many different dates, none of which were correct" (160:43).

In every era of history, false astrological prophecies can be found. During World War II, astrologers constantly failed in their predictions. The August 27, 1939, column of astrologer "Lyndoe" confidently predicted concerning the invasion of Poland, "Hitler will not do it." Four days later Hitler invaded Poland (98:21). Similarly,

English astrologer Naylor said in his column of August 27, 1939, "... for years I have constantly belabored these points: Hitler's horoscope is not a war horoscope..." (98:21).

Now briefly consider the astrologers' dilemma in prediction. The "aspects" in a chart are often deemed vital for correctly interpreting the horoscope. Yet one astrologer will find the "aspects" valuable and another, such as the following, will find them useless:

> My friends insisted I do their charts. In doing so, I quickly discovered that much of the material on planetary aspects didn't fit the experience of my friends or my knowledge of them.... It was hard for me to accept that most of the information in these books wasn't pertinent to the lives of those I knew, but it was true (126:i).

This astrologer notes correctly, "There is currently much confusion both among students and professional astrologers regarding the quality and power of astrological aspects (126:1). The dilemma is obvious: Is the astrologer who uses or ignores aspects going to be more successful in prediction?

Yet all of the scientific disproof of astrology still cannot explain how astrologers can sometimes provide accurate disclosures to their clients (information they have no way of knowing), or how in rare cases they are accurate in their predictions. As we shall see in chapters 12-15, it "works" for reasons unrelated to astrology itself. Some of these reasons are natural and some are supernatural, but in no case are they astrological.

But next we will examine the response of the astrology community to the scientific invalidation of their craft. Are astrologers honestly facing the facts or are they stubbornly refusing to accept the facts and promoting a system many of them know is false?

8

The Response of the Astrological Community

The astrological community has been acting as the physician who discovered that the drug he has been prescribing widely is increasingly harmful to his patients—causing cancer, severe depression, and paralysis in some, and slow death in all. But knowing this, the doctor continues to prescribe the drug, giving absolute assurances of its safety and health benefits. Astrologers, likewise, have ignored the scientific evidence and continue to promote the benefits of their craft in glowing terms as if nothing at all has happened.

Perhaps the extremely conclusive nature of the scientific evidence against astrology has sent the astrological community retreating to its own private world, impervious to all assaults. Notes the proprietor of Australia's largest computerized chart calculation service:

> I often get the feeling, after talking to astrologers, that they live in a mental fantasy world, a kind of astrological universe where no explanations outside of astrological ones are

permitted, and that if the events of the real world do not accord with astrological notions or predictions, then yet another astrological technique will have to be invented to explain it (172:178).

Astronomers Culver and Ianna argue that because astrology is *not* science, it is never subject to the same restrictions that every scientific discipline is subject to, nor is it subject to the restrictions those in the scientific community place upon themselves:

> As scientists, we do not have such freedom, since we are of necessity constrained by facts. ...The "popular" and "serious" astrologers almost without exception, continue on their merry way, all but oblivious to the empirical assaults that have been made in recent years on some of their most cherished articles of faith (96:XI).

They also point out that astrologers' willingness to suppress scientific evidence "is not the road to the scientific credibility and respectability that so many astrologers for so many years have complained about not having" (96:179).

Instead of embracing the scientific method, the astrologers jump on the promotional bandwagon and simply claim scientific proof for the slightest hint of a positive result, all the while ignoring the massive weight of negative scientific results (96:149-50).

Take, for example, the response of astrologer Francis King. Oddly enough, this astrologer finds in Gauquelin's *disproof* of astrology, the *proof* of its truth: "His results showed that the classic astrological theories appeared to have been scientifically vindicated" (96:149). But even astrologer Richard Nolle concedes that astrologers have ignored Gauquelin's research for two decades and:

...we can't have it both ways. We cannot in good conscience accept empirical findings when they [allegedly] confirm our traditions, while at the same time rejecting whatever findings run against the grain of astrological tradition (84:75).

Concerning the Gauquelin research, Nolle exhorts his fellow astrologers, "...whether the Gauquelins are right or wrong, it is utterly wrong not to be aware of their findings and their methods, or to practice astrology in total ignorance of the Gauquelin work" (84:92-93).

Nolle also grants that "using empirical methods to expose astrological nonsense is a worthwhile imperative in its own right" (84:93). Still, in spite of such statements, 99.9 percent of the astrological community considers this a waste of time. This kind of response by the astrological community borders on personal and social irresponsibility.

Swindlers and practitioners of quack medicine are vigorously prosecuted by society because their deception and lies bring harm to people. Whether swindlers believe in their own scheme is irrelevant, for the public cannot and will not tolerate fraud. In its own sphere, astrology is a swindle, equivalent to quack medicine.

The current effort by astrologers to have their craft legitimized must be rejected. Astrologers are confronting city councils and local ordinances, demanding that restrictions against them be dropped or that society be redefined in more positive terms. Because the astrologers inaccurately portray astrology as a science and/or a psychology, they are demanding the word "astrology" be removed from local ordinances prohibiting palmistry, mediumship, fortune-telling, witchcraft, etc. (e.g., 144:16-19).

In Atlanta, Georgia, for instance, the first vice president of the AFA, Maxine Taylor, spearheaded a successful movement to legalize astrology in Georgia. It is now a fully legal practice and astrologers are licensed by their own board which is certified by the state of Georgia (329).

Astrologers have succeeded because they have foisted a deception upon the public that astrology is a science, and not an occult art, and therefore worthy of social respect. Astrologers say that they "function legitimately as prescriptionists for the human condition—to help folks deal with the real as well as the spiritual world..." (144:18). Their ultimate goal is seeing astrology educationally institutionalized—placed in the schools, colleges, and universities. If they succeed, this one step alone "would circumvent the effects of all existing [anti-astrology] legislation" (144:19).

But the scientific evidence shows astrologers do not function legitimately as prescriptionists for the human condition. Astrologers do not help people deal with the real world or with spiritual truth. Therefore, the efforts to make astrology respectable and professional should be vigorously opposed.

Yet, response to the scientific disproof of astrology underscores a more fundamental problem within the ranks of this modern myth. This is what astronomers Culver and Ianna have labeled "The Gemini Syndrome." This is the tendency for astrologers to mimic the characteristics said to be typical of the Gemini personality: the propensity to speak out of both sides of the mouth. At its core it concerns astrological self-deception, the "confident use of glaring inconsistencies" (173:265), the refusal to face the facts, the justification of astrology by any means. Even though facts constantly fly in the face of the theories of astrology, the facts continue to be distorted or ignored and false theories continue to be promoted. For example:

Thus a Sagittarian calvary officer will be seen as confirming astrology (the centaur, symbol of Sagittarius, is half-man, half-horse) even though the occurrence is at a chance level and everything else in his chart says he should be a banker (173:265).

Note the comments of the chairman of the United Kingdom Astrological Association, who is critical of the astrologers' inclination toward excuses. He is describing what an astrologer can do to "harmonize" astrological predictions with a person who does not match them (in this case, a person who is very meek, but who astrology predicts should be aggressive):

> If I found a very meek and unaggressive person with five planets in Aries, this does not cause me to doubt that Aries means aggression. I may be able to point to his Aries Ascendant, or to his Sun conjunct Saturn, or to his ruler in the twelfth house; and, if none of these alibis are available, I can simply say that he has not yet fulfilled his Aries potential. Or, I can argue (as I have heard argued) that, if a person has an *excess* of planets in a particular sign, he will tend to suppress the characteristics of that sign, because he is scared that, if he reveals them, he will carry them to excess. But if on the next day I meet a very aggressive person who also has five planets in Aries, I will change my tune: I will say that he *had* to be like that because of his planets in Aries (172:173).

Leading astrologer Richard Nolle comments, "If you're confused [about astrology] it's a sign of spiritual growth—an indication that you're on the right track" (84:114). But confusion exists in astrology because it is irrational and contradictory. When an astrologer discovers this fact, is it wise to tell him confusion is a sign of spiritual progress and evidence he is "on the right track"?

Astrologers reason that because astrology works or seems to work, it therefore must be true. But the shaky assumption is that when it works, it is working on the basis of the stated principles of astrology rather than through psychological principles or spiritistic powers. Because the astrologer reasons astrology is true, there- fore every argument against it must be false—and counter arguments must be drafted no matter how inane. Former astrologer Charles Strohmer confirms this process of self-deception:

> Now astrologers have set replies to such arguments [against astrology]. And I don't blame them. Their sanity is at stake.... His experience proves that it works; therefore he feels these arguments must be wrong. So he must build a case to refute each argument. ... He is forced, by the silences of the practice, to manufacture a seemingly satisfactory reply to each question, almost in order to keep his sanity. For he cannot understand how the sys- tem can work apart from the way he has been taught. Since he believes that the books can- not be wrong, he feels the opposing arguments must be incorrect. And so he must out-argue the arguers. But in all honesty, these refuta- tions are imaginary, too ... (81:37).

Astrologer and parapsychologist Philip Sedgwick is president of Delta Dynamics, an astrological research and consulting company that includes Fortune 500 cor- porations among its clients. He says that the "black hole" 3U1617-15, which he calls "Scorpio X-1," indicates a person should "allow yourself to be naturally guided in the way of the Higher Directive without knowing what it means" (144:185).

When astrologers allow themselves to be guided or led by some higher source without knowing what it means, perhaps this is one reason the astrological community ends up with so much astrological confusion. Astrologers appeal to endless different factors—all irrelevant—and to endless unknown influences in the attempt to "explain" astrology. Lawrence Jerome observes, "By the time the astrologers get through explaining away all their failure due to outside 'influences,' there's little left to the stars but random chance" (102:105).

The astrologers will thus invent an answer to explain any factual error or inconsistency within astrology. When the facts deny astrology, so much worse for the facts. Astrology must survive at all costs. Former 12-year astrologer, Karen Winterburn, agrees, "How true it is. I amused and abused myself for years running on this treadmill. Astrologers will not face reality" (202).

9

The Alleged Evidence for Astrology in the Bible

Astrologers often claim the Bible teaches and supports their views. Listen to some of their statements.

Joseph Goodavage, author of *Astrology: The Space Age Science* and *Write Your Own Horoscope*, says "the Bible is full of" the philosophy of astrology (14:XI).

In his *Astrology of the Old Testament* (p. 10), K. Anderson refers to the Bible as the "greatest of all astrological works" (97:197).

Jeff Mayo, founder of the Mayo School of Astrology in England, remarks, "The Bible is full of astrological references" (3:7).

Nicholas de Vore goes so far as to argue, in his *Encyclopedia of Astrology,* "Either the Christian religion is Astrology, or Astrology is the source of the Christian religion; for there is no conflict between them. Both Old and New Testaments abound in astrological symbology and teachings" (42:VII).

The following are views of the Bible commonly held by astrologers. We have supplied a brief comment after each statement.

1. *The Bible is not the Word of God, but the words of great men of history.* What is forgotten is that the Bible claims repeatedly to be the Word of God (2 Timothy 3:16,17, cf. 330).

2. *The Bible has been corrupted over the years; thus many of its alleged astrological and reincarnation teachings have been deleted.* The same could be said about the teachings of "Martians." Where is the proof that shows such material was once in the Bible?

3. *Parts of the Bible were written "in code" and only astrologers understand that code.* But most scholars still believe it was written in Hebrew and Greek, because the nation of Israel and the early Christians would have had a hard time deciphering a "code."

4. *Because the Bible was written by great men and because it has been so influential throughout history, some of these men must have been astrologers. Astrology itself is so important and influential, it is difficult to believe none of the biblical authors practiced this great art.* (Therefore, various astrologers claim the patriarchs, prophets and even some of the apostles were astrologers!) That is like saying that, because football is so important and influential, in fact, America's number-one sport, it is difficult to believe the patriarchs weren't football players.

Moreover, astrologers approach and read the Bible with the following assumptions (again, we have supplied brief comments):

1. *Obscure (unclear) passages are to be stressed.* But then, since these passages are unclear, it is easy for those who *want* to see astrology in them to do so.

2. *Contrary passages are to be ignored.* But since the Bible clearly rejects astrology, such passages *must* be ignored, falsely reinterpreted, or considered "corrupted."

3. *Every biblical passage that "teaches" astrology is misinterpreted.* But since no Bible passage teaches

astrology, by definition it must be misinterpreted in order to make it teach astrology.

4. *Astrologers are to read between the lines.* For example, they say that even the simple mention of the stars and constellations is deemed "astrological," but just because the Bible describes clouds and wind, do we assume it is speaking about meteorology?

5. *Preference is given to marginal or heretical Christian or Jewish writings over the Bible.* But these writings support not only astrology, but paganism, and heretical philosophies which are incompatible with the Bible.

But now let us consider concrete examples from the Bible itself. In the material below, first, we will quote the passage alleged to teach astrology; second, we will examine the astrologers' claim about the passage; and third, we will give the Christian response to the astrologers' claim. (Note: All references in this section are from the NIV.)*

Genesis 1:14—"And God said, 'Let there be lights in the expanse of the sky to separate the day from the night, and let them serve as signs to mark seasons and days and years....'"

Astrologers teach that the word "signs" here indicates heavenly bodies (planets) given by God as astrological signs. Thus, they claim the Bible is affirming astrology. Some astrologers confidently assert that these "signs" are Pisces, Aries, Gemini, etc.

But in the biblical text, the word "signs" cannot refer to the astrological signs in any sense, for such assertions ignore the context of Genesis 1:14-19 where the word is defined: "...to separate the day from the night, and

---

*The authors would like to thank Dr. Sherman Kanagy of Purdue University for some helpful comments in this section.

... to mark seasons and days and years, and let them be lights in the expanse of the sky to give light on the earth." The words in these verses define the function of the sun and the moon as signs of the passing of day and night. This is why the NIV study note here states that "signs" are not mentioned "in any astrological or other such sense." Moreover, how could Moses, who authored Genesis, teach astrology in Genesis 1 and then condemn it later in Deuteronomy 18 (another book he wrote)? He would be condemning his own teachings!

Genesis 1:16—"God made two great lights—the greater light to govern the day and the lesser light to govern the night. He also made the stars."

Astrologers claim the word "govern" or "rule" means God made the sun and moon to govern or rule over the lives of men, but the meaning of the Bible text is entirely different. God made the sun to govern "the day," not men's lives; He made the moon to govern "the night," not the affairs of men. Govern or rule here means the dominance of the sun during the day, as compared to any other heavenly body—and likewise the moon at night.

In addition, in verses 17 and 18, God says the purpose of the sun, the moon, and the stars is "to give light on the earth, to govern [separate] the day and the night, and to separate light from darkness." Also, Psalm 136:9 indicates the stars help the moon "govern the night," which means "shine in the night." In the context of Genesis 1, no other meaning or other influence is suggested or intended. These passages have no astrological meaning whatsoever.

Genesis 37:9-11—"Then he [Joseph] had another dream, and he told it to his brothers. 'Listen,' he said, 'I had another dream, and this time the sun and moon and eleven stars were bowing down to me.' When he told his father as well as his brothers, his father rebuked him and said, 'What is this dream you had? Will your mother and I and your brothers actually come and bow down to

*the ground before you?' His brothers were jealous of him,
but his father kept the matter in mind."*

Astrologers believe the reference to the sun and the
moon and the 11 stars proves Joseph and his brothers
believed in astrology. Admittedly, these verses do refer
to the sun, moon, and 11 stars, but there is no
indication they have anything to do with astrology, or
even astronomy. The sun, moon, and 11 stars are used
symbolically to refer to Joseph's parents and his brothers.
This is the clear statement of the text itself.

Genesis 49:3-27—Jacob's blessing of his sons.

Here astrologers overzealously identify the 12 sons of
Joseph with the 12 astrological signs. But in doing so,
they add to the text what is not there. Their correlation
of Joseph's sons to the astrological signs is arbitrary and
without basis. Then in typical fashion, astrologers disagree with one another as to which son was related to
which sign.

*Numbers 24:17—"A star will come out of Jacob; a
sceptre will rise out of Israel."*

Astrologers claim the reference to a star coming out of
Jacob proves there was astrological belief in the days of
Moses, but the reference here has nothing to do with
astrology. The word "star" is metaphorical for a person,
the Messiah, who will be a descendant of Jacob. Additional proof of this is that the text says that not only a
star will come out of Jacob, but a sceptre (a ruler) will
rise out of Israel. In other words, the same person who
comes from the line of Jacob will also be a ruler (331).

*Daniel 4:26—"Your kingdom will be restored to you
when you [Nebuchadnezzar] acknowledge that Heaven
rules."*

Astrologers claim that this passage shows that
"Heaven" (the stars and planets) "rules" over (influences) the affairs of men. But this passage teaches no
such thing. The word "Heaven" here is used as a symbol
for God. And Daniel was no astrologer, for he states to

Nebuchadnezzar, *"The God of heaven* has given you dominion and power and might and glory; in your hands he has placed mankind and the beasts of the field and the birds of the air. Wherever they live, he has made you ruler over them all . . ." (Daniel 2:37,38). If it was the God of heaven who gave Nebuchadnezzar dominion over the Babylonian Empire, it could not have been the stars.

Jeremiah 10:2—"Do not learn the ways of the nations or be terrified by signs in the sky, though the nations are terrified by them."

Astrologers claim the phrase "signs in the sky" is an astrological reference. Admittedly, this passage is speaking about astrology; the problem for astrologers is that the passage condemns it. The Bible specifically condemns "the ways of the nations," referring to their astrological practices.

The text also implies the nations were terrified by *literal* signs in the sky, not *symbolic* signs in the astrological charts. The ancients were terrified by eclipses since they thought the moon was being "eaten" by demons. Meteors and comets were also considered portents of evil. But in the Bible God tells His people not to be terrified by such events in the sky because they are merely things that He has made. He is in control over all. The very context of Jeremiah 10 is to exalt the true God over the false idols that men worship, and the superstitious fears (such as astrology) that control their lives.

Job 9:9,10; 38:31-33—"He is the Maker of the Bear and Orion, the Pleiades and the constellations of the south. He performs wonders that cannot be fathomed, miracles that cannot be numbered."

" 'Can you bind the beautiful Pleiades? Can you loose the cords of Orion? Can you bring forth the constellations in their seasons or lead out the Bear with its cubs? Do you know the laws of the heavens? Can you set up God's dominion over the earth?' "

Astrologers claim that the mere mention of the constellations here is evidence that the Bible is teaching astrology. But this is nonsense. Job 9:9,10 refers to God as the Maker of various constellations. The ancient Israelites had limited astronomical knowledge but they were nonetheless aware that God had created the constellations and was in charge of the universe.

In Job 38:31-33, God is speaking to Job, asking if he is powerful or smart enough to know how to "bind the beautiful Pleiades," or "loose the cords of Orion," or "bring forth the constellations in their seasons," etc. This has nothing to do with astrology. God is showing Job's utter impotence in comparison with His almighty power. Job has no control over the constellations, but God does. Job cannot bind them or loose them or bring them forth in their seasons.

God concludes by challenging Job, "Do you know the laws of the heavens? Can you set up God's dominion over the earth?" (38:33). The obvious answer is, "No." Only God has power to control and regulate all the heavens. That is why men are to worship Him. Men are to acknowledge His power and sovereignty rather than question Him over issues too deep for human understanding. God Himself commands people not to worship or seek spiritual advice from the things (e.g., the stars and planets) He has created (Romans 1:15-21).

Judges 5:20—"From the heavens the stars fought, from their courses they fought against Sisera."

Astrologers claim this refers to the influence of the stars on Sisera, the commander of Jabin's army, but to do this, they interpret a poetic or figurative passage literally. These words occur in the "Song of Deborah," which is a poetic victory song describing Israel's victory over her enemies.

In Judges 4:7, God says He will lure Sisera, the commander of Jabin's army, to the Kishon River and give him into the hands of the Israelites. The NIV study note explains:

> With the Israelites encamped on the slopes of Mount Tibor, safe from chariot attack, the Lord's strategy was to draw Sisera into a trap. For the battle site, Sisera cleverly chose the valley of Jezreel along the Kishon River, where his chariot forces would have ample maneuvering space to range the battlefield and attack in numbers from any quarter. But that was his undoing, for he did not know the power of the Lord, who would fight from heaven for Israel with storm and flood (see 5:20-21), as He had done in the days of Joshua (10:11-14). Even in modern times storms have rendered the plain along the Kishon Valley impassible. In April of 1799 the flooded Kishon River aided Napoleon's victory over a Turkish army.

Accordingly, "From the heavens the stars fought, from their courses they fought against Sisera. The river Kishon swept them away, the age-old river, the river Kishon" (Judges 5:20,21), is nothing more than Deborah's poetic way of singing about the powers of the heavens God used to fight in Israel's behalf. There is no reference to astrology in this text. The only way a person can find an astrological reference here is to impose it from outside the biblical text.

Psalm 121:6—"...the sun will not harm you by day, nor the moon by night."

The King James Version says "the moon will not smite you." Astrologers claim this proves the Bible teaches the moon will "smite" some men, and further, that this refers to the moon's alleged influence in crime and insanity. The promise of the sun not harming by day, however, is an obvious reference to the sun's power to naturally burn and dehydrate men. This passage affirms God's protection, not astrological influences.

Verse 5 teaches the Lord watches over His people, that He is their "shade" at their right hand; verses 7 and 8 say, "The Lord will keep you from all harm—he will watch over your life; the Lord will watch over your coming and going both now and forevermore." The references to the sun and the moon are in agreement with the "shade" metaphor, and serve as figures of speech for that which threatens any person (all the distresses of life), day or night.

The words "sun" and "moon" then must be metaphorical for distresses and threatening events in life. The use of the word "sun" for a day would have special meaning to the Israelite who lived in the desert. Since the passage is obviously figurative, there need be no fear of literal harm done by the moon at night or the sun by day.

Isaiah 13:10; Joel 2:31; Luke 21:25—"The stars of heaven and their constellations will not show their light. The rising sun will be darkened and the moon will not give its light."

"The sun will be turned to darkness and the moon to blood before the coming of the great and dreadful day of the Lord."

"There will be signs in the sun, moon and stars. On the earth, nations will be in anguish and perplexity at the roaring and tossing of the sea."

These references to the sun and moon being darkened, not giving their light, and turning to blood are thought by astrologers to prove the people in the Bible believed in astrology. But all of these references refer to the Day of the Lord, the Second Coming of Christ. These events have nothing to do with astrology. If astrologers claim them today, it is obvious that the sun and the moon are not darkened and have not turned to blood. Also, Isaiah 13:7 points out that in that Day of the Lord the stars and constellations will not show their light. Would any astrologer claim this occurs today?

Matthew 2:1-11—"After Jesus was born in Bethlehem in Judea, during the time of King Herod, Magi from the east came to Jerusalem and asked, 'Where is the one who has been born king of the Jews? We saw his star in the east and have come to worship him.'

"When King Herod heard this he was disturbed, and all Jerusalem with him. When he had called together all the people's chief priests and teachers of the law, he asked them where the Christ was to be born. 'In Bethlehem in Judea,' they replied, 'for this is what the prophet has written:

" ' "But you, Bethlehem in the land of Judah, are by no means least among the rulers of Judah; for out of you will come a ruler who will be the shepherd of my people Israel." '

"Then Herod called the Magi secretly and found out from them the exact time the star had appeared. He sent them to Bethlehem and said, 'Go and make a careful search for the child. As soon as you find him, report to me, so that I too may go and worship him.'

"After they had heard the king, they went on their way, and the star they had seen in the east went ahead of them until it stopped over the place where the child was. When they saw the star, they were overjoyed. On coming to the house, they saw the child with his mother Mary, and they bowed down and worshiped him."

Astrologers claim this is proof of astrology in the Bible, but a careful examination of this passage reveals:

1) The star actually moved because it preceded the Magi.
2) In some unknown manner the star was able to indicate the exact place Jesus and His parents were staying.
3) The star apparently was lost from sight for a period of time, and then became visible again.

4) The star seems to have been visible only for the Magi, as apparently no one else noticed it (including Herod and the religious leaders in Jerusalem).

The evidence shows this was not a normal star but a miracle from God to guide and direct the Magi to Jesus. This was a temporary phenomenon and seems to have had no other purpose than stated. Certainly it had no astrological meaning.

Astrologers have claimed the Magi were astrologers, but this conclusion is not substantiated by many scholars. The fact that these men are mentioned favorably and that God deals with them especially in relationship to His Son indicates it is more certain that they were *not* astrologers. The term "magi" originally referred to a group of Medes who were Zoroastrian priests for the Persians (69:59). Zoroastrianism, originally a mono-theistic religion, possibly had Judaistic influences.

The term "magi" primarily means "wise men" and astrology was part of the practice and interest of some "wise men." Examples of such men who did use astrology include the "magicians" in Pharaoh's court (Exodus 7:11) and the wise men in the court of King Nebuchad-nezzar (Daniel 2:2ff.). In these instances, the Bible accurately records that some people who did not know or follow God did practice astrology.

But the Bible also is clear that not all "wise men" were astrologers. A clear example is Daniel (see discussion below), a godly man promoted to the inner circle of the counselors to the king. The Scriptures indicate, "In every matter of wisdom and understanding about which the king questioned them, he found them [Daniel and his friends] ten times better than all the magicians and enchanters in his whole kingdom" (Daniel 1:20).

Like Daniel, it is possible that the Magi who followed the star to Bethlehem were themselves Jews who had remained in Bablylon after the captivity, and they, as seekers after truth, had attained a high station. As Jews, they would not only have been acquainted with the biblical prohibitions against astrology, but also with the biblical messianic prophecies concerning the coming "King of the Jews."* Their scripturally based faith in God would thus have provided them a "context" for the miraculous phenomena which they followed to the place where Jesus was.

But it is also possible that the Magi were Gentiles. Even as Gentiles, the Magi could have learned about the coming Jewish Messiah through the influence of Daniel, who lived in Babylon in the sixth century B.C. Daniel's influence was so great that King Nebuchadnezzar sent out at least two proclamations to the entire known world, commanding that all men honor Daniel's God. The king even declared that Daniel's God was the supreme God (Daniel 3:28–4:3,34-37).

Because of Daniel's influence, many people, perhaps thousands, probably believed in the God of Daniel and in the Jewish Scriptures. The Magi of Christ's time may have been descendants of such peoples, or may have been following a tradition kept alive from the time of Daniel. What is clear is that these men are not condemned as astrologers or as pagan unbelievers. In fact, the Scriptures relate that they worshiped Jesus when they found Him. Nothing in this passage in Matthew condones or approves the practice of astrology.

The Book of Daniel

Astrologers often say the Book of Daniel is proof of God's acceptance of astrology because God made Daniel

---

*See the authors' *The Case for Jesus the Messiah: Incredible Prophecies that Prove God Exists* (331).

the head of the astrologers and magicians in Babylon (Daniel 2:48). They also assert that because Daniel was the head of all the Babylonian "wise" men, he was proficient in astrology. After all, Babylon was widely known for its astrological practices.

But this is not true. First, the biblical account of Daniel explicitly attributes all of Daniel's success to God alone, not to his alleged practice of astrology or to the stars (Daniel 1:17; 2:27,28; 4:17,18). Second, Daniel was a godly man who, according to his own testimony, abhorred the idolatrous and evil practices of Babylon (Daniel 1:8; 4:27). Third, it is unthinkable that God would have permitted Daniel to engage in the very practices He condemned and for which the nation itself was now in judgment (astrology, idolatry, etc.). Fourth, proof that Daniel did not embrace astrology can be seen from the fact that he constantly compared the failures of the Babylonian astrologers with the true knowledge given by God.

So, far from endorsing astrology, Daniel rejected it and pointed men to the one true God. The entire Book of Daniel reveals and stands against the uselessness of astrology. It shows astrologers to have a failure rate of 100 percent when compared with the words of the one true God (Daniel 2:27,28; 4:7; 5:7-9,12,13,17).

In the Book of Daniel, God is the One who is sovereign. When the Babylonian kings turned to the stars for advice and ignored God, they encountered trouble. For example, in Daniel 5 God pronounces judgment upon the Babylonian ruler's son, Belshazzar: "But you his son, O Belshazzar, have not humbled yourself, though you knew all this. Instead, you have set yourself up against the Lord of heaven.... You praised the [astrological] gods ... which cannot see or hear or understand. But you did not honor the God who holds in his hand your life and all your ways" (Daniel 5:22,23).

When divine glory and power are ascribed to the heavens and not to the God who made the heavens, God says they have "exchanged the truth of God for a lie, and worshiped and served created things rather than the Creator—who is forever praised" (Romans 1:25). Astrology is one reason why God's judgment comes. It comes because men ignore Him and suppress the truth. The apostle Paul wrote,

> The wrath of God is being revealed from heaven against all the godlessness and wickedness of men who suppress the truth by their wickedness, since what may be known about God is plain to them, because God has made it plain to them. For since the creation of the world God's invisible qualities—his eternal power and divine nature—have been clearly seen, being understood from what has been made, so that men are without excuse.
>
> For although they knew God, they neither glorified Him as God nor gave thanks to him, but their thinking became futile and their foolish hearts were darkened. Although they claimed to be wise, they became fools and exchanged the glory of the immortal God [for false idols] (Romans 1:18-23).

This passage shows the very practice of astrology, a form of idoloatry, is already under divine judgment—"But God turned away [from them] and gave them over to the worship of the heavenly bodies" (Acts 7:42).

Astrology is rejected in the Bible because it 1) is futile and worthless, 2) constitutes involvement with occult powers, and 3) is a form of idolatry (exchanging the heavens for God). Astrology is seen to have no power to save men from their sins, instead it opens men to demonic deception, and robs God of the glory that is due Him.

Here are a number of biblical passages that prove God clearly and strongly condemns astrology. (Note: In several of the Scriptures below, the pagan gods Molech, Astarte [the Asherah pole], and Baal were associated with worship of the heavens and with human sacrifice.)

Leviticus 18:21—"Do not give any of your children to be sacrificed to Molech, for you must not profane the name of your God. I am the Lord."

Leviticus 20:1-6—"The Lord said to Moses, 'Say to the Israelites: "Any Israelite or any alien living in Israel who gives any of his children to Molech must be put to death.... I will set my face against that man and I will cut him off from his people; for by giving his children to Molech, he has defiled my sanctuary and profaned my holy name.... I will set my face against the person who turns to mediums and spiritists to prostitute himself by following them, and I will cut him off from his people." '"

Deuteronomy 4:19—"And when you look up to the sky and see the sun, the moon and the stars—all the heavenly array—do not be enticed into bowing down to them and worshiping things the Lord your God has apportioned to all the nations under heaven."

Deuteronomy 17:2-5—"If a man or woman living among you in one of the towns the Lord gives you is found doing evil in the eyes of the Lord your God in violation of his covenant, and contrary to my command has worshiped other gods, bowing down to them or to the sun or the moon or the stars of the sky, and this has been brought to your attention, then you must investigate it thoroughly. If it is true and it has been proved that this detestable thing has been done in Israel, take the man or woman who has done this evil deed to your city gate and stone that person to death."

Deuteronomy 18:9-11—"When you enter the land the Lord your God is giving you, do not learn to imitate the detestable ways of the nations there. Let no one be found among you who sacrifices his son or daughter in the fire, who practices divination [astrology is divination] or sorcery, interprets omens, engages in witchcraft, or casts spells, or who is a medium or spiritist or who consults the dead."

2 Kings 17:16—"They forsook all the commands of the Lord their God and made for themselves two idols cast in the shape of calves, and an Asherah pole. They bowed down to all the starry hosts, and they worshiped Baal."

2 Kings 21:3-6—"He rebuilt the high places his father Hezekiah had destroyed; he also erected altars to Baal and made an Asherah pole, as Ahab king of Israel had done. He bowed down to all the starry hosts and worshiped them. He built altars in the temple of the Lord, of which the Lord had said, 'In Jerusalem I will put my Name.' In both courts of the temple of the Lord, he built altars to all the starry hosts. He sacrificed his own son in the fire, practiced sorcery and divination, and consulted mediums and spiritists. He did much evil in the eyes of the Lord, provoking him to anger."

2 Kings 23:4,5—"The king ordered Hilkiah the high priest, the priests next in rank and the doorkeepers to remove from the temple of the Lord all the articles made for Baal and Asherah and all the starry hosts. He burned them outside Jerusalem in the fields of the Kidron Valley and took the ashes to Bethel. He did away with the pagan priests appointed by the kings of Judah to burn incense on the high places of the towns of Judah and on those around Jerusalem—those who burned incense to Baal, to the sun and moon, to the constellations and to all the starry hosts."

2 Kings 23:24—"Furthermore, Josiah got rid of the mediums and spiritists, the household gods, the idols and all the other detestable things seen in Judah and Jerusalem. This he did to fulfill the requirements of the law...."

Jeremiah 7:18—"The children gather wood, the fathers light the fire, and the women knead the dough and make cakes of bread for the Queen of Heaven [a feminine deity, probably related to star worship]. They pour out drink offerings to other gods to provoke me to anger" (cf. Jeremiah 44:17-25).

Jeremiah 8:1,2—"At that time, declares the Lord, the bones of the kings and officials of Judah, the bones of the priests and prophets, and the bones of the people of Jerusalem will be removed from their graves. They will be exposed to the sun and the moon and all the stars of the heavens, which they have loved and served and which they have followed and consulted and worshiped. They will not be gathered up or buried, but will be like refuse lying on the ground."

Jeremiah 19:13—"The houses in Jerusalem and those of the kings of Judah will be defiled like this place, Topheth—all the houses where they burned incense on the roofs to all the starry hosts and poured out drink offerings to other gods."

Ezekiel 8:10,11,16—"So I went in and looked, and I saw portrayed all over the walls all kinds of crawling things and detestable animals [possibly a reference to Zodiac creatures] and all the idols of the house of Israel. In front of them stood seventy elders of the house of Israel, and Jaazaniah son of Shaphan was standing among them.... Between the portico and the altar, were about twenty-five men. With their backs toward the temple of the Lord and their faces toward the east, they were bowing down to the sun in the east."

Amos 5:25,26—"Did you bring me sacrifices and offerings forty years in the desert, O house of Israel? You have lifted up the shrine of your king, the pedestal of your idols, the star of your god—which you made for yourselves."

Zephaniah 1:4-6—"I will stretch out my hand against Judah and against all who live in Jerusalem. I will cut off from this place every remnant of Baal, the names of the pagan and the idolatrous priests—those who bow down on the housetops to worship the starry host, those who bow down and swear by the Lord and who also swear by Molech, those who turn back from following the Lord and neither seek the Lord nor inquire of him."

Acts 7:42—"But God turned away and gave them over to the worship of the heavenly bodies. This agrees with what is written in the book of the prophets: 'Did you bring me sacrifices and offerings forty years in the desert, O house of Israel?' "

1 Corinthians 10:20—"No, but the sacrifices of pagans are offered to demons, not to God, and I do not want you to be participants with demons."

Galatians 5:19-21—"The acts of the sinful nature are obvious: sexual immorality, impurity and debauchery; idolatry and witchcraft; hatred, discord, jealously, fits of rage, selfish ambition, dissensions, factions and envy; drunkenness, orgies, and the like. I warn you, as I did before, that those who live like this will not inherit the kingdom of God."

Colossians 2:8,20—"See to it that no one takes you captive through hollow and deceptive philosophy, which depends on human tradition and the basic principles of this world rather than on Christ.... Since you died with Christ to the basic principles of this world, why, as though you still belonged to it, do you submit to its rules?"

We can see that the Bible clearly condemns astrology as not only a futile and worthless activity, but as an activity so evil that its very presence precipitates God's judgment.

Throughout Old Testament history, divine judgment fell upon Israel and Judah often as a result of their astrological and other idolatrous practices. This was because, as both a philosophy and practice, astrology rejects the truth concerning the living God. Instead of leading people to God, it led them to dead objects, the stars and planets. Moreover, just as the Bible mocks idols, the Bible mocks astrologers and their practice (Isaiah 47:13).

The assessment of Drs. Bjornstad and Johnson is correct: "Absolutely NO scriptural passage supports astrology, although several indicate awareness of its existence and that of the accompanying astral worship. Moreover, not a single reference even indicates tolerance of this art" (69:43).

The usual response of astrologers to such biblical passages is that certainly God condemns *worshiping* the stars, as that would be idolatry, but astrologers do not advocate worshiping the stars; rather, they are simply taking advantage of the help and information God has made available through the stars.

Honestly, though, isn't the practice of astrology really worshipful behavior that should be considered as idolatrous behavior? In considering Exodus 20 (the Ten Commandments), astrology violates the first two commandments: "You shall have no other gods before me," and, "You shall not bow down to them or worship ["serve," NAS] them."

Throughout history, some astrologers have actually bowed down to the stars and worshiped them. Even today this occurs in various non-Western nations. But those astrologers who do not literally bow down before the stars nevertheless do "serve" them, and this is specifically a violation of the second commandment.

By definition, worship includes religious devotion and reverence for an object, whether living or dead. Many astrologers believe the universe *is* living—it is divine. The stars and planets are revered as part of the larger universe which itself is believed to be one with God. The alleged power of the stars and planets over human lives evokes feelings of religious awe and devotion. These special objects in the sky (the stars and the planets) are, in one sense, also served by the astrologers. To serve means "to perform duties for, to give obedience and reverent honor to, to wait upon." All astrologers serve the heavens in this manner. That is, the positions of the stars are dutifully recorded and the information derived from them is carefully analyzed and religiously obeyed. The heavens are honored for their power as the obedient astrologer waits upon their advice.

But in addition to all of this, there are three primary reasons that the Scriptures oppose astrology. First, the Bible explicitly rejects astrology by name. In Isaiah 47:13,14, God declares:

> All the counsel you have received has only worn you out! Let your astrologers come forward, those stargazers who make predictions month by month, let them save you from what is coming upon you. Surely they are like stubble; the fire will burn them up. They cannot even save themselves....

Here God condemns the counsel of the Babylonian astrologers because it accomplishes nothing and only wears out people physically. Then, God says the astrologers' predictions based on the stars will not save the people from what is coming: God's divine judgment. Finally, He says the counsel of the astrologers cannot even save the astrologers themselves.

The second biblical reason astrology is rejected is because God forbids occult practices. Astrology is basically the occult practice called "divination," defined by *Webster's New Collegiate Dictionary* (1961) as "the act or practice of foreseeing or foretelling future events or discovering hidden knowledge." This is exactly what astrology does. It foretells future events or uncovers hidden influences by the stars. In *Webster's New World Dictionary* (1962), divination is defined as "the art or practice of trying to foretell the future or the unknown by occult means."

God strongly condemns divination as evil, as an abomination, and says it leads to contact with evil spirits called demons (Deuteronomy 18:9-13; 1 Corinthians 10:20).

The third reason the Bible rejects astrology is because it leads people to transfer allegiance from the infinite God of the universe to the things He has made. This is like seeking advice from, and ascribing all the credit, honor, and glory to, a masterpiece of art, while forgetting the great artist who made it. Who would seek advice from a painting of Rembrandt or Picasso, when they could talk to the master himself? Yet those who seek advice from the stars routinely do this with God, though He is infinitely more worthy of honor than men, the God who "made heaven and earth" and in whose hands is their very life's breath (Genesis 1:1; Daniel 5:22,23).

10

Are Astrology and Christian Doctrine Compatible?

We have seen that astrologers have misinterpreted most Bible passages "proving" astrology, and that the Bible does not support or advocate astrology; rather, it strongly condemns it. It therefore is logical to conclude that Christian doctrine is not compatible with astrology. In this chapter, therefore, we shall see that whenever astrology confronts Christianity, the end result is astrology always reinterprets and rewrites Christian doctrine, or rejects it as a "lower" form of spirituality (144:22).

Astrology has not been content to just misinterpret individual verses; it has tried to reinterpret the entire Christian faith into an occultic spirituality. This is evident in the "esoteric astrology" of Alice Bailey's Lucius Trust (55), Rudolph Steiner's anthroposophical teachings (332), as well as other astrological views proposing a new, occult, and pagan Christianity (23:20; 12:359-60; 92:1; 93:11,39,106; 144:20-21; 151:13-19, etc.).

But when astrology has reinterpreted Christianity,

all that remains is a system of occult teaching that utilizes a thin veneer of Christian words. For example, if "the Bible is written in code" (162), then it is the astrologer who provides the proper "code" for correctly interpreting it. The results of such interpretation are anything but Christian.

In addition, astrologers believe Christian history must also be rewritten to conform to astrological and occult beliefs. Professional astrologer Terry Warneke claims, "Original Christianity had reincarnation built into it" (168). Jesus is viewed as a master teacher of occult wisdom who taught that within men existed that which would save them (162; 120:XXIV)—a direct contradiction of Jesus' real teachings (Mark 7:20-23; John 5:24; 6:29,39,40).

Astrology today perceives the Christian faith as an inferior faith largely because it is a *theological* faith. Some astrologers are teaching that the "god that can be known is not God" (120:4), and "God is not interested in theology" (120:54).

Moreover, some astrologers are suggesting that the Christian faith is inferior, that it is a perverted and harmful faith. Here are two examples taken from astrology books advocating this:

> It is the creed of a crucified and dead Christ which rules Christianity and not that of the risen Master [the occult Christ]. One of the reasons for this travesty of the truth [is] ...Saint Paul [who was] potently under Martian influence and was born in Scorpio [and therefore slanted] Christian teaching into channels of teaching which its Founder never intended.... Saint Paul misinterpreted... the New Testament message (55:213,215).

> These are the individuals who hide behind a puritanical shell, and then proceed to betray

those who follow them. These natives are heavily involved in religion and philosophy that betters humankind. They preach the love of God and humanity and pray for others continually; however, they create prejudices, ignorance, guilt and fear behind their puritanical sermons. They follow all the rituals of their religion or philosophy and condemn all those who do not accept their faith (129:83).

Further, astrology today considers Christianity to be a harmful religion because of its insistence on teaching that Christ is the only way to God. Astrologers are offended when Christians engage in evangelistic activity to bring this good news to the world. Astrologers believe:

All religions are but roads to the same Place. It is only when people say "my road is the *only* road" that the pathway to the Place becomes blocked (2:84).

The negative manifestation of this evolutionary condition is what I call the "Billy Graham archetype"—the need to convert others to one's own point of view. In a delusive way this need is called teaching but it is really indoctrination....The stated goal of Christianity has been to "convert" those of other religions to the Christian faith. Thus we have missionaries (131:168).

Astrology and God

Astrologer Barbara Clow goes so far as to say that the biblical God is a demon god. She believes we may now "choose our freedom without the interference" from such gods (130:24). Former AFA vice president, Edward

Doane, described the Christian God as an invention of men, and claimed the biblical teaching on God was "a lot of poppycock" (143:69, cf. pp. 9, 17). One influential astrology text teaches "the Father, Son and Holy Ghost are [the pagan gods] Isis, Horus and Osirus" (142:36).

Many astrologers agree with the principle of "the Fatherhood of God and the Brotherhood of man" (143:57). For them, being atheist, Hindu, Buddhist, or Moslem, or holding to almost any other view of God, is not a problem. As long as a person is open to astrology, astrologers do not care what that person believes about God. But astrologers usually oppose anyone believing in a God who defines certain actions and deeds as wrong or sinful. Obviously, they oppose anyone who believes in a God who condemns the practice of astrology.

Finally, like the majority of people in our world, astrologers do not accept the view of our Lord Jesus Christ, "No one comes to the Father except through me" (John 14:6). In other words, astrologers usually do not believe that Jesus is the Savior of the world, the only One who can forgive sins (John 3:16; 5:24; 6:47; Acts 4:12; 1 Timothy 2:5,6).

Many astrologers define God in such a way that their belief easily blends with an occult view of the world. God is seen as a divine power, and in some sense all life and all nature are seen as divine (7:130,136)—a religious belief called "pantheism" (God is all and all is God).

Astrologer and witch Sybil Leek writes, "God is in everyone," including nature. She sees no conflict between her view of God and her use of astrology as a major means of witchcraft (149:19,202).

Another astrologer has expressed his belief that astrology is an "affirmation of the Divine order in the universe" which enables one "to align oneself with the energies of Nature" and realize that the "planets are our sources of energy..." (22:348-49). Others believe that true astrologers are spiritually oriented "healers" who know that they are "only the channel through which the Power [inherent in creation] flows" (36:275-76).

Unfortunately, for astrologers who look to the creation for divine wisdom, "nature" often becomes a smoke screen (a disguised world view) that allows spirits or demons to provide occult answers and power to them. This occult power includes personal revelations, the ability of the astrologer to give startlingly true information to a client by looking at the horoscope. But when astrologers give this kind of information, they are emulating spiritists who give information to people through the power of their spirit guides. (See chapters 14-15.)

The following are brief statements about God made by astrologers. Astrologer-occultist Thomas Burgoyne refers to "the one great occult fact, viz.: *The Divine Oneness of Life*" (142:10). Astrologer Mae Wilson-Ludlam states, "Nothing in the universe is independent or separate because of the One Life pervading all. The life within a Tibetan is the same life within an American, or a plant, or an animal" (151:3). Other astrologers teach, "God dwells in you as You" (120:73); "... nature herself, [is] God ..." (125:83); "God is life itself" (151:122); "...*everything, everything is God!*" (120:xviii).

So, astrologers have redefined God as nature and in the process made Him impersonal energy. Once God is interpreted as impersonal energy, He becomes indistinguishable from occult energies in general. Astrologers and occultists claim to use these energies to develop psychically, or to achieve "higher consciousness" (e.g., 137).

Astrologers claim:

> Just as the planet is evolving, so are we, and astrology gives insight into the evolutionary cycles of the individual and collective [reality]. Astrology is a language of symbolism based on Nature. To align oneself with the energies of

Nature facilitates growth, change, and trust
in evolution as an ongoing rhythmical process
(22:348-49).

Such statements are indistinguishable from the philosophy of spiritism and witchcraft.

According to astrology, God never created and nurtured us, the universe did. It is the universe we must look to for help. Weingarten believes, "It is the *total* state of the solar system at the moment you are born that indicates your personality characteristics" (5:29), and, "...the events of life are 'programmed' more or less in a given sequence. If you were born at a different time, even a few seconds early or later, than each event would occur at a different time and different events would unfold" (5:76).

To summarize, astrology has rejected God for His creation, and has abandoned the idea of a personal creator. Therefore, men are no longer responsible to God, but only to themselves and to some impersonal force. Astrology has rejected the biblical teaching about God and adopted an occultic view that gives to the creation the glory due to God alone. As Robert Morey has said, "It is idolatry to ascribe to the stars that which belongs *only* to the God who created them" (70:54).

Astrology and Jesus Christ

Astrology accepts every view of Jesus Christ except the view that Jesus taught. Astrologers typically adopt an occultic view of Christ (for example, that Jesus was a man who evolved into God through self-perfection and reincarnation, and that "Christ" is our "higher self").

Leading astrologer and spiritist Alice Bailey taught that Christ "achieved [his own] divinity" (55:315). Ronald Davison, "England's foremost living astrologer" and editor of *The Astrologers Quarterly* since 1959, says about Christ, "The story of the most perfect Being who ever incarnated on earth tells of the ultimate sacrifice on the cross . . . for the purpose of paying off any remaining debts [karma] of his own to the past . . ." (9:94). Note that this prestigious astrologer believes Jesus was just another spirit who was reincarnated on the earth. and that His death on the cross was necessary for paying the price of His own "sins" (karma), not ours.

Marcus Allen, another professional astrologer who defends an occult view of Christ, says Christ is now "everyone's higher occult self," and further declares:

> Christ had all seven ancient planets . . . all conjunct in Pisces . . . so he was the supreme, the ultimate Pisces . . . and so he initiated the Age of Pisces which is now coming to an end with the dawning of the Age of Aquarius, which is initiated by the second coming of the Christ Life within *all* of us. . . . In the Age of Aquarius, everyone is the Avatar [God], everyone is tuned into their higher self . . . (137:117).

What Allen believes is that Jesus Christ was the supreme illustration of the Piscean temperament or personality. However, since the Age of Pisces is now passing and the Age of Aquarius is started, the Second Coming of Christ is supposedly the beginning of a period of higher "consciousness" for all men, leading them to realization of their own divinity.

In other words, this professional astrologer has determined that Christ through His "return" is really the beginning of the emerging occult consciousness of all humanity.

But none of these views are taught in the Bible. The Scriptures clearly teach that Jesus Christ is fully man and fully God in one Person. He is the only begotten Son of God and Savior of the world, who will return someday, physically and visibly, to the earth (Matthew 24:1-35; John 1:1; 3:16; 10:30; Acts 1:11). Astrology and Christianity are not compatible in their teachings about who Jesus Christ is.

Astrology, Salvation, and the Death of Christ

The basic belief of astrologers concerning salvation is that man is his own savior. Astrology in general rejects the atonement of Christ and proclaims a "salvation" based on the realization that "all is One," i.e., that man is already one with God or the universe.

When astrology does refer to Christ or to His salvation, it reinterprets it in astrological (non-Christian) terms. For example, professional astrologer Irene Diamond boldly teaches that "being born again" is rebirth "into a heavenly state of consciousness" that can unashamedly state, "I am God" (74:15; 162).

Joan Hodgson is founder of the spiritistic White Eagle School of Astrology. She insists that Jesus, as many other great men of history, was a "God-man" who helped men to realize that they are one with God. "These God-men...demonstrate the spiritual power and perfection which every soul will in due time learn to manifest, for the seed of this God-power is hidden within every human being" (94:13).

It is not uncommon to find influential astrologers instructing their followers that salvation lies within, that to "bring forth the Christ [spiritual perfection] in every man is the ultimate goal of humanity. Astrology charts the path" (23:20); "...humanity as a whole IS the Messiah..." (2:25); and "the transforming power of Christ-consciousness lies in the...power of the heart" (136:192).

Since astrology teaches that man is his own savior, it should be no surprise that astrology rejects the atonement of Christ. Astrologers must deny that Christ is the only Savior of the world if they are to maintain their own beliefs. Proof of this is Edward Doane, a former AFA vice president (160:46), who admits, "...there is no vicarious atonement...[this is] a philosophy which advocates [an] escapist method of using a scapegoat [for salvation]..." (143:45).

Professional astrologer Jane Evans is also not reluctant to disagree with Christian beliefs. She confesses:

> I have always felt that the Church erred in stressing the crucifixion of Jesus Christ as a historical happening...and [teaching the] vicarious atonement, all of which have caused so much trouble and confusion in the ensuing centuries. It obscured the deeper meaning of the cross symbol, which is the crucifixion of the spirit, i.e., every soul is "crucified" in matter for evolutionary purposes and is his own savior, not just one man [Jesus] in one point of time (140:140-41).

Thomas Burgoyne, a spiritist and early founder of The Church of Light (200:4-5), a leading astrological and occult society, refers to "the path of Christ (Truth) which leads up to salvation; [but] not [by] a vicarious atonement, but gaining [salvation by personal effort]" (142:82).

Astrologer-occultist Louise Huber accuses Christians of selfishness and naiveté which has resulted in their believing and teaching the idea that Christ is the only Redeemer and Savior. She writes:

> Thus in the Christian age in particular the belief has arisen that redemption may be attained through the vicarious sacrifice of one who has borne the burden of the sins of others. Many think that it is merely necessary to

believe in the Redeemer showing personal
devotion to him and to pray to him in order to
achieve in this way redemption and to be
accepted into paradise. This is a naive idea of
the true nature of the Redeemer (136:228).

A leading astrologer and Jungian psychologist thinks
the concept of New Testament salvation preached by
Paul was really "Christ or Krishna consciousness." This,
she believes, is what Jung refers to when he speaks of
"the process of individuation" (140:42).

Most astrologers believe man's main problem is that
he is out of harmony with the divine forces of the universe, and must become united with this harmony.
Therefore, for many astrologers, salvation is not forgiveness from sin (most astrologers do not believe in sin in
the biblical sense) but rather an enlightenment as to the
underlying divine pattern they assume governs the universe.

"Salvation" for them is awareness of the powerful
effect of these celestial patterns and incorporation of
them into one's life. Many astrologers believe that
"higher consciousness," which is supposedly a joining of
man with the divine evolutionary "impulse," will eventually bring a mystical Oneness with ultimate reality.

Astrologer Dane Rudhyar argues that anyone who
accepts astrology "...learns to identify his consciousness and will with the 'celestial' patterns and rhythms."
A person "becomes one with the principles of universal
order, which many call 'God' " (7:8). Rudhyar assumes
astrology provides "the path to our immortality" through
our diligent effort and cooperation with nature, because
"...man has everything he needs WITHIN HIMSELF—
as potential, as divine seed. All he has to do is TO USE
IT." This occult process is falsely termed "divine grace"
(7:113,135,138).

Obviously, astrology is a system of self-salvation

based upon personal merit and worth, not upon faith in Christ's atoning death on the cross. For example, within their view of salvation, a belief in reincarnation is necessary for most astrologers because, "one lifetime could never be enough to reach perfection" (23:21). Thus we are told, "Each soul is an independent entity working out its own salvation..." (143:68). Reincarnation is the view that over many lifetimes a person will eventually evolve back into the state of his original oneness with God. Astrology is believed to be a guide and a tool to enlighten a person during each lifetime so he will avoid adding more karma. This in turn will hasten the day when he will fully attain his true divine nature.

The incompatibility between astrology and Christian doctrine is evident when astrologers caution not to look to the biblical Jesus Christ for salvation. A former AFA vice president sternly warns, "... so long as you depend upon something or someone outside of yourself [e.g., the Christian God] to be the supreme authority in anything...you will fail to make progress and fail to develop and realize the vast potentials in your Divine Self. Authority equals stagnation" (143:93-94).

The Bible completely rejects such teachings, maintaining that we are rebellious creatures who willfully ignore God and disobey Him. Salvation is a free gift that delivers us from God's wrath against our sin. It is based on our believing Christ died for us and personally asking Him to appropriate His free gift of salvation to us (John 3:16; Romans 5:1-10; Ephesians 1:7; 2:8,9; 1 Peter 2:24).

Astrology and Man

Astrology teaches that man's basic problem is not realizing he is part of God, for man controls his own fate. All that is needed is for "astrology [to] give the evolutionary keys, and act as a guiding body of light to lead man to his rightful power of total control over his own destiny" (56:back cover).

Louise Huber has written, "I am That." What she is referring to is the Hindu belief that she and all men are God [Brahman, or absolute consciousness] in their true natures (136:103). Other astrologers teach men are evolving into gods:

> Each man has ingrained in his higher consciousness a part of the word as set down in the gospel of John. "In the beginning was the Word, and the Word was with God, and the Word was God."... We are, as all else is in the universe, but thought forms of the Absolute [God] ... (56:6,59).

> God lives in you as you (120:7).

> Few of mankind have as yet realized that they are a god.... Like God, man is eternally creating through utilizing his creative powers of thought.... Like God, he is a ruler and creator within his own lesser sphere ... (143:42).

At the 50th Anniversary (1988) AFA Convention in Las Vegas, Nevada, astrologers repeatedly expressed the belief that they were God. In all of the classes we attended, as well as in all of the personal conversations we had with dozens of astrologers, this was the common view.

In one class, taught by spiritist and professional astrologer Irene Diamond, the entire class was led through a chant in which they repeated, "I am God, I am God, I am God." The class was titled, "Let's talk about God" (which really meant, "Let's talk about ourselves").

Diamond, who claims to be a Catholic, taught, "I know who I am, and I am God." Pointing to the audience she emphasized, "I am looking at God" and "I have found God." As to her being God, she assured listeners she had "researched it, created it, tested it and proven it!" (162).

Psychotherapist-astrologer Capel McCutcheon explained, in his seminar on "Esoteric Astrology," that every person was God, but they were God at different levels (164).

In her class entitled, "Can I Rise Above My Chart?" psychic and current first vice president of the AFA, Maxine Taylor, declared, "Who we are is God in an earthbound body," and, "you are God... why not create?" (167).

Astrologer Terry Warneke, in his class entitled, "The Archetype of Planets," spoke confidently of "the God within" all men. He admitted that astrology had given him a belief in God in a pantheistic (everything is God) sense (168).

But the Bible rejects astrology's view. The Bible teaches that man is the creation of God, not God Himself, and is in a fallen condition, separated from God. Man needs to realize his condition and turn to the one true God for mercy and salvation.

The Bible strongly warns, "Stop trusting in man, who has but a breath in his nostrils. Of what account is he?" (Isaiah 2:22).

Jeremiah wrote:

> This is what the Lord says: "Cursed is the one who trusts in man, who depends on flesh for his strength and whose heart turns away from the Lord. He will be like a bush in the wastelands.... But blessed is the man who trusts in the Lord, whose confidence is in him. He will be like a tree planted by the water ..." (Jeremiah 17:5-8).

Likewise, the Bible strongly condemns those who teach they are "God" or "a god." Such men are said to be opposing God and preparing the way for their own judgment:

> In the pride of your heart you say, "I am a god; I sit on the throne of a god...." But you

> are man and not a god, though you think you
> are as wise as a god.... Your heart has grown
> proud.... Will you then say, "I am a god," in
> the presence of those who kill you? (Ezekiel
> 28:2,5,9).

Astrology and Life After Death

Seventy-five to 80 percent of all astrologers believe in reincarnation (10:12). That being the case, death is assumed to be merely a transition for man, bringing him to a higher state of existence. Death is therefore something good, something to be looked forward to.

One astrologer expressed his conviction this way: "... death is no more than the change into another state of consciousness in which new life presses toward unfoldment" (136:229). Another has written, "Death is a fulfillment one step closer to perfection" (151:18). Or, as another astrologer has said, "There is no death!" (143:126).

Reincarnation can be proven to be an extremely consequential philosophy. Reincarnation provides a seemingly "logical" justification for many individual and social evils, including occult practices, religious intolerance and persecution, divorce, abortion, etc. (307).

But astrology's belief in reincarnation only places one more nail in a coffin already six feet under. An astrology that believes in reincarnation must chart the "path" of the soul, not just the current personality. The difficulties raised by this are insoluble.

In *Astrology and Past Lives,* Mary Devlin admits, "There are no hard-and-fast rules regarding astrology and reincarnation; and, unfortunately, it is not always easy to read karmic implications in a person's chart" (92:3). That is an understatement! Stephen Arroyo correctly concludes that once an astrologer accepts the belief and implications of reincarnation, "all of the traditional labels, meanings, and interpretations of event-oriented astrology are turned inside out" (135:xiii).

In addition, the belief in reincarnation typically leads the astrologer into other occult philosophies. For example, "Many of today's astrologers move into the world of Theosophy due to its doctrine of reincarnation..." (56:6).

By the same token, astrology has rejected the biblical teaching of divine judgment and eternal punishment in hell, saying: "...man has invented...hell. He has also invented a devil..." (143:69, cf. Matthew 25:46; Revelation 20:10-15).

In conclusion, we have now compared the beliefs of astrology and traditional Christian teachings. Astrology contradicts virtually every major tenet of the Christian faith.

11

Astrology and the Occult

"*Astrology is the key that opens the door to all occult knowledge*" (142:1).

—Thomas Burgoyne
Astrologer and occultist

The Occult: An Introduction

In a televised debate (October 1988) with two professional astrologers from the American Federation of Astrologers, Dr. Weldon briefly defined the occult as "any involvement with demonic activity."

Maxine Taylor, the first vice president of the AFA, was quick to respond, "*That's* not astrology!" But as we shall see, that *is* astrology.

Ms. Taylor's difficulty in equating astrology and demonism is common to all astrologers. Indeed, it is a difficulty faced by most people in our modern Western culture, for there is simply very little awareness or understanding about the reality of the demonic realm (190–197). One reason is that most of what is really demonic activity and power has been *redefined*. Today, astrologers and others label occult activity as new "human potential" or as divine activity, but not that which deals with the demonic realm.

Most people probably consider the demonic as an extremely small part of a much larger occultic realm. They limit the demonic to a few things such as Satanism, black witchcraft and black magic (white witchcraft and magic are put in another category), voodoo, etc.

But the fact is that the demonic realm covers a vast expanse of territory. To illustrate, imagine a golf ball on a football field. The golf ball represents what most people think of as "demonic activity." Yet the entire football field actually encompasses true demonic activity.

The word "occult" is defined by *Webster's Third New International Dictionary* as "of, relating to, or dealing in matters regarded as involving the action or influence of supernatural agencies or some secret knowledge of them" (p. 1560).

The occult has been with man from the beginning, for it was the true "father" of the occult, Satan, who presented to our first parents three basic lies that still form part of the foundation of occultism today. They are: 1) "You shall not die"; 2) "You shall be like God, knowing good and evil"; and 3) "Has God said?"—planting doubt in man's mind about something God had clearly stated.

In these three lies the devil promised Adam and Eve a self-achieved or self-induced personal immortality ("You shall not die"), forbidden power ("You shall be like God"), and forbidden knowledge (knowing evil—"good *and* evil").

Not much has changed since then. Throughout history, the essence of occultism in its myriad forms has remained the same. It still comprises the acquisition of forbidden supernatural power and knowledge via occult technique to enable the individual to realize the supposed truths about good and evil and to increasingly gain an alleged mastery over creation through functioning as a "god in embryo," as an evolving deity. From Eastern religions to mind science cults, from magic to witchcraft the alluring promise is the same: With the proper knowledge you can discover the secret power that will allow you to unravel latent divinity inside of yourself and become like God.

The essence of occult involvement includes three related and supernaturally derived experiences. First, the *reception of secret knowledge*—information normally unavailable through the five senses. Second, the *contacting of the spirit world* in various forms and at various levels. And third, the *acquisition of power* to manipulate or control the creation, animate or inanimate. Whether a person perceives it or not, these three experiences cannot successfully be achieved without the supernatural.

But the realm of the supernatural, particularly the idea of the *satanic*, is scoffed at today. That is why those embarrassed by the accusations of supernatural have tried to redefine these three categories into more "natural," more "normal," more acceptable terms.

In the first occult experience we listed, it is now supposed that occult knowledge originates within men (called the "higher mind," etc.), rather than from demonic revelation.

In the second experience, which is contact with the spirit world, this is now perceived as man tapping into his own unconscious powers, archetypes, inner self, inner advisers, etc.—anything but the evil personal beings the Bible refers to as demons.

In the third experience, the acquiring of psychic powers is now presumed to result from "latent human potential" available to all men, not something produced in conjunction with demonic power. In this way, those who have difficulty accepting the concept of a real supernatural, can still frequent the occult by merely redefining every experience in human or naturalistic terms (195: 273-89,319-99).

In a similar fashion, those removing the label of "evil" from demonic activity are now attributing this activity to God Himself. Today, occult knowledge has been redefined as divine revelation; contact with the spirit world has been redefined as contact with benevolent spirits (saints, angels); and the use of occult powers has been redefined as the use of divine power. Nonetheless, for those willing to examine the evidence surrounding occult phenomena, neither the genuinely supernatural nor the truly evil nature of the occult can be denied (189–197; 300; 309).

From a biblical perspective, the source and motivation behind occult activity is very clear. The vast amount of occult evidence, exhibiting endless hostility toward God and Jesus Christ, speaks volumes. The antagonistic nature of occult spirits to biblical revelation suggests that the entire occult realm lies under the domain of the fallen angels (demons) and their leader, Satan.

The Bible exposes the goals of Satan and his demons as part of a plan to oppose God, to deceive men, and to build a rebellious kingdom. Scripture teaches that Satan does have a kingdom (Matthew 12:26) and even refers to him as the "god" of this world (2 Corinthians 4:4, Revelation 12:9).

The Bible discloses that Satan is the mastermind behind the occult realm (1 Corinthians 10:20; 2 Corinthians 11:11-14; 2 Thessalonians 2:9). Yet, in spite of his great power exercised everywhere by his angels in occultism, judgment and disaster will ultimately fall upon Satan and his angels as well as those who disregard God's warnings about occult involvement (Isaiah 47:8-15; Deuteronomy 18:9-12; Revelation 12:9; 20:3-15).

In occultism, we find a partnership of cosmic and human rebellion—two classes of created beings (fallen angels and fallen men) who continue to assert their sovereignty against God's. Dr. Ronald Enroth, a sociologist at Westmont College states:

> The ultimate objective of psychic/occult power is to validate the lie of Satan—that man is God and that death is an illusion. In the deceptive quest for godhood and power, men and women are brought under the power of Satan himself. They are able to manifest a degree of counterfeit power by engaging in occult experiences. Such paranormal manifestations represent an imitation of authentic spirituality and demonstrate Satan's true nature as the arch deceiver (217:788).

The occult world comprises a sizable number of practices and phenomena. Below is a brief and selected listing of relevant illustrations.

General Occult Categories

Magic
Witchcraft
Sorcery
Voodoo
Satanism
Spiritism
Divination
Astrology
Necromancy
Shamanism

Occult Related

Parapsychology
Mysticism
Holistic health
Meditation [Eastern & Western occult traditions]
Yoga
Visualization
Hypnotism

Occult Practices

Seances
Magic ritual, spells, curses, charms
Various "automatisms" (writing, typing, dictation, painting, etc.)
Astral travel
Psychometry/ radionics
Psychic diagnosis/ healing/surgery
Water dowsing (323)
Pendulums
Crystal-gazing
Ouija board
Tarot cards
I Ching

Occult Phenomena	Occult Religions
Ectoplasmic manifestations	(Almost all major religions and cults are occultic to one degree or another.)
Materializations/ apparitions	
Telepathy	
Telekinesis	Rosicrucianism
Apportation	Scientology
Clairvoyance/clairaudience	Theosophy
Poltergeists	The Church
Trance	Universal and
Spirit possession	Triumphant
Psychic transference of power	The Association for Research and
Levitation	Enlightenment
Polyglot mediumship	(Edgar Cayce)
Altered states of consciousness	Silva Mind Control
	Astara
Spirit guides, fairies, nature spirits, UFO entities, ascended masters	Eckankar
	Children of God
	Anthroposophy
	Mormonism
Precognition	"New Age"
Reincarnation phenomena	Movement
Most near-death experiences	
UFO experiences	

Astrology employs all three of the principal occult experiences mentioned earlier—secret knowledge, spiritism, and power to manipulate or control the creation. Astrologer Jeff Green acknowledges, "Astrology is an aspect of the metaphysical [occult] tradition known as the Ancient [secret] Wisdom" (131:XIX). Astrologers Zipporah Dobyns and William Wrobel affirm that secret knowledge and power are both inherent aspects of astrology:

> Astrology is highly pragmatic.... Our expanded knowledge will also help us to better *predict and control* future experiences and to produce more satisfying experiences for ourselves and our world.... Astrology, numerology,

palmistry and graphology are pragmatic tools
of divination which serve as lights or "cosmic
lanterns" along the path of unfoldment....
Here astrology and other *gnostic* tools can be
invaluable aids, but any system of unfoldment
can apply to the principle of power-bestowing
knowledge.... The psychic sciences or *gnostic*
tools, as well as all other exploratory techniques, serve as entry doors to unfoldment,
personal development and knowledge. It is the
knowledge of your power: the power of your
consciousness creating effect and form (appearance).... Ultimately, as mystics tell, it is the
knowledge of Consciousness (God, macrocosm) manifesting as you (human being, microcosm), the energy of which you direct as you
freely choose (146:2,184-85, first and third
emphases added).

Astrology also conforms to another characteristic of
the occult in its fundamental hostility to biblical truth
(see chapter 10). The very essence of the occult is the
assertion of human sovereignty against divine sovereignty, man's will against the will of the one true God.
Occultism incites fallen man's pride to further rebel
against his Creator—in refusing to accept his own crea-
turehood, God's rightful rule over men, and in exalting
one's own divinity in the face of God. It is not surprising
that occult practice invariably brings people into contact
with like-minded entities.

Astrology and the Occult

Astrology is related to the occult in four major ways.
First, astrology is defined as an occult art (Webster's
Dictionary). Accordingly, astrology employs the occult
practice of divination. We may define this as "the art of

obtaining secret or illegitimate knowledge of the future by methods unsanctioned by and at variance with the holiness of God" (192:119) and which involves contact with evil spirits. Significantly, many astrologers admit to spirit contact (298–299).

Second, astrology appears to work best when the astrologer himself is psychically sensitive, what most astrologers term "intuitive" (43:16-18).

Third, prolonged use of astrology often leads to the development of psychic abilities. This was admitted by the majority of astrologers we interviewed (299).

Fourth, due to its history and very nature, astrology often becomes the introductory course to a wider spectrum of occult practices.

In spite of these occult connections, modern astrology, as we have seen, wishes to be considered a science. Time and again, we are told that astrology has nothing to do with the occult. For example, influential astrologer Carroll Righter "feels strongly that astrology should not be considered [part of] the occult" (255). Because of his practice as an astrologer, he even "regards himself as a scientist..." (255).

Another well-known astrologer, Charles E. O. Carter, asserts, "Astrology does not involve any form of psychism..." (28:14). And practicing astrologer Colette Michaan argues, "Astrology is magical only in the sense that insight is magical" (22:350).

These statements echo the pronouncements of parapsychologists who similarly claim that when they study psychics and mediums they are only studying "natural" and "normal" human powers, nothing occult, supernatural, or spiritistic (cf. 195). But such claims are false, whether made by parapsychologists or astrologers. Astrologers, wishing to be seen as truly scientific, obviously do not want to admit their craft is part of the occult.

So, is there evidence that astrology is by nature part of the occult? To begin with, there are historic ties between the rise of astrology on the one hand and the corresponding turning to the occult on the other. It can also be shown that where there has also been a rise in the occult, there has also been a corresponding turning to astrology.

One example is Helena P. Blavatsky, a medium and a virulent antagonist of Christianity, who founded one of the most influential occultic movements in modern Western culture, known as the Theosophical Society. Astrologers West and Toonder wrote of her influence, "It is to Mme. Blavatsky and the Theosophical Movement she founded that astrology owes its revival..." (12:107-08). (In fact, Theosophy and two other occult societies— modern Rosicrucianism and Rudolph Steiner's Anthroposophy—are responsible for America's renewed passion for astrology in the twentieth century.)

It is an open fact that most occultists today use astrology, and many astrologers practice other occult arts. For example, astrologer Daniel Logan admits he is involved with mediums and spirits (256:63-66,169-70); astrologer Marcus Allen is involved with a spirit guide and studies such esoteric disciplines as yoga, Zen, Tibetan Buddhism, and the Western magical traditions (137:2-6).

Both astrologers and occultists openly admit astrology is a pillar of occultism. In *A Manual of Occultism,* prominent astrologer Walter Gorn Old ("Sepharial") states, "The astrologic art is held to be the key to all the occult sciences" (257:3). Even famous "black occultist" Aleister Crowley was an avid believer in astrology (160:74-75; 313).

In her book, *My Life in Astrology,* witch Sybil Leek testifies, "Astrology is my science, witchcraft is my religion..." (149:11). She calls the horoscope "a magical document," and believes astrology is "a vital tool" for using magic, relating its connection to numerology, phrenology, palmistry, and witchcraft (149:12,19,31,48).

In *An ABC of Witchcraft Past and Present,* witch Doreen Valiente observes, "Astrology.... is another of the fundamentals of magic. It is studied by witch and magician alike" (147:21). Valiente reveals:

> [When] a witch wants to select an herb to use for a magical purpose, she has to use one whose astrological rulership is correct for the work in hand.... the Moon rules psychic things, and an herb of the Moon, mudwort, ... is used to make an infusion or tea which many believe is an aid to clairvoyance (147:23).

Many astrologers have also acknowledged that astrology is an occult practice. For example, the practice of "humanistic" or "transpersonal" astrology combines astrology with Eastern philosophy, the occult, and Jungian psychology. Theosophist Dane Rudhyar, the leader in this field, writes, "The astrologer has authority as one who deals understandingly and effectively with ... the occult." He also says "astrology is threshold [meaning occult] knowledge" (7:21).

Henry Weingarten, director of the National Astrological Society in New York, and author of the multivolume series, *The Study of Astrology,* has concluded that astrology is related to palmistry, numerology, and Tarot cards. He testifies that "almost all occultists use astrological timing [the best time as set by astrology] in their work ..." (33:77). But he adds, "Most astrologers are not occultists," thus allowing his philosophical "slip" to show. The plain fact is, astrologers have traditionally advised other occultists concerning the best time to practice their craft. In sixteenth- and seventeenth-century England we discover:

The links between magic, astrology and witchcraft were both intellectual and practical. On the intellectual level, astrology provided a coherent justification for geomancy, palmistry, physiognomy and similar activities. "All these skills of divination are rooted and grounded upon astrology," declared Cornelius Agrippa. By postulating correspondences between the heavenly bodies and earthly substances, the palmist and physiognomist assigned different parts of the face or hand to different signs of the Zodiac. Geomancy employed the 12 astrological houses and, according to the leading textbook on the subject, was "none other thing but astrology." Alchemy also divided up the metals between the planets. ... *The astrological choice of times was important, not only for alchemical operations, but also for the ritual gathering of magical herbs and the conjuration of spirits* (46:631-32, emphasis added).

This interaction continues today. A former astrologer told us how this process could work: "An astrologer would want to determine which sign or nativity structure would lend to a person being capable of mediumistic experiences, and would want to elect the most favorable time for that kind of [spirit] contact..." (205:4-5).

Astrologer Jane Evans, refers to one particular astrological combination that supposedly indicated in past history when people's receptivity to spirit contact was opportune. She writes, "This conjunction [of Uranus-Neptune] indicating a union of positive intuition and receptive mediumship was frequently found in the charts of those who were adult when the spiritualistic [spiritistic] movement began after 1846" (140:178).

Not only do many astrologers, and virtually all occultists, admit that astrology is part of the occult, but so do objective scholars who have studied the subject. Richard Cavendish, the main editor of the 24-volume encyclopedia, *Man, Myth and Magic,* and also of the *Encyclopedia of the Unexplained: Magic, Occultism and Parapsychology,* was educated at Oxford University and considered a leading authority on the history of magic and occultism. In *The Black Arts* he expressed his own conviction that "astrology is essentially a magical art.... astrological considerations have always been extremely important in magic. ... some magical textbooks classify the 'spirits' ... in terms of their planetary affiliations" (145:219, 222,225).

In his definitive study of sixteenth- and seventeenth-century English occultism, *Religion and the Decline of Magic,* Oxford-educated historian Keith Thomas also documents the strong intellectual and practical links between magic, divination, astrology, and witchcraft (46:631-40). He shows that much of occultism is actually undergirded by an astrological world view, and documents that some medieval astrologers claimed to get their knowledge of astrology from the spirit world. One example he mentions was a spirit named Bifrons that made men "wonderfully cunning" in the subject of astrology (46:634).

In *Astrology Disproved,* engineer and science writer Lawrence Jerome maintains that of the occult "sciences," astrology appears most scientific, but is really "nothing more than a magical system for controlling others" (102:225). He concludes, "Astrology, then, has played a major role in all the magical 'sciences,' alchemy, black magic, the conjuring of spirits, necromancy, and even in the simpler magical practices such as the use of talismans" (102:76).

Historian and philosopher, Dr. John Warwick Montgomery, discovered that astrology is "found virtually everywhere occultism is to be found" (72:96).

Other scholars believe that among certain people, astrology provides a logical connection for a conversion to the occult practice of Satanism. Sociologist Edward J. Moody explains there is a certain psychological need for control and power in many whom (because of their disposition) he classifies as "pre-Satanists." He shows how this need naturally finds its expression first in astrology, then logically progresses into Satanism which provides a "more powerful means of control" of one's fate. Notice Moody's frightening conclusion: "... those who eventually become Satanists usually have begun with astrology ..." (133: 362-63).

The evidence shows that no matter where we find astrology—geographically or historically—we also find occultism. These facts incriminate astrologers *as* occultists, no matter how loudly and sincerely they may deny it.

From the Latin *Matheseos Libri VIII* (the Eight Books of the Mathesis, i.e., theory of astrology) by Firmicus Maternus (A.D. 334), the final and most complete work on astrology of the classical world, to William Lilly's classic 1647 text, *Christian Astrology,* one will find astrology mixed with paganism in abundance.

In 1854, the first American text on astrology was written by Dr. Carl Roback, president of the Astrological College of Sweden. In *The Mysteries of Astrology and the Wonders of Magic: A History of the Rise and Progress of Astrology and the Various Branches of Necromancy,* he discussed his involvement with numerous forms of nineteenth-century American occultism:

> At the age of fourteen I began diligently to apply myself to the study of the liberal and occult sciences, devoting especial attention to Astronomy, Mathematics, Geometry, Astrology, Geomancy, Physiognomy, Phrenology, and every species of Magic. The investigations

I then commenced were continued for 17 years, during which I visited various parts of Europe, Asia and Africa, for the purpose of perfecting myself in magical science, and practicing the arts of Divination, for which my family had so long been famous.... In America, *I have cast not less than thirty eight thousand nativities* [birth charts], and have given audience to more than two hundred thousand applicants for magical information.... My occult powers ...have been employed to heal the sick, cheer the desponding, foretell peril, and suggest the means of escaping it, detect crime, aid faithful lovers, make friends of foes, [etc.]... (199:XI, XIII, emphasis added).

Roback also expressed his conviction that there is a "hereditary predisposition" in the transferring of the occultic powers involving astrology. This hereditary transference leads to the horoscope being "readily interpreted by those who possess the requisite occult knowledge, and those peculiar natural or supernatural gifts which are transmitted from generation to generation in the families of astrologers and magicians..." (199:79).

In *The Psychic Yellow Pages* (1977), 17 of 31 astrologers willingly admitted they were interested in the occult. Of these, some were psychic and others had studied under occult teachers (138: 109-44). The occult activities these astrologers were involved in included: Tarot cards, occult/Eastern meditation, psychic development, kundalini yoga, mandalas, past life hypnotic regression, numerology, palmistry, crystal work, alchemy, holistic health practices, and altered states of consciousness. Their teachers included occultists Alice Bailey, Edgar Cayce, H. P. Blavatsky, and others.

While attending the 1988 American Federation of Astrologers Convention in Las Vegas, Nevada, we examined over 300 astrology texts on display and found occult philosophy or practice in almost all of them. (In the convention program, dozens of advertisements for occultic practices and services were offered by professional astrologers [161].)

From the same program, consider the following brief listing of classes offered by professional astrologers at the convention, and the listing of astrologers who were on record as practicing other occult arts:

CLASSES OFFERED BY ASTROLOGERS

"Astrology/Palmistry—Clues to Counseling"

"New Age and Astrology"

"The Crystal and Astrology"

"Esoteric Astrology"

"American Indian Astrology"

"Astrology and the Chakras"

"Yogananda—Spiritual Pioneer/New Awareness"

"Astrology and Spiritual [occult] Healing"

"Past Lives and Major Aspects"

"Astrological Rule Over Tarot Cards"

"Astro Physiognomy"

"The Goddess and You"

"Astrology, Tarot and Alchemical Process"

"Ancient Astrology—Afterlife Traditions"

"Transcendental Astrology"

PROFESSIONAL ASTROLOGERS AND OTHER OCCULT INTERESTS

Rene Anderson—medium, psychic healer, Tarotologist

Bonnie Armstrong—palmist

P. M. H. Atwater—numerologist, rune caster

Brett Bravo—psychic

Stacey Dean—psychic healer

Arlene de Angelus—medium, healer

Narendra Desai—palmist, numerologist

Robert Donath—Theosophist and Mason

Wendy Hawks—occultist, Zen practitioner

Joy Kate Kajan-Basile—psychic healer

Frank Kegan—I Ching diviner

Glenn Malac—witch

Randall Leonard—crystal healer

Joan Fitzworth—hermetician

The AFA publishes *Astrological Pioneers of America* (1988), documenting that many leaders in astrology today, including many presidents, vice presidents, and officers of the AFA, are clearly occultists. Past and present leaders who are identified as occultists are also termed "pioneers of astrology" (160).

As examples from that text, consider the following persons, all of whom have exerted a significant to profound effect within modern astrology:

Evangeline Adams practiced palmistry and was for a time an associate of the infamous black occultist, Aleister Crowley (p. 2).

Elbert Benjamine ("C. C. Zain") was a spiritist and past president of the spiritistic Church of Light and channeler of its lessons (p. 13).

Doris Chase Doane, leading American astrologer and spiritist, is the current AFA president. She admits to being a Tarot reader, psychic, and past secretary, editor or instructor in the Church of Light for 30 years (pp. 44-45, cf. 166).

Howard Duff, former AFA president, was a Rosicrucian and member of the Church of Light (pp. 48-49).

Ernest A. Grant, "the single most important figure" in AFA history, an AFA founder, was a Rosicrucian and Mason (p. 63).

Max Heindel, is an admitted spiritist and founder of The Occultic *Rosicrucian Fellowship* (p. 75).

Marc Edmund Jones, vice president of the Astrologers Guild of America, occultist, spiritist, was founder of Sabian Astrology (pp. 88-90).

Charles E. O. Carter, the "dean of British astrologers," was president of the Astrological Lodge of the occultic Theosophical Society (p. 176).

Ronald Davison, editor of the *Astrological Quarterly,* succeeded Carter as president of the Astrological Lodge of the Theosophical Society (p. 182).

Brigadier Roy Firebrace was an occultist and leading authority on sidereal astrology (p. 186).

Alan Leo, "the most famous and influential of the modern English astrologers," was a devoted Theosophist and founder of the magazine, *Modern Astrology* (pp. 200-02).

Richard Morrison ("Zadkiel"), a famous English astrologer, was a spiritist and crystal gazer (pp. 210-12).

Walter Old ("Sepharial"), a member of H. P. Blavatsky's "Inner Group," was a Cabalist and numerologist.

Many other individuals in *Astrological Pioneers of America* are also listed as graduates of "The Church of Light," itself an official affiliate of the AFA (160:13). This spiritistic organization offers 21 courses (210 lessons) on astrology and occultism, dictated (channeled) by the spirits through C. C. Zain (200/143:22,116,120), and grouped into three basic categories, each with seven courses: 1) Astrology, 2) Alchemy, and 3) Magic.

Under Alchemy, the courses offered include "Occultism Applied" and "Cosmic Alchemy." Under the category of Magic we find courses such as "Laws of Occultism,"

"Esoteric Psychology," "The Next Life" (reincarnation), "The Sacred Tarot," "Divination," "Imponderable Forces," and "Ancient Masonry" (201).

In light of the content of AFA's literature, it is surprising to find that the stated "aims and objectives" of the AFA are: "To clarify astrology ... *as a science* ... for professional use ... to give astrology the prestige and standing to which it is entitled *as a science*" (210, emphasis added).

But who would claim that the above courses and activities are science, or even touch on being scientific in any sense? Only astrologers.

The evidence reveals astrology is an occult art. In fact, few occult practices are so widespread and powerful in America today as astrology. Astrology is the most publicly accepted occult practice, and perhaps no other activity today provides an introduction to occultism so easily. Astrologers' claims that their craft has no associations to the occult are misleading, for astrology is an occult practice that bears great responsibility for the spread of the occult in our society. Thus, "While astrologers today will strenuously object to the inclusion [of astrology] with the other occult 'sciences,' there can be no doubt that belief in astrology has greatly aided and spread the more esoteric forms of occult magic..." (102:172).

12

Making Astrology "Work"

Astrologers claim no need to examine the scientific evidence for the simple reason they *know* astrology works. They contend that if the scientific evidence disproves astrology, yet astrology works, then there must be something wrong with the scientific evidence. For this reason alone, astrologers such as Edith Custer have remarked, "Whether the scientific world accepts or rejects astrology makes it no less a valid tool for me to work with.... I know it works and I am satisfied with that" (172:176).

But astrologers everywhere admit they don't know *why* it works. One such psychiatrist and astrologer, Harry Darling, M.D., concedes that the horary astrologer "often tells you ... he doesn't quite know how he gets his results" (95:V). At the 1988 AFA Convention, professional astrologers privately disclosed to us, "Any astrologer who tells you they can explain how it [astrology] works is lying. No one knows how it works."

Understanding how and why astrology works, however,

will enable us to answer the question of whether or not astrology *should* be practiced. (In the modern world few people would eat, drink, or use any product whose ingredients were unknown—even if it worked for some people.) And what if the reason astrology "works" has nothing to do with astrology itself?

Astrological "data" must be explained by known astrological facts or theories that have been proven true. But if no astrological theories have been proven to be true, then there can be no astrology. And there can be no demonstrable astrological truth that explains why it "works."

In the next four chapters, we will approach the crucial question, "Does astrology work?," and show why astrology *seems* to work, and why it *really* works. We will show that the real reasons astrology seems to work are the very reasons why people should avoid it like the plague.

It was P. T. Barnum who once said, "There is a sucker born every minute." The task of the con artist is relatively easy; all he has to do is be convincing. Truth need not enter the picture. Given human nature, a smart con man can always fool some of the people some of the time.

Today, there are con artists who rake in millions of dollars a year from land, gold, and other swindles. These men all claim their schemes will work legitimately, but they really work illegitimately. Once a "good" con job is invented, it may continue as long as the real reasons for its working are never discovered.

There exist other fraudulent practices, however, that work almost indefinitely because the truth about their "effectiveness" is never discovered, yet the practice claims to meet the endless needs of human nature. Astrology is one of these practices. It claims to meet a wide range of psychological needs that, given the human condition, will never be exhausted (such as the need for self-esteem, friendship, ultimate meaning, etc.).

Below we cite three illustrations that prove astrology need not be true in order to work. Theoretically, the combination of elements in these three illustrations covers every basic claim promoted by astrology. These illustrations are given in order of increasing absurdity to amplify our point. It should be obvious that these three practices all offer the exact same claims and proofs as astrology.

Astrology and Phrenology

Phrenology, which promised character could be analyzed by the shape of the head, was more popular in the 1830s and 1840s than astrology is today. The practice was based on particular assumptions which, like astrology, claimed to be scientific, and also claimed ability to read a person's character or future from the brain development—as revealed by the shape of the head.

Like astrology, phrenology had sufficient complexity to fascinate people and was related to similar arts such as physiognomy (a diagnosis made by reading the body, especially the lines of the face) and metoposcopy (the judgment of a person's character by the features of the forehead). Phrenology included analyzing a person's character and, like astrology, it encouraged self-assessment on the basis of its principles. It also encouraged people to strive for inner harmony with the world. As such, it appealed both to the average person and the intelligent—as does astrology.

Phrenology developed a vast literature that vigorously attacked every criticism, and it flourished because, like astrology, phrenologists claimed it "worked." Phrenology was believed to work because it had great antiquity and durability, and because many scholars said they believed in it. These claims led many to believe

it was true, and it was further substantiated by supposed observation and "proven research" (172:177-78).
Though it all sounded good, nevertheless phrenology
was a fiction.

Character is not determined by the shape of the head,
nor its bumps, nor can the future be divined by examining the bumps on someone's head. Today no one believes
in or practices phrenology—except for a few astrologers
(113)! Nevertheless, multitudes once accepted it, and
they did so for the very same reasons that millions of
people now accept astrology.

Most astrologers believe that the phrenologists were
wrong, so why then do astrologers never consider they
might also be wrong? For the very reasons the phrenologists never did. Phrenologists were satisfied because
their art "worked," their clients were happy, they made
money, and they had power over their clients. All objections therefore seemed irrelevant.

Interestingly, the Chinese divine the very same things
astrologers do, except they use *birds* rather than stars
and planets. They suppose that a bird's color, behavior,
flight, and sounds all have special meanings (57:16).

Ancient peoples such as the Greeks and Romans performed divination by interpreting bones, the liver, en-
trails, smoke patterns, the rustling of leaves, the shapes
of tortoise shells, or the movement of sacred animals—
as well as unusual occurrences. The term for this kind of
divination is "augury."

Moreover, there was divination by interpreting significance from the movement of liquids in a vessel, the
pecking behavior of sacred chickens, and the flight of ar-
rows. Astrology, which is divination by the use of stars
and planets, is only one of hundreds of forms of divination used throughout history.

In fact hardly any phenomena in nature has not, at
some period, been used by people anxious to know their
future or the future of others (318:648). But perhaps one

of the most novel forms of divination of recent date is the "science" of earology.

Astrology and Earology

Earology is the invention of a Hindu, J. K. Karmakar. Having researched his "science" for 30 years, he claims to be the world's leading authority on the subject (88:36). Karmakar thought the world would be impressed to know he had enough credibility to "deliver a lecture on earology in London on the 28th of August, 1980" (88:93) and so he expounded on the importance of this in his book. He is now the director of the Research Institute of Earology in Calcutta. His other claim to fame is his authoritative text, *Earology*.

This "science," like astrology and phrenology, divines things, but earology uses the human ears. Following are ten similarities between earology and astrology (nine of these characteristics also perfectly fit the debunked practice of phrenology).

1. *Earology and astrology each claim to utilize the knowledge of other sciences.* Karmakar boldly asserts:

> Earology is a new discipline of science. ...The students of earology have to acquire sound knowledge of the science of ear. They should have sound knowledge of human physiology. They have to study various books on "ear" published so far. They have to develop the power of observation and analysis.... an earologist should not forget that it is in an accurate science, as astrology is.... The earologist should also understand human psychology (88:24-25).

2. *Earology, like astrology, is complex and detailed.* Each claims to provide "the capacity to determine an

individual's character" (88:85) by studying certain objects (in earology, the ears; in astrology, the stars and planets). As Karmakar explains:

> It may more precisely be reckoned as an applied science, based on the study of external morphological features of human ear.... There exists positive associations between the expressed character variations of external ear and the nature, quality and content of human traits. The scope of the subject is rather enormous and far-reaching (88:36).

Earology utilizes complex scientific language:

> The carnial surface of the auricle presents elevations which correspond to the depressions on its lateral surface, and after which they are named, e.g., eminentia conchae, eminentia triangularis, etc... (88:37-38).

Karmakar explains that at least two dozen morphological and metric measurements must be understood (88:39-40), and details the fact that the ear itself is plotted on a chart with 40 distinct divisions. Just like the astrological horoscope, the ear is divided into 12 main parts. Each of these parts is supposed to have at least a dozen possible combinations offering different meanings.

In addition, several possible physical characteristics require an interpretation from the earologist. According to Karmakar, the ear lobe has 27 possible combinations relating to its thickness, curvature, etc. Like the astrological "house," the ear lobe is assumed to represent departments of life: "The lobule relates to all earthly affairs, like success, failure, to barriers, obstacles, etc...." (88:56).

3. *Earology and astrology each offer glowing testimonies that it works.* One satisfied customer testified of earology, "Whatever has been predicted to me and my family members by Mr. Karmakar, after thoroughly seeing the ears, it has become 100 percent fact and true [sic]" (88:86).

4. *Earology, like astrology, claims to provide all the knowledge and wisdom necessary for complete accuracy.* "Actually everything is found in the ear. An earologist has the confidence in his science. There is no scope for mistakes and pitfalls in the science of earology" (88:26).

5. *Earology, like astrology, claims to have great significance.* "An earologist can be of immense help in the administration of a state or a business. He can profitably help the administration in the selection of the personnel by means of examining their ears" (88:26).

6. *Historically, earology, like astrology, has been fatalistic* (although most astrologers today say the stars impel but do not compel), because the physical shape of the ear determines one's fate.

> [The] Earologist boldly proclaims that fate is inevitable, and that no amount of human endeavor can modify or nullify it. It is simply foolishness to say that the course of fate can be altered by the exercise of free will. An earologist firmly believes that fate reigns supreme in human life (88:26-27).

7. *Earology, like astrology, claims to give psychological insight.*

> The study of this subject will help the curious and energetic readers to get the idea of one's aptitude, adaptability, personality, and other psychological factors which influence human activities and achievement (88:24).

8. *Earology, like astrology, claims it can be combined with other sciences, such as medical diagnosis (88:44).* Karmakar insists it "will undoubtedly benefit astrology and futurology" (88:90).

9. *Earology, like astrology, claims it can accurately predict the past, present, and future.* Says Karmakar, "With the help of this science it is possible to depict a vivid picture of one's past, present and future life" (88:24).

Here is an example:

> If the lobe is thin and straight the native will have to pass [experience] a very curse [cursed] life. From morning to night he has to work hard for his livelihood. He does not get a peaceful hour in his lifetime. Sometimes his mental position turns bad. The native will suffer from blood oozing diseases from time to time. He has to suffer a long period of his life from intestinal troubles (88:59).

10. *Earology, like astrology, argues its case despite the evidence.* "To be a successful earologist one should be able to argue, to convince and to establish the correctness of the predictions" (88:25).

Here is Karmakar's prescription for success in earology: One must accept failures, be discreet, not offend others, follow many different methods—and know some astrology. He should not be over-confident but calm. He should apply correct principles and not exaggerate facts "and thereby invite trouble" (88:25).

As its chief proponent, Karmakar believes earology to be the solution to the world's problems—just as head bumps, birds, and tortoise shells are all purported to contain the same great power that the astrological planets and signs contain.

Astrology and Itemology:
Planets, Signs, Houses—and Spoons?

Itemology does not exist in reality. It is the view that one can plot the locations of common household objects or children's toys as they move in their "orbits" about the house, just as an astrologer can plot the stars and planets on his chart. Also, if itemology were employed among the gullible, it would have the same rate of success as any other method of divination.

One could develop a set of very complex theories and interrelationships said to exist among household items: tables, chairs, beds, knives, forks, spoons, spatulas, etc. One would note their spatial relationship to the cupboard, refrigerator, fireplace, etc., carefully plotting angular relationships, times of placement, etc.

Kitchen towels could be said to have a "good aspect" when found on their rack, but an "evil aspect" when found on the floor. The ringing of the telephone could have many symbolic meanings or portents. If the butcher's knife were found in the TV room at 8:00 P.M. on December 13, it would mean the person must exert care the next day to avoid an accident. The relationships between various objects in the refrigerator, such as the mayonnaise and pickle relish, or the lettuce and rhubarb, would undoubtedly be significant in their shelf life, food values, combination with other foods, etc. If the peanut butter were found next to the pickles, this could signify intestinal troubles.

Children's toys could be labeled as having a beneficent (good) influence when found in one part of the house, or a malefic (bad) influence when found somewhere else. If Ken and Barbie were found unaspected in the hallway, this could indicate a significant relationship would soon develop.

In a similar manner, each room in the house (as with an astrological house) could represent a different "department" of life. The living room could represent finances; the TV room, entertainment; the bedroom, sex and procreation; the bathroom, health; the garage, vocational aptitude; etc. Thus, whenever the dog or other object crossed from the kitchen to the dining room and into the TV den, it would magically relate to a certain department of life.

Like the astrological chart, the stationary backdrop of all this activity (the house floor or the yard) could be used to carefully plot the actual and potential consequence of the moving objects in relationship to one another.

The point to all this is that any set of imaginary factors and theories can be developed into a complex set of rules and "meanings"—and they will all "work" in a certain number of cases. Phrenology examined bumps on the head and foretold all sorts of things. Geomancy examined meaningless combinations of dots and did the same (199:86-87). Earology predicted character and destiny. These and hundreds of other divinatory arts all "worked." That they were falsehoods was irrelevant.

The simple truth is that astrology also is false. It only *appears* more valid because of its claimed association with astronomy. It lives off astronomy and yet denies the very life of astronomy, thus making the relationship parasitic.

Few would really believe that ear size or shape, head size or shape, or the movements of objects around a house in the course of a day, year in and year out, could really foretell the future. But millions believe that the movements of planets around the sun foretell the future. It is true the planets invoke awe, are powerful and mysterious, and that we have no control over them. But this gives them no necessary control over us.

13

Psychological Factors That Make Astrology "Work"

Astrologers continue to insist that astrology works for more reasons than those we have already stated. Therefore, in this chapter we will examine psychological factors that make it work. Still, after we have examined all of these categories, we shall see that it is not astrology that works but something else. Therefore, it is dangerous.

1. *Astrology seems to work because clients want it to work.* No believer in astrology wants his faith in astrology shaken, so he looks for ways to confirm astrology. Common coincidences become astrological confirmation for him. Chance events become imbued with cosmic meanings.

Clients often read relevance and "meaning" into a chart even when it is not there. For example, a person may accept general or vague statements as applying uniquely to him when they would apply equally well to most other people. People who believe astrology often fall into the trap of self-fulfilling prophecy. This takes

185

place when seeds are planted in the person's mind by the astrologer (for an example, see chapter 16), and resultantly the client "arranges" or permits the events to be fulfilled. If the astrologer's words are positive, as they often are, this provides all the more incentive to fulfill the prophecy. Given a poor self-image, pessimism, or a fatalistic outlook on life, even the negative prophecies of the astrologer can become positive when they are self-fulfilling.

Whether the astrologer's words are positive or negative, in neither case is the astrologer successful. The client himself has fulfilled the astrological prediction.

Richard Nolle concedes that astrologers can take advantage of most clients' faith in astrology—"Most people who come to an astrologer want the astrologer to succeed in reading their charts. They are therefore generally sympathetic and cooperative" (84:83).

But what do astrologers and their clients do when the astrological information does not come true, or worse, is contradicted? They tend to remember the things supportive of astrology, while ignoring or rationalizing the rest. For the most part, someone who desires to believe in astrology will not listen to criticism because of the strong emotional investment he has made in astrology. That is why even basic commonsense advice, wholly unrelated to astrology, will be seen as evidence of astrological "truth."

2. *Astrology seems to work because it satisfies the human need for friendship, personal security, or dependence on others.* Given the fact of psychological needs and insecurities that all people experience, astrology can prey upon every person's need for certainty about the future and control of one's life. Many people use astrology as escapism; they ask astrologers for advice, thus letting someone or *something* else (the stars) make the important or painful decisions for them. They prefer

to depend on another's advice rather than living independently.

Other people are just lonely or insecure and desire the friendship of someone who seems privy to cosmic or divine wisdom. They attain a feeling of importance from association with someone of such importance. They are attracted to the astrologer more than to astrology itself.

3. *Astrology seems to work because it can help justify wrong behavior.* Astrology is without moral values. Any person seeking justification for selfish or sinful behavior can find a "logical" reason for it in astrology. Astrologers seem willing to tolerate, rationalize, or even encourage any behavior the client deems personally important. They desire to please the client's wishes, and amazingly the stars often agree! If a person convinces himself the stars have either compelled or impelled his wrong action, he may feel he can dismiss his guilt because he was not fully responsible for his behavior.

In our pleasure-oriented society, if astrology advocates anything it advocates a way of life devoted to integration with the client's world view. Thus astrology will never condemn any form of behavior in which the client is involved. That is why astrology is without moral value.

4. *Astrology seems to work because it is made to appear as a science.* Astrologers utilize bits and pieces of astronomy and mathematics to draw up their charts, giving the impression they are being scientific, yet the conclusions given are neither scientific conclusions nor based on true science. Though claiming to draw from thousands of years of empirical observation, no astrologers can point to one authoritative interpretation of that long history of observation that all other astrologers agree upon and use. The reason for this is that there is no one conclusion.

Astrology also has a convincing array of technical terms and specialized language, but so do the mystery religions of Egypt. But this validates neither the mystery religions nor astrology. Using complex rules and a complicated chart with impressive symbols, the astrologer impressively calculates. But so do those who believe in a flat earth.

Most people assume something so complicated and scientific-looking must be true. (The same was said about phrenology in the nineteenth century.) The fact is that astrology is no more a science because it uses math and astronomy than is the Flat Earth Society, which does the same.

Astrologers confuse the mere *use* of scientific information (such as astronomical calculations) with the *practice* of science (such as the use of the scientific method). For these reasons, astrology only gives the impression that it is a science, though it really is not.

Astrology can work even when astrologers give advice using wrong information based on true scientific facts. For example, astrology teaches that a person with "Libra rising" will be artistic. The astrologer believes that this tenet of astrology is true because the information surrounding the charts points to this. In fact, Libra spends more time on the ascendant than most other signs, so more people are born under this sign than any other sign. But the astrologer is wrong because most of the people born under "Libra rising" are not artists and do not have any unusual artistic ability. Thus, as one astrologer admits, ". . . more people are born with Libra on the ascendant than practically any other rising sign. And this holds true not only for artists, but for any group of human beings you may care to name" (84:78).

The astrologer has used a fact of science—namely that Libra spends more time on the ascendant. To him it means people born during this time should have artistic abilities, but reality proves this is not true. Thus, what at first seems to give astrology credibility (citing some scientific and mathematical facts), upon closer examination proves to have been a misinterpretation or misperception on the part of the astrologer.

5. *Astrology seems to work because astrologers make interpretations that are, or can be made, universally applicable.* The chart of any person is potentially relevant to every other person. For example, all Sun-sign traits are universal in that they apply to all men. The reason a client fits a given Sun-sign trait is for the simple reason that everybody has some of the traits listed for every sign. As a result, no matter *what* your sign, it will already agree with a trait you possess or will someday possess. And this is true for each of the 11 other signs.

In addition each chart has hundreds of factors, each with many possible different meanings. All the astrologer needs to do is keep probing until the person responds in a positive manner. One astrologer has explained how astrologers "feel out" clients:

> How do we know when an interpretation resonates with our client's experience and is being fully received by him? First, he may indicate by gestures or facial expressions that he has been touched and affected. Second, he may respond verbally with associations and further elaborations. If he does not react at all, we may be inaccurate in our interpretation... (86:164).

This technique is no different than the "cold reading" professional magicians use. It is also used by fortune-tellers to give clients information based on body language. So in other words, astrologers have endless possible interpretations available to them in any chart, and they need only to keep probing until their client responds positively through body language.

Former astrologer Charles Strohmer has disclosed that most chart interpretation involves two basic methods: *speculation* and *generalization.* An astrologer's speculations are simple guesses using safe, abstract language. These guesses potentially apply to anyone. Strohmer explains:

> Using only a person's Sun sign, Moon sign, or ascendant, astrologers make vague and open-ended guesses, using ambiguous terms about why people are the way they are, or what they should or should not be doing, or what may or may not be currently happening to them (81:39).

Generalizations, more detailed guesses than simple speculation, are the next step that astrologers use. This can be made after an astrologer has done 20 or 30 charts, for such practice enables him to give general astrological answers that he has learned from the entire mythic and symbolic substructure of astrology. The bottom line for astrology is that astrologers apply most of their time and energy to generalizations, but they still let their clients decide what these generalizations mean and how to interpret them (81:40). Practice has simply made the astrologer a better salesperson.

Because human beings are so complex, virtually any system of symbols (astrology being one) may be used to provide "insight" for a client. For example, Sabian astrology (from an astrology school in Stanwood, Washington, that borrows its name from an ancient gnostic sect existing in Southern Iraq) uses many additional symbols to interpret a chart and finds all of them useful—"The symbols open a door to new levels of insight of high value.... The symbol operates in a more abstract way to reveal a general concept of high importance to the native" (58:12). But how does the symbol reveal this to the client? By guessing. The Sabian Assembly argues, "To have these symbols at your command at any time when you look at a chart, is to give your mind something it can work with to enhance your delineations" (58:14). In other words, the astrologer should always be able to find something that fits the client.

Astrology "works," then, because the astrologer provides information the client deems relevant, thus "confirming" astrology. Clients will actually find relevance in an astrologer's statement, even when it's not there. When the astrologer tells his client that he is influenced by Neptune and that "Neptune allows the soul to leave the body" (131:XVI), one person will feel astrology confirms his practice of astral projection. Another person, more philosophically inclined, will see his commitment to exalting spiritual over material values in his life. Yet another person will see his love for the arts and poetry. Obviously, such vague statements can be interpreted by many different people in many different ways. How can the astrologer help but succeed with such a system?

6. *Astrology seems to "work" because astrology is applicable to almost every human situation in life.* Astrology can speak to almost everything and usually does. Whatever a person's interests or needs, astrology has something "important" to say. Astrologers Sakoian and Acker have correctly stated, "There is no area of human experience which is not touched upon in some way by astrology" (34:XII). The reason for this is simple: By its very nature astrology is all-inclusive. Thomas reports concerning the sixteenth century:

> Nothing did more to make astrology seductive than the ambitious scale of its intellectual pretensions. It offered a systematic scheme of explanation for all the vagaries of human and natural behavior, and there was in principle no question which it could not answer. . . . Every

> earthly occurrence was capable of astrological explanation.... There was no other existing body of thought, religion apart, which even began to offer so all-embracing an explanation for the baffling variousness of human affairs (46:324).

But just because it touches each of these areas does not mean the information astrology is giving is true. Christian Science, for instance, touches many of these same topics and gives completely different advice. One or the other could be true but they can't both be true at the same time if they give conflicting statements. And of course, there is one more option: They could both be wrong. The question is not how many areas do they touch upon, but how do we know that the advice they give is true?

Most astrologers practice other disciplines (such as holistic health methods, modern psychotherapies, and other forms of divination) that offer additional false viewpoints or information for the client. This has always been true. Keith Thomas illustrates with the case of medieval England:

> The astrologers themselves were often men of wide-ranging activity. Forman practiced astrology, geomancy, medicine, divination by facial moles, alchemy and conjuring [spirits]. Ashmole's activities were equally diverse. Richard Saunders wrote a series of textbooks on chiromancy and physiognomy. Even Lilly, who did more than anyone to "purify" astrology, also practiced conventional medicine, spirit-raising, treasure hunting and the conjuration of angels and fairies (46:632).

7. *Astrology seems to work because it changes a person's world view.* Whether a person is a materialist,

nominal Christian, or anything else, astrology can change his outlook on life. The astrologer can mold his world view toward astrology merely by interpreting his chart:

> What the astrologer tells to his client will build in him a complex picture. This picture will act upon his consciousness.... It establishes a new allegiance, a new polarization of the will ... perhaps a new faith.... The astrologer discussing the client's birth chart is thus responsible for helping him to establish a new relationship between his conscious ego and the potentialities latent in his total nature (7:94-95).

If one embraces the idea of astrology, the universe takes on new meaning, even though the new meaning given by astrology is scientifically, theologically, and psychologically false. Astrology presents the old occultic axiom that in the world, "as above, so below." Because the universe is seen as being somehow interconnected, it becomes infused by the astrologer with design and meaning, thus leading to the conclusion that it is somehow designed and ordered that way by God. Once God is introduced as the power behind astrology, the universe is thus infused with spiritual meaning and implication.

No wonder a person with no interest in religion suddenly finds himself becoming religious. A materialist who finds no logical meaning or value in life suddenly has a reason. A person who thinks he is a Christian because he grew up in the church but doesn't really know what a true Christian is can easily believe in some higher power called God who has provided astrology for mankind. Astrology infuses this person's "faith" with specific content for his beliefs. Therefore, a misrepresentation of reality leads people to misperceive how the world operates.

8. *Astrology "works" because it traps people.* Most people who first visit an astrologer are at a crisis in their life and are thus vulnerable. As one astrologer concedes, "Eighty percent to ninety percent of the people who come to me are really at a crisis point in their lives" (138:110). If the astrology "helps" the client, it becomes accepted and trusted.

This ability of astrology to meet a person's need in a crisis situation is made especially evident by examining how famous astrologer Carroll Righter became the personal astrologer to so many movie stars and other prominent people, such as Ronald Reagan. The famous astrologer Evangeline Adams was a friend of Righter's parents, and in 1923, when Righter was 14, Adams read his horoscope. "She told him that his chart indicated an exceptional talent for celestial divination. . . . A few years later, he began to study astrology in his spare time" (160:134). Eventually he stumbled into prominence:

> [In 1939] he met the actress Marlene Dietrich at a party and read her chart. She had been down on her luck for sometime, and Righter told her that things were about to look up. Shortly afterward they did. She became a devoted client and recommended him to her friends among the movie stars. He soon became the leading astrological advisor to film notables (160:134).

If Dietrich had remained down on her luck, Carroll Righter's life could have been vastly different. Righter became an astrologer to important people because of good timing, not because of any truth in astrology.

It is interesting to note what first sparked Carroll Righter's interest in becoming an astrologer: the prediction of an astrologer. Many astrologers have seen in a client's charts "excellent potential" to become an astrologer. Whatever the initial response, the idea remains and often germinates.

At the 1988 AFA conference, many of the astrologers we talked with attributed their careers as professional astrologers to such an event. Their chart had been read when they were younger, and an astrologer had predicted they would become an astrologer, psychic, etc. Eventually they did.

Astrology also has the power to trap the curious. "I wonder what would happen if I tried it once?"; or, "If the president uses astrology some part of it must work"; or, "What's behind these thousands of newspaper horoscopes anyway?"; or, "My friend Susan just raves about what astrology has done for her"; or "I certainly need something new in my life. I wonder what would happen if I tried doing what an astrologer says?"

The experience of the famous astrologer William Lilly could be multiplied a thousand times over. Zadkiel writes of Lilly's experiences:

> In the year 1632 he began to study Astrology.... Lilly tells us that he applied himself to these interesting studies "many times, twelve, or fifteen, or eighteen hours day and night"; adding, "I was curious to discover whether there was any verity in the art or not" (48:3).

Lilly came to believe astrology "worked" for him as a result of initial curiosity, and thus became one of the most renowned astrologers in English history. Lilly even cast horoscopes for King Charles I (48:5). Eventually astrology turned Lilly to other occult practices such as spiritism (46:632).

Below are a few modern-day illustrations of people getting hooked on astrology and becoming professional astrologers.

One day I was browsing through a stack of books and came across one on astrology by Evangeline Adams, the famous New York astrologer. I was curious, so I started reading about my Sun sign Leo. The book knocked me over, because it fit me so well. That episode piqued my curiosity and resulted in my astrology study for the past 15 years.... From that experience I have expanded my work, doing astrology charts and teaching classes for the public (138:109-10).

Keith told us that he "fell into astrology, like everyone else!" He was introduced to astrology while a student at the Harvard School of Design.... He has been studying astrology and metaphysics ever since, a period of 20 years (138:113).

Tony Joseph's interest in astrology was initiated by a reading he received from an astrologer. He had been very skeptical about the subject prior to that time, but was so impressed that he decided to study with a teacher (138:130).

Whether curious or skeptical, those who set out to examine or disprove astrology may become hooked themselves. In the case of Jungian psychoanalyst Alice O. Howell, when she was 21 her father experienced a period of "considerable distress." On the recommendation of a good friend, he decided to visit an astrologer. After returning from the visit, the father was "visibly shaken and affected" and he "absolutely insisted" that both Alice and her mother also have their charts done. So the very next day they visited the astrologer. The mother's chart was done first, and then Alice's.

The more he talked, the more devastated I became. All the pride of a 21-year-old convinced that no one could be capable of understanding her vanished into thin air. He penetrated my soul deftly.... The more Hermes [the astrologer] talked, the more insightful he became, and the more I began to wonder and question the basic premise of astrology. Something was ringing true, and convincing me that my prayers had been heard (120:XIX-XX).

Eventually Alice was led to a spiritual teacher who encouraged further studies in astrology with Marc Edmund Jones (120:XXI). Jones and astrology led her into alchemy; alchemy found its meaning in Jungian psychology, where she "kept seeing the parallels to the premises and foundations of astrology" (120:XXIV).

Today Alice O. Howell is a leader in the integration of astrology and psychology. Her background in astrology led to her present belief in a "wholly new approach to the understanding of the individual horoscope.... Someday it may be a perfectly natural occurrence for a therapist to consult the chart of a patient.... It could serve all the helping professions, including pastoral counseling" (120:XXV-XXVI). All of this was the result of a sequence of events that began when a troubled father sought out an astrologer on the advice of a good friend.

Or, note the impact of an astrologer on New York psychiatrist Bernard Rosenblum, who, at 41, was convinced that astrology was "a pseudoscience filled with interesting generalities and unfounded predictions . . . [not] hard facts and realities" (118:3). Rosenblum describes his first meeting with an astrologer:

I introduced myself to the astrologer as "mister," not "doctor," and took note that she was not observing me for clues [about himself]. After 15 minutes or so, during which time she [accurately] described my personality patterns,

she went on to say that I was, or should be,
a psychoanalyst or psychiatrist. She even
described something more specific about the
type of therapy or analysis I would likely practice, which corresponded exactly to the orien-
tation I had as a psychiatrist! (118:3-4).

The astrologer's uncanny accuracy had exploded
Rosenblum's perception of astrology as dealing only in
vague generalities. He was converted. He went on to
integrate astrology with his psychiatric profession and
now refers some of his clients to astrologers.

Former astrologer Strohmer concludes from such testimonies, "I cannot remember anyone who became less
interested in astrology when it touched upon, not generalities, but obvious personal facts" (81:41).

(We admit that many astrologers have the uncanny
power to reveal information about people, but we insist
that power neither comes from astrology, nor is it based
on astrological symbols. For a comprehensive discussion
of what frequently causes accurate interpretation, see
our next two chapters.)

9. *Astrology seems to work because astrologers always
have "reasonable" explanations for failures.* Within
astrology exists an inexhaustible reserve of material for
explaining the failures of astrology without threatening
astrology itself. Some of the excuses astrologers have
given are: The client did not really "know himself"; the
time of birth must have been inaccurately recorded; the
stars "impel," they do not "compel"; the person's free will
countered the astrological prediction; astrologers aren't
perfect; the client never fulfilled his "astrological potential." A thousand and one excuses are given except the
right one: Astrology itself is a falsehood.

10. *Astrology seems to work because of the astrologer's
attentiveness or seductiveness.* Like the professional psy-
chodramatist, some astrologers are quite adept at

"reading" a client. This means that by observing unintended clues the client gives (physical or verbal), an astrologer is able to feed back accurate information to the client.

Some astrologers are also skilled in manipulating to make an otherwise marginal or meaningless session seem wonderfully meaningful. This same technique may be used by a skilled actor to bluff his audience. Geoffrey Dean reports the following amusing story:

> Dr. Fox was an actor who was coached to give a highly entertaining but otherwise meaningless one-hour lecture on games theory to various professionals such as psychiatrists and social workers. They found his talk to be clear and stimulating, and nobody realized it was nonsense (173:273).

Likewise some astrologers are so skilled in communication they can make astrological nonsense seem stimulating.

11. *Astrology seems to work because it is increasingly a psychology.* Astrologers who become good counselors, but attribute their success to astrology, are wrongly accrediting their success to astrology rather than to good counseling procedure. Still, many astrologers encourage other astrologers to take courses in counseling. One astrologer has confided, "Any astrology student planning to use astrology directly with people is advised to enroll in one or more counseling courses, to read books on the counseling process itself, and to gain experiential supervised practice with counseling skills" (86:143).

Anyone who daily interacts with people in a counseling session is going to learn about people, and this knowledge will help in choosing the appropriate or relevant elements in a chart. This type of activity is neither occultic nor astrological, but simply observational. The difference is that the insight of the astrologer (which at best is no different from that of the psychologist) is attributed to the planets and the stars. Therefore astrology leads to its own form of psychological knowledge.

Some astrologers betray themselves by saying it "makes better sense" to first understand a person's background—heredity, upbringing, marital status, occupation, etc.—than to begin by merely using a chart. This is because the chart itself is so complex and subjective it is "extremely difficult" to interpret it accurately (86:87; 131:20-21). This is more psychology than astrology, but astrologers do it every day. To attribute one's success in psychology to astrological theory is deceptive.

14

Astrology and Spiritism

"For most adherents of astrology, it is enough that it 'works.' There is a fascination with the power, without a suspicion as to the nature of that power" (81:42).

— Charles Strohmer
Former astrologer

If spirits are the power behind astrology, then its acceptance in society is opening the doors for millions of people to potentially contact the spirit world. But according to the Scriptures, this means they are really contacting the world of demonic beings (189–197; 309; 333–342). Astrologers deny this, of course, but we intend to demonstrate in the next two chapters that wherever astrology exists, spiritism [demonism] exists alongside it. As far as we know, no one else has thoroughly documented if there is a connection between astrology and spiritism.

The average person believes astrology is either a harmless pastime, a helpful activity, or an innocent superstition. If spirits (demons) are often the real source of power behind astrology, however, then the advice of an astrologer may really be the advice of demons. Such advice may lead to spiritual deception as well as to physical destruction. As we shall see, listening to the spirit world is dangerous. We shall now proceed to document four converging lines of evidence that have convinced us of the real connection between astrology and spiritism. Then, in our next chapter, we will examine the evidence linking astrology and spiritism in four additional ways.

Historically, astrology is connected to pagan gods and the spirit world.

Astrology has always been connected to spirits through its contact with supernatural spirit beings who were held to be "gods" (47; 53; 65–66; 148; 303). In every civilization, the acceptance of polytheism, and the contacting and worship of the gods, has been a fundamentally spiritistic phenomenon (343; cf. 1 Corinthians 10:20). Astrology has historically been connected to the gods and therefore to spiritism.

Tracing astrology through the different civilizations of the ancient world and through the Middle Ages will reveal a variety of direct associations between astrology and the spirit world. Aztec astrology, for example, contained barbarous and evil rites of human sacrifice, regulated totally by the gods and spirits of ancient Mexico (53:11-16,73-81,91-92). The ancients believed the gods exerted great influence over the lives and affairs of men. These people reasoned that if the stars were the gods, the stars would exert an influence over the affairs of men. They also believed people could contact the gods (spirits). In his comprehensive critique of astrology, Robert Eisler comments:

> It is important to understand that the Babylonian, Greek, and Roman belief in myths and

in gods being associated with the Sun, Moon and planets was not a game designed for amusement. . . . They believed that the stars and planets were associated with gods, or *were* gods, and that it was possible for the gods to communicate with men; it then followed that the stars and planets could influence the lives of men (99:45).

If the stars were actually gods, or associated with the gods, there was good reason to worship the stars. One of the greatest astrologers of the Classical World, Firmicus Maternus (A.D. 334), argued for the deity of the stars: "Let us therefore worship the gods, whose origin has linked itself to us through the stars. Let the human race regard the power of the stars with the constant veneration of a suppliant. Let us call upon the gods . . ." (50:20). The influence of the sun and the different planets, which directly relates to astrology in the past as well as today, is made especially evident when Maternus states:

O Sun, best and greatest, who holds the middle place in the heavens, Mind and Moderator of the universe, leader and Princeps of all who kindle forever the fires of the other stars; and you, Moon, who, placed in the farthest reaches of the sky, shines with holy rays and ensures with your monthly office the continuation of human procreation, ever increased by the light of the Sun; and you, Saturn, who, set in the highest point of the sky, carries the leaden light of your planet in sluggish revolution . . . (50:30).

A scholar closer to our own time, Franz Cumont, curator of the Royal Museum of Antiquities at Brussels, was recognized as the leading authority on Greek astrology and Mithraism. In 1912 he wrote a classic text,

Astrology and Religion Among the Greeks and Romans, in which he cogently argues that astrology or star worship was the most influential and widespread cult of all history. He documents how it rose to become the strongest of all the various forms of deity worship in the ancient world, how it infiltrated Greek paganism; influenced Israel, Syria, and Egypt; and was eventually proclaimed the official religion of the entire Roman Empire. He explains, "The stars are not only eternal gods, but also universal, their power is unlimited in space as in time" (47:63). History records that the astrological powers attributed today to the planets stemmed from the personalities and powers of the ancient gods themselves, whether from Assyrian, Babylonian, Roman, Greek, or other beliefs (99:77; 39:85,106-28; 140:167).

Former astrologer Charles Strohmer explains that modern astrologers, attempting to be scientific, have replaced the ancient gods with planetary nomenclature. But nevertheless they counsel their clients with advice based upon ideas surrounding the ancient gods. Astrologers today do not cite the personalities of "the gods" or talk about the gods' influence or advice. Instead they cite the "personality," influence, or advice of "the planets." Strohmer has correctly revealed that, even though astrologers are trained to think and talk only of *planets*, the influence attributed to the planets is no different than the influence once attributed to the gods. He writes:

> Principles of astrological interpretation are clearly excerpted from ancient myths, updated, and have absolutely nothing to do with planets but with superstitions and imaginings related to mythical deities. This literature, therefore, should not use the material word *planet* because in fact the studies bear upon the elaborately devised intrigue of the gods ... (81:22-23).

For some ancient astrologers the stars and planets were the bodies or homes of the invisible gods, but for others the stars and planets were the gods themselves. The Sumerians believed the sun, moon, and stars were actually gods who had personal feelings and could be grieved or angered (99:32). A modern astrologer acknowledges:

> In the age of the gods and goddesses all things were alive.... Jupiter was not out there to be studied as a foreign object. It was here in our world, in our bodies where it could be felt directly. Even as late as Ptolemy, in the second century A.D., the planets were not seen as symbols or even as the homes of gods. They were seen as the living gods themselves (144:130).

Because they believed the planets were the homes of the gods, or ruled by the gods, or were the gods themselves (in each case, directing earthly affairs), it is easy to see why the ancients made careful observations of the motions of the stars and planets. In this way astrology and astronomy were joined. This is why many ancient astronomers were also astrologers (99:35-37).

For still others in ancient history, the stars became either living men or the homes for the souls of the dead. Falling stars were believed to be the descent or fall of human souls to the earth (99:29; 98:65). The Druids, for example, worshiped the stars and moon, believing they housed the souls of the dead. In the afterlife or through reincarnation, a soul could progress from star to star and so increase in glory (99:29). Some believed the dead actually became the stars and so were worshiped (98:56-69; 97:123).

Not only were the stars and planets associated with the gods, but even the astrological signs themselves were believed to be the gods or related to them. Modern astrological signs were derived from what the ancients considered to be the nature of the gods (98:91-107). Thus, Aries was related to Zeus; Taurus was Zeus in disguise; Leo was related to Hercules; Virgo was the daughter of Jupiter and the goddess of justice; Sagittarius was the father of Zeus; etc. (39:106-28).

The logical consequences of the ancients' belief are obvious: polytheism, idolatry, and necromancy (contact and/or worship of the dead). Since the stars and planets were believed to be gods and spirits of the dead, one could worship them, contact them, or sacrifice to them. In this way, astrology, spiritism, and even necromancy were intertwined.

As the influence of ancient paganism has revived in our culture, we find adherents of astrology returning to a belief that the planets are gods, or are related to them. Sometimes the planets are seen as literal gods (powerful spirit beings) and at other times they are seen as psychological constructs (e.g., archetypes) that embody or symbolize the ancient character and teaching of the gods. For example, in *Asteroid Goddesses,* astrological counselor Demetra George discloses that the asteroids are gods and/or psychological archetypes whose ancient teachings are relevant to modern chart interpretation as well as psychic development (128:XVI-3,58-59,97, 130,165-66).

Astrologer Stephen Arroyo, a leader in the field of "energy astrology" (see chapter 15), seeks to develop awareness of, and attunement with, "universal forces." He believes and teaches, "The gods of mythology (just like the planets in astrology) represent *living* forces and principles in the universe and in the lives of each of us" (116:28).

The goal of some contemporary astrologers today is to experience and absorb the god or gods into one's own being. By this process the astrologer will partake of the god's power. That is why one astrologer has explained,

"Each planet represents, exteriorly, a stupendous being or intelligence which is part of the consciousness of the Absolute. Interiorly, we are striving to absorb that part and principle of divinity which a planet represents" (56:2).

Kathleen Burt, who teaches astrology at Mira Costa College in Del Mar, California, reveals, "As C. G. Jung has stated, the gods and goddesses are all within us. These planets represent our contact with the sacred, so it's good to get to know them" (144:88).

Astrologer Jeff Jawyer is a pioneer in "Astrodrama," which seeks, in part, to reintroduce ancient and spiritistic astrology to modern astrologers. Through Astrodrama he is referring people back to the spirit contact (144: 131), pantheism and polytheism of ancient astrology. "Astrology," he says, "is...a tool for personal transformation. When we connect with the planetary archetypes, we train ourselves to use their qualities. We discover the essence of the planetary gods within" (144:136).

Jawyer holds to the belief that modern astrology can become reconnected to the ancient gods through the use of magic ritual. As an example, he cites the Findhorn community in Scotland, a spiritistic community that has embraced the ancient ritualistic connections between astrology and spiritism (344:33). According to Jawyer, any astrologer may perform the appropriate rituals:

> There are quite a number of books available on the subject of rituals to assist you if you don't have a tradition or method of your own. What is most important is the spirit of openness....When the heart is open, magic happens. When we align ourselves with the cosmos we open and become magical. This is the astrology of our ancestors (144:144-45).

In Theosophical circles the spirits that spoke through medium Helena P. Blavatsky recorded, "The Planetary

Spirits, are the informing spirits of the stars in general and of the planet [earth] especially. They rule the destinies of men who are all born under one or other of their constellations" (55:644). In spiritist Alice Bailey's *Esoteric Astrology*, her spirit guide confided to her that every planet constitutes the incarnation of "an Entity or Being" (55:651).

But other forms of astrology today (particularly in Asia) need not return to ancient times, for these practices never changed. Hindu astrology, for example, has not "progressed" and substituted sophisticated scientific/psychological terms for its dealings with the gods and spirits. Today, as in the past, the elephant-headed god of knowledge, Ganesh, is still a principal deity "to whom Hindu astrologers devote their prayers and salutations" (62:back cover).

In sage Mantreswara's astrology text, *Jataka Phaladeepika,* one can discover how to invoke the gods and spirits for assistance in astrological work. This text begins with a salutation to Lord Vasudeva. The author also explains how to pray to the sun god and invoke his blessings and gives obeisance to the goddess of speech; his family deity; his guru; the nine planets; and the god Siva (61:1-2). He believes the nature of the planets is ultimately derived from the nature of gods (61:8-11).

Another Hindu astrologer who exemplifies those who follow the ancient paths is Dr. Gouri Kapoor, author of *Remedial Measures in Astrology*. His "how to" book gives the most appropriate methods for protection from "malevolent planetary effects." Because the planets are gods, he concludes that they may be good or evil; inflict disease, pain, or pleasure; help or destroy. Kapoor makes it clear he is dealing with living spirits, not dead planets. He advises astrologers to use lengthy rituals and rites involving mantras, yogas, rosary beads, amulets, and fasting to propitiate the "planet." He sees the planets as deities that must be worshiped, sacrificed to, obeyed, feared, and propitiated. For him, one's life and well-being depend on the planetary gods being kept happy. Otherwise, "the results are disastrous" (52:204). For example, he writes:

> Prayers to the planets and other deities are very often resorted to in times of trouble. ...From our personal experience we can say that prayers, if offered with faith and due reference to the deity, act as a very effective remedial measure in everyday life.... [Thus] when we recite the *mantra* of a planet who is giving us trouble, we actually pray to him to bestow upon us his mercy and save us from his evil rays (52:11-14).

Depending upon the individual's need, Kapoor proscribes various rituals to the planetary gods. For instance, he advocates that to regain health, one must burn incense before the idol of the Goddess Durga and then recite the appropriate mantra (52:209). Likewise, to solve financial problems, "The following *mantra* should be recited 25,000 times in front of the picture of *Anjali* (mother of [the monkey god] Shri Hanumann) after observing the usual rituals" (52:211).

It is clear that some modern astrologers have never left the ancient ways and beliefs. Other Western and European astrologers are openly returning to the spiritistic beliefs of ancient astrology. The question is, why?

The spirit world is interested in promoting astrology.

The spirits intentionally promote astrology. As we have seen, history shows astrology has been tied to the world of magic, spiritism, paganism, and the occult from the beginning. This remains true today.

Spirits are writing books through human mediums in which they are promoting astrology. Many people do not realize that we have today over 1,000 channelers in the city of Los Angeles alone, and their popularity grows. Tapes, literature, and seminars form a hundred-million-dollar enterprise. Celebrities are acknowledging the counsel of channelers (309:7-8).

But what is the connection between the spirits' speaking through the channelers and the practice of astrology? Astrology is being connected to spiritism by the spirits themselves. The following examples illustrate this connection.

First, one of the spirits who communicated through mystic and occultist Alice Bailey (founder of Lucius Trust), telepathically transmitted many books to her, including *Esoteric Astrology.* In this text, a third volume of a larger treatise on occultism, the particular spirit (demon) said astrology is very important to the welfare of mankind and to its spiritual evolution. The spirit also disclosed to Bailey that "intuitional astrology [astrology using psychic or spiritistic help]... must supercede" the non-psychic variety (55:3). Finally, he told Bailey that astrology is important because it is "*essentially* the purest presentation of occult truth in the world at this time..." (55:5). (As we will see later, one of the goals of the spirits' use of astrology is to gain possession of the astrologer.)

A second example of spiritistic literature promoting astrology can be seen in the writings of Edgar Cayce, one of the most powerful and influential mediums of our era. The spirits speaking through Cayce endorsed the practice of astrology. The 14,000 readings he gave in trance are considered the largest single body of psychic information in the world, and over 2,500 of them deal with what were termed "life readings" and "almost all [of them] refer to past incarnations and specific astrological or planetary influences bearing on the present"

(51:VIII). When asked if it was right and proper to study astrology, the spirits that spoke through Cayce said, "Very, very, very, much so" (51:15).

At the 1988 AFA Convention, astrologer Irene Diamond told students in her seminar (titled "Let's Talk About God") that all her books on astrology (including her *Astrology in the Holy Bible)* were produced by spirit dictation and/or automatic writing (162; 74:VI).

Astrologer Cynthia Bohannon, the "channel" for the astrology text *The North and South Nodes: The Guideposts of the Spirit—A Comprehensive Interpretation of the Nodal Placements,* dedicates the book to two of the many spirit guides who dictated the text:

> This book was written by the twin spirits, Ovensky and Lester, who have given us this divine gift of love from God. It is their contribution to the great spiritual science of astrology for the time had come for this information to be known (16:V).

Her book contains statements from about a dozen different spirits, with names such as Father Malachai and Orthrocar.

Still another book written by various spirits is Ted George and Barbara Parker's *Sinister Ladies of Mystery: the Dark Asteroids of Earth.* In this text, the spirits provide astrological interpretations for the invisible asteroids (dark moons) surrounding the earth (129:III, 117).

Remember that these books are claimed to be totally dictated by the spirits. But the connection between astrology and spiritism can also be seen by astrologers who admit astrology depends upon or is heavily influenced by the spirits. Doris Chase Doane, the current president of the AFA, the largest astrological society in America (a society that claims astrology is scientific), personally told us after her seminar titled "The Art of

Transmutation" that the spirits who work through the Church of Light are "very important to the work of astrology." During her seminar, the two books Doane recommended as being key to the study of astrology were C. C. Zain's *Occultism Applied* and his *Spiritual Alchemy,* both spiritistically-inspired texts.

Spiritistic societies promote astrological goals. When we examine the claims of these religious groups, we discover that their literature is said to have been revealed by the spirit world.

These societies include various religious sects begun by Eastern gurus, as well as various occult and Rosicrucian groups. For example, the Eastern gurus often have courses on the subject in their spiritual programs; Max Heindel's Rosicrucian Fellowship publishes many books on astrology; and the spiritistically-founded Theosophical Society also publishes numerous astrology texts (321).

Another example is the White Eagle Lodge. This allegedly Christian society was begun by the spirit entity called "White Eagle" through the English medium Grace Cooke (320:7,71). Cooke's daughter Joan Hodgson founded the White Eagle School of Astrology. Hodgson is a spiritist who specializes in presenting New Age teachings to children in such books as *Hullo Sun!*, *Angels and Indians,* and *Our Father* (94:138-39).

In this category of spiritistic societies with astrological goals, we shall discuss two groups: the Sabian Assembly in Stanwood, Washington, and The Church of Light in Los Angeles, California. Both societies consider it important to promote astrology. In fact, a sizable number of professional astrologers formally associated with the American Federation of Astrologers, are graduates of The Church of Light (160/161).

1) *The Sabian Assembly:* Marc Edmund Jones (1888-1980) formed the Sabian Assembly in 1923. The goal of the society is to educate its members in a comprehensive

occult world view through dissemination of some 3,000 "Sabian lessons" that cover a great variety of subjects from astrology to philosophy to biblical topics (60:266-80).

Jones is best known for his influence on the astrological community, partly because astrology plays a key role in the activities of his society. Approximately half of its students engage in astrological studies (60:24). Jones himself served as vice president of the Astrologers Guild of America from 1941 to 1942, and authored over 25 books on astrology and the occult, including *The Counseling Manual in Astrology; How to Learn Astrology; Occult Philosophy;* and *The Sabian Manual,* which discusses the spirits who founded and who help guide the assembly (60:21-22,83-84).

Although Jones was raised as a child in the occult practices of Theosophy, he began his astrological studies in 1913 at the age of 25 (60:21,23). Jones had chanced upon an astrologer and decided to have his chart done. The astrologer's interpretation of his chart led him into the study of astrology (60:21). Within a year Jones had encountered a spirit guide (60:21).

Eventually, the Sabian Assembly was founded. At first, the emphasis was upon astrology, but "before long the scope of attention broadened to embrace virtually every phase of occultism" (60:22). Soon Bible studies were added, and in San Diego, in 1926, a spiritistic church was begun. Medium Elsie Wheeler pastored the church while Jones assumed the role of president (60:23).

From its inception, the spirits guided the assembly. They helped produce its occult lessons, the emphasis on astrology (60:24), and the specific rituals and Eastern/occultic practices—such as yoga, meditation, breathing exercises, etc. (60:88-90,172). The official history of the assembly records:

> During these sessions the author became aware of an effective and living contact with

intelligences of long prior generations and proceeded to enlist them in what gradually became
identified as the Sabian project.... This new
mode of research... was largely of a spiritualistic [mediumistic or spiritistic] nature...
(60:22,83-84).

According to the history, "All its rituals were developed at the specific request of the sponsors constituting the invisible council [the spirits]..." (60:110).

Because the spirits are so vital in the work of the
assembly, each student is encouraged to establish a
personal relationship with the spirit world. Thus, "the
initiate-to-be and his invisible fellowship must serve
each other equally and in an identity of creative potential if the Sabian project as a whole is to have any
spiritual actuality..." (60:80). The student is told:

He is preparing himself for service and fellowship with the Great Ones [the spirits].
... The real life and being of the Sabian Assembly are in the necessarily intangible par-
ticipation of its members collectively in what
occultism knows as an invisible fellowship.
... [a] continual relationship [is] maintained by
the aspirant with the Great Ones... (60:14,29).

Even the members' own children are dedicated to the
spirits (60:196-97). In addition, the alleged dead are
contacted; the student is taught that "contact with the
deceased can be quite personal" (60:203). There are special
ceremonies for dead members of the assembly. In these
ceremonies the student is dedicated to the service of the
dead and to keeping them "present among us" (60:206).

Such contact with the spirit world often leads to mediumship—a form of voluntary spirit possession. The
Sabian aspirant is told he must dedicate himself to

helping the spirits experience "vicarious embodiment" or the inhabitation of the physical body. The seeker "first of all must be willing to dedicate himself to facilitating the vicarious embodiment of the Great Ones in this manner as need and opportunity arise..." (60:74).* Spirit possession is implied by the description of a person permitting an unembodied spirit to "dwell within him" (60:74).

The Bible, however, strictly forbids mediumism and all forms of contact with the spirit world (Deuteronomy 18:9-12), because the indwelling by spirits is really demonization—possession by an evil spirit or demons who seek to imitate benign spirits or the dead in order to deceive men spiritually (333–340).

2) *The Church of Light:* The Church of Light is an affiliate society of the American Federation of Astrologers, with similar goals (160:13). For example, as noted, many AFA members are graduates of The Church of Light's 210 course lessons on the occult (160–161).

The Church of Light claims to be the preserver of the occult knowledge of a sect of ancient Egyptians (200:3-5). This knowledge allegedly has been transmitted throughout history (since 2400 B.C.) by an occult hierarchy/brotherhood of spirit beings known as "The Brotherhood of Light." (Note: The *Church* of Light refers to the earthly organization of *humans* directed by the hierarchy of *spirits* called the *Brotherhood* of Light.)

In America, The Church of Light can be traced to the medium Thomas H. Burgoyne, a Mason and "natural born psychic" in contact with the spirit world for over 20 years (141:V-VII). "Through his [Burgoyne's] seership [mediumship] he contacted the Brotherhood of Light on the inner plane" in order to produce the two-volume text

---

*Since there are levels of initiation, this is not to say every Sabian seeker becomes indwelt by spirits, but that they must apparently dedicate themselves to its facilitation whenever necessary.

on astrology and the occult, *The Light of Egypt or the Science of the Soul and the Stars* (200:5). This material, published in 1889, provided the occult teachings for the modern Church of Light.

In this text we are told that astrology is very important to the spirit world. For example, it is stated that the spirit world works through many classes of occultists but "especially those devoted to alchemy and astrology" (141:84). (Perhaps this is one reason why the current AFA president, Doris Chase Doane, told us that "the work of the spirits" through the Church of Light was "very important" to the cause of astrology [166].)

Occultist Elbert Benjamine was one of its three founders and served as its president until his death in 1951.

In 1898, he "began his occult studies which led to his contacting the Brotherhood of Light [the spirit world] in 1900 and commencing studies under its tutelage" (200:6). The spirits instructed him "to prepare a complete system of occult education" (200:6). Thus, through Benjamine, the spirits produced the 21 courses offered by The Church of Light. (These are the courses taken by many professional astrologers associated with the AFA.)

Elbert Benjamine is not listed as the author of these lessons because they were really the work of the spirits (200:6-7). As a result, the pen name, C. C. Zain, was placed on the 21 courses in order to acknowledge the fact that the material originated from the spirits and not from the human instrument they worked through. Benjamine was only the "physical channel" or medium (200:7;143:22,114-121).

These lessons given by the spirits reveal both the importance the spirits attach to astrology and the importance of astrology for the occult. For example, the 21 courses are arranged into 210 individual lessons "comprising the 21 branches of occult science known as the religion of the stars [astrology]" (201:1).

The 21 courses are divided into three main categories: astrology, alchemy, and magic. Each main category is subdivided into seven major lessons (201:1). For example, in Course 1, *Laws of Occultism* (lessons 39-45), the student is immediately introduced to such subjects as "Doctrine of Mediumship," "Spiritism," and "Phenomenal [i.e., physical or material] Spiritism" (the branch of mediumism concerned with producing physical manifestations by the power of the spirit world).

In Course 11, *Divination and Character Reading,* we find such subjects as "Doctrine of Divination" and "Divining Rod and Other Divination." In Course 20, *The Next Life* (reincarnation), we find lessons on "Turning the Dial to Inner Planes" and "Astrological Influences in the Next Life."

The courses given by the spirits on astrology include: spiritual astrology; horary astrology; natal astrology; horoscope progression; divination and character reading; mundane astrology; stellar [psychic] healing; etc. (201).

The 21 courses cover an extremely wide range of occult and astrological subjects, and over 4,500 pages! With some 1,800 pages devoted to astrology itself, it should not surprise us that the Church of Light would be an affiliate of the American Federation of Astrologers. What is important to realize is that these 210 lessons, with their 1,800 pages of instruction on every facet of astrology, originate from the spirit world.

The astrological research conducted by the Church of Light from 1920-1950 was specifically carried out under the direction of the spirits. This spiritistic astrological work "has become [the] standard reference for many astrologers" (200:6), but astrologers who study these lessons do not realize that they may encounter spiritistic assistance. For example, Edward Doane, a former director and vice president of the AFA, stated that in the course of studying the lessons with his wife, they realized that the spirits had been "watching over us," guiding them and impressing their minds with thoughts and convictions. He confesses, "we were directly tuned in on the minds of our inner-plane tutors" (143:119-21).

One can but wonder how many astrologers acquire spirit guides by taking courses such as those offered by The Church of Light.

Spirits may deliberately lead their contacts to study astrology. Another indicator of the spirits' interest in promoting astrology can be seen in the fact that many people who contact the spirit world are led by the spirits to begin the study of astrology (151:56,126). For example, again at the 1988 AFA conference, we talked with several people whose initial contact with the spirit world resulted in the spirits personally leading them to become professional astrologers. Among these was Irene Diamond, author of *A New Look at the 12 Houses* and other astrological books. As with literally thousands of people today, an occultic "near-death" experience resulted in an occult initiation and her receiving spirit guides (345; cf. 322). In a gravely ill condition, she encountered spirits while out of the body. These spirits then directed her into astrology.

Before the spirits contacted her, she had no interest whatever in astrology, but since her contact with the spirits she now lectures throughout the country on "God and Astrology," assuring audiences the occult art is divinely endorsed.

Initially, at least, the spirits will sound Christian for one with a Christian upbringing. (Irene Diamond has a Catholic background.) For example, one spirit revealing astrological knowledge started by saying, "in the name of the Father, the Son, and the Holy Ghost, I come in the name of the Lord" (16:46). This is a typical ploy, a ruse to make the contact believe the spirit is sent from God.

So how does one know these spirits are *not* from God? Because no matter how spiritual they sound, they always proceed to deny what God has revealed in Scripture.

Eventually the spirits teach the same old pantheism—"everything is God and you are God also." This was the message of Irene Diamond's class at the 1988 AFA congress (162).

Many astrologers promote spiritism.

We have documented that the spirit world is interested in promoting astrology, but the reverse is also true: Many astrologers promote the practice of spiritism. Both facts indicate that spiritism and astrology are more closely linked than most people realize. Below we cite brief illustrations of astrologers promoting spiritism.

The American Federation of Astrologers 1988 Convention: At random, we selected and attended nine seminars given by professional astrologers. We discovered that seven of the instructors claimed spirit guides or were spiritists, and another was involved with spiritistic literature (219; 298–299). In addition, approximately one-fourth of the astrologers we talked with at the convention freely admitted to contacting the spirit world. Many others were evasive, hesitant, or refused to answer.

Perhaps the reason for this reluctance is that members realize the AFA claims to be a scientific organization and that contacting spirits is not exactly a scientific practice. By talking to family members of the astrologers, we found that some astrologers deliberately hide their spiritism from their clients.

Astrology Texts Dedicated to the Spirits: In addition to the many astrologers who are openly mediums or spiritists, there are also a number of astrology books actually dedicated to individual spirit beings, or which acknowledge their assistance. Examples include Marcus Allen's *Astrology for the New Age: An Intuitive Approach*. He gives special thanks to "my spirit guide for his insight, clarity and presence" (137:6). Demetra George, author of *Asteroid Goddesses*, dedicates the text to "the Mother Goddess in her emanation as Tara" (128:V). And Joan Hodgson, author of *Reincarnation Through the Zodiac*, dedicates her book "with deep love and gratitude to [the spirit] White Eagle" (94:4).

One reason astrologers contact and endorse these spirits is that astrology blends so easily with ancient or modern spiritistic tradition, cults, or religions. For example, a large number of spiritistic Hindu cults and sects practice astrology because most of traditional Hinduism encourages it (144:12). Witchcraft is another tradition that easily blends spiritistic practice with astrology (147; 149). Shamanism is one more example of many additional practices or traditions that could be cited (144:234-41).

Many former astrologers concede their power was spiritistic (demonic).

It is significant that many former astrologers have concluded the power behind astrology does not come from the stars. Rather, after objectively examining both astrology and the powers they exercised as astrologers, these professionals concluded that the real power in astrology originates from the spirit (demon) world.

1) *Karen Winterburn—12 years:* Karen was a professional astrologer schooled in humanistic astrology, but even as an astrologer she admitted, "I was convinced it [the astrological information] wasn't from me..." (202).*

---

*This is a common observation of many astrologers. For example, Barbara Clow, an astrologer who has written on the "planet" Chiron, was converted to astrology in 1969 after studies in Reichian, Freudian, and Jungian psychology. Yet, "as she read charts from 1973-1981, she did not believe it was possible to be obtaining the results she got from any known source" (130:II).

Winterburn observes that it is irrelevant whether or not the humanistic (or scientifically oriented) astrologer claims that astrology *isn't* spiritistic—because it still is. Winterburn became a spiritist and channeler as a result of her involvement with astrology, and, after commitment to astrology for 12 years, she is now convinced it was a demonic activity. She describes her spiritistic involvement in the following prepared statement (signed October 11, 1988):

> The 12 years I spent in the occult involved a logical progression from humanistic astrology to spirit channeling to cult involvement. Astrology as a divination tool was the perfect entrance. It appeared to be secular, technical and humanistic, a "neutral" tool. In addition, its occultic presuppositions were not immediately apparent. When it began to "work" for me, I became hooked. I became driven to find out the "hows" and the "whys."
>
> This led me right into channeling, a sanitized term for spirit mediumship. In 12 years of serious astrological study and professional practice, I never met a really successful astrologer—even the most "scientific" ones—who did not admit among their professional peers that spiritism was the power behind the craft. "Spirit guide," "higher self," "ancient god," "cosmic archetype," whatever name is used— the definition points to the same reality: a discarnate, personal intelligence claiming to be a god-in-progress. Such intelligences have access to information and power that many people covet and they have a desire to be trusted and to influence human beings.
>
> Once the astrologer becomes dependent upon one or more of them, these spirit intelligences

(the biblical demons) lead the astrologer into forms of spiritual commitment and worship. This is the worst kind of bondage. Seasoned astrologers who have experienced fairly consistent and dramatic successes in character reading and prognostication invariably become involved in some form of worship of these demons.

I have seen this occur in myriad forms— from the full-blown revival of ancient religions (Egyptian and Chaldean) to the ritualization of Jungian psychotherapy. The bottomline reality is always the worship of the spirit personal intelligences (demons) the astrologer has come to rely on.

2) *Charles Strohmer—seven years:* In his critique of astrology, *What Your Horoscope Doesn't Tell You,* Strohmer discusses the fundamentally spiritistic nature and power of astrology:

But as we look honestly at astrology, we begin to see that adherents of this system— without knowing it—are banging on the door through which communication is established with knowledgeable but yet deceptive spirit beings. Eventually that door opens. And the opening produces an appalling development in the adherent's life. He or she matures in the craft in a most unthought-of manner: as a spirit medium. . . . In much the same way that the palm of the hand or the crystal [ball] is "contact material" for the fortune-teller—the horoscopic *chart* is used by the astrologer. It is the mediumistic point of interaction. Get rid of the contact material with the visible world and the spirits have no point of contact to make the psychic connection, to seep information through the spokesperson to the client. ... What matters is that "contact material" (horoscope) and a medium are present. The spirits will show. Self disclosures will come (81:51,54).

Strohmer concludes, "Without contact with spirit beings, there would be no astrological self disclosures. Or if they did come, it would be almost entirely from guesswork: they would be very rare" (81:51).

3) *Dr. Atlas Laster—13 years:* Dr. Laster received his Ph.D. from the University of Pittsburgh for his work on astrology and was an active astrologer for 13 years. He observed that, as an astrologer, "I did not feel that astrology was an occult art" (205:4). Yet after he renounced astrology, he came to realize that "there are certain rituals and knowledge associated with astrology which may attract spirits of divination" (204:4). Although he had no (conscious) contact with the spirit world, he nevertheless felt the need after conversion to Christian faith to request "prayer and the laying on of hands in order to exorcize, as it were, any spirits of divination and the like that may have lingered" (205:5).

There is absolutely no doubt that astrology and spiritism are historically connected; that the spirit world has a definite interest in promoting and nurturing astrology; that many astrologers are spiritists and mediums; and that many practicing and former astrologers admit their real power comes from spirits. These four lines of evidence reveal that spiritism and astrology are interconnected.

15

Spiritism and Chart Interpretation

Some astrologers openly confess they are assisted in chart interpretation by spirit guides. But usually the influence is indirect and less obvious. For example, an astrologer may report feeling somehow "directed" to certain chart symbols or factors—or that something in a chart will suddenly "jump out." Distinguishing spiritistic assistance from normal human intuition is not easy, so the fact that these areas can be blurred presents a dilemma for the astrologer. How is it possible for him to know his "intuition" is truly human and not from another source? Most astrologers today stress the necessity of intuition for proper chart interpretation, but in most "New Age" thinking the word "intuitive" often includes the word "psychic"; the line between them is blurred (346).

The spirit world itself often encourages the development of "intuition" as a means to induce psychic powers in an individual and establish spirit contact (347:304-07). In such cases, "intuition" becomes a euphemism for psychic development. Thus, the spirit author of *Esoteric Astrology* stated, "It is intuitional astrology which must eventually supersede what is today called astrology" (55:3). And texts such as Marcus Allen's *Astrology for the New Age: An Intuitive Approach* reveal that the result of "intuitive astrology" can help the astrologer become a channel for spiritistic guidance (137:9-16, 29-53,65-70).

If startling self-disclosures can help convert a person to astrology, and if this is one goal of the spirit world, then it is logical to assume that when astrologers speak of being "directed" or of symbols "jumping out" at them, that they may indeed be supernaturally, though inconspicuously, guided in the process.

Since astrologers use charts, the spirits must have a way to direct their minds to relevant chart factors. Former astrologer Charles Strohmer discusses this phenomenon, which he attributes to spiritistic guidance (81: 45-56):

> You have a new horoscope before you. You begin to notice that a certain item in the chart gets your attention. It sticks out in your mind, softly glaring at you. You then begin to dwell upon its meaning. Perhaps a particular aspect of the chart pops into view, one you had not noticed before. It becomes difficult to shake off this impression that you "see" in the chart. After some consideration, you feel that this has relevance for your client. So you begin to discuss it with him or her (81:53).

> What is occurring? The [astrologer's] mind is becoming focused upon a portion of that client's life. [As in mediumism] this is a detail that a familiar spirit is privy to. It is the spirit that is somehow doing the "focusing" (81:53-54).

Astrologer Tracy Marks, an award-winning author

and recipient of a Carnegie Fund grant, has also observed this "jumping out" factor. After explaining that the "rational" approach to chart interpretation is "usually not sufficient for conducting meaningful readings," she goes on to stress the intuitive approach:

> Only by drawing upon our intuition as well as our intellect can we penetrate to the essence of the chart and interpret it in a vital and relevant manner. As we study a chart, perhaps even as we calculate it, several of its features may "jump out" at us (86:86).

Marks goes on to state that "if we feel our attention pulled in one direction or another, we should go with the pull, letting foreground and background [of the chart] shift accordingly. Eventually . . . new insights will emerge from the depths of our consciousness" (86:87).

Marks emphasizes that these experiences lead to those issues especially significant to the client, as well as to the astrologer (86:86). Thus she concludes that once the inherent wisdom of the intuitive process is recognized, the astrologer can "begin to consult it on a regular basis" (86:87). In order to do this, the astrologer must develop intuitive or psychic abilities "by relaxing and emptying our minds as we look at a chart, [so] we can gaze at it as we would a mandala or painting, communing with it . . ." (86:87).

Former vice president of Professional Astrologers Incorporated, Gray Keen, also describes this process:

> When the new astrologer reaches a point of perception—a sudden awesome insight like a large wave engulfing him on a beach—when the chart has talked, giving him a conclusive truth—he knows he has seen beyond himself. As the hair prickles his neck and coldness

runs his back, he knows he has stepped across a divide that separates the material from the mental or unknown [spiritual] world—the discovery of an unseen latent power that has been looming in existence for eons of time. ...He will attempt to develop some form of association with this unseen magical power that resides within, around and above the horoscope he holds in his hand (144:19-20).

Other astrologers emphasize learning to trust the images "floating up" to them from the chart. However unlikely or irrelevant the image may initially seem, it may produce surprising insights for a client (120:59-62). Some astrologers even psychically "enter" the chart as a dream world where information about the client is supernaturally revealed to them (140:194-96).

Whether the astrologer "enters" the chart, whether images "float up" to him, whether he is "led" in a particular direction, or whether something "jumps out," we cannot rule out the possibility of a spirit using the chart to place images or information into the mind that only the spirit knows are relevant to the client. A number of former professional astrologers insist this does happen (81:45-56). Many other astrologers will strongly disagree with such a conclusion, but this possibility of inconspicuous or unnoticeable spirit contact makes denials of spiritistic associations by astrologers difficult to assess. Like Dr. Laster, many astrologers do not feel astrology is an occult art or that it has anything to do with spiritistic guidance.

Because of this denial of astrologers, we will present four lines of evidence suggesting that the spirit world can indeed be active in helping astrologers to interpret their charts:

1. *The chart is a vehicle to "higher" (psychic) consciousness and personal transformation typically promoted*

in spiritism. Astrology affects more than the client; it may also affect the astrologer in ways he never expected. The construction and interpretation of the astrology chart may produce results similar to many methods of mystical or psychic development (84:110; 143:29-34). For example, the chart can be employed as a mandala (a geometric form used for meditation) to break down the door of normal consciousness. In other words, the astrologer's personality is temporarily set aside and the consciousness is turned inward. This permits development of a "higher" or altered consciousness—an alleged contact with a "high self" which then supposedly provides the key to proper chart interpretation. Thus, through the symbology of the chart, the astrologer can "be taken out of his personality inward to realization.... A door opens to communication with the Inner Self, whether your own or that of the person whose horoscope is being studied" (140:5).

Many astrologers view the practice of astrology as a powerful method for occult transformation. This transformation process involves a radical shift in consciousness and perception, and a typical indoctrination into a New Age world view (309).

As one astrologer observes, "Man can achieve some magical transformation of himself and Astrology can show how this may be achieved" (140:8). This same astrologer goes on to state, "Like Theosophy, its [astrology's] purpose is the ultimate [i.e., occult] transformation of the individual" (140:19). Another astrologer reveals "...everything in the chart is to be used for [self i.e., occultic] transformation" (117:44).

In *The Astrologer's Guide to Counseling,* psychiatrist and astrologer Bernard Rosenblum discloses that once the client is ready to seek out an accomplished astrologer, the client is now willing to be "educated by the teachings of an archetypal psychology, a 'wisdom school,' so to speak. The client...becomes sensitized to the nature of universal forces and principles and how they are manifesting in his or her psyche and life" (118:14).

Humanistic astrologer Dane Rudhyar defines astrology's purpose as developing sensitivity to "spiritual inner promptings"; as "calling down divine [i.e., occult] power"; as transmitting "celestial" messages; and as leading a client into the development of higher consciousness (117:40-41,60).

New Age occultist/astrologer Barbara Clow emphasizes that astrologers have the power to make their clients "alive" to the psychic realm, much as the Hindu and Buddhist gurus give *shaktipat* in Eastern forms of initiation. (Shaktipat is the transference of occult power from master to disciple in order to generate occult transformation.) Clow states, "Astrologers have been given stellar divination so that they can initiate clients into the powers of the outer planets.... This is a great power indeed" (130:11).

These disclosures by professional astrologers reveal that astrology involves much more than predicting the future and counseling a person by the stars. It also involves the possibility of an occult transformation of the astrologer and client. But how does this relate to spiritism? Because the history of the occult reveals that where altered states of consciousness and occult transformation are encouraged, the spirit world is also found (348).

In the citation below, a professional astrologer is discussing how various astrologers interact with the chart. Significantly, these astrologers speak of being "given" occult information and of receiving communication from other "personalities." But who exactly is giving the information, and who exactly are the other personalities?

> Mrs. Elliot tells of concentrating on the center of the chart, as one would with a mandala. The center

becomes a golden orb and she begins to feel as if she is inside the chart, standing in the center, with all the planetary forces playing around her like the rays of the sun. . . . As she reaches a certain point of transcendence the central golden orb where she stands seems to open out and she finds herself in a corridor. . . . From this "present" point she can look back down the corridor into the past, and forward into the future. She can also see rooms which open off the corridor and light up, allowing her to see within them. She relates that as she peers into these lighted rooms she sees pictures, like a cinema portraying incidents in the past—perhaps in this life, perhaps in a past life—and certain incidents in the future. These always have a bearing on the chart and, she feels, are shown her only if it will help her client to understand more about himself and the reasons for certain karma in his life. . . . My own method of "going through the horoscope" to make contact with the Soul may differ from that of Mrs. Elliot. I see the birth chart as a mandala expressing symbolically the character of the Soul. . . . So, after carefully studying the whole chart I meditate upon those factors I feel tell the most about the past. . . . I will myself to enter the horoscope and open up to whatever the Soul within and behind this personality can communicate to me. Perhaps it is only my own Soul or Higher Self that I hear, or perhaps it is our Souls speaking to one another, it hardly matters. . . . What happens next is usually a vivid unrolling of certain past scenes, personalities, and relationships. Like Rose Elliot, I feel I am only shown those fragments of the past that have relation to the present life and knowledge which will be of help to the person whose chart I am reading (140:194-96).

This illustrates that astrologers can gain occult information by entering altered states of consciousness and being "open" to receiving communication. Astrologers say this information comes from their charts and/or their "higher self." But what if the chart is merely a tool for a spirit to work through? What if the "higher self" that gives the astrologer occult information is really an unannounced spirit guide? These questions take us to our next topic.

2. *The astrology chart can become a "living" power (a focusing agent) through which other powers can work.* Astrologers often speak of the "power" or "energy" within their charts. Like a living being, the chart "speaks" to the astrologer. Images rise to the mind (120:58-65), the astrologer is directed to certain aspects of the chart, psychic information or visions are received, etc. It is as if a living power either resides within or works through the chart.

Barbara Clow observes, "Something magical happens when the astrologer carefully draws out the natal chart and meditates on the symbols. Suddenly a whole [realm of] energetics comes alive.... Astrology is alchemical [transformative]..." (130:10).

Consider the following descriptions of the astrologer's chart:

- ...a unified energy field of consciousness ...(130:XV).

- To me the chart is a *temenos,* a sacred precinct, a holy place...(120:7).

- The construction and interpretation of the horoscope is a *ritual,* carrying a magic dimension. All ritual, all magic embodies certain steps of circumscribing the area of work, the words, chant, or hymn setting the stage for the manifestation of power or acquisition of knowledge. Setting up the horoscope is the ritual that puts the astrologer in tune with the [power and] the individual to be studied (140:7).

This emphasis on occult power and knowledge is why the chart can become a vehicle through which a power outside the astrologer lends its assistance to the astrologer's task. In this respect astrological charts are similar to many other occult devices—Ouija boards, amulets, mandalas, yantras, etc., all known to be vehicles through which the spirit world functions to impart information, transfer occult power, or even to possess an individual (348).

While an amulet is believed to be simply an object of occult power (for protection, etc.), a yantra (a picture of the disciple's guru upon which he meditates and communes with the guru) and a mandala are focuses for concentration and meditation whereby communication can be established with spiritual powers.

This is why many astrologers actually speak of their charts as mandalas—because the chart functions as a means to contact spiritual powers that guide and direct a person. Astrologer Jane Evans refers to the mandala as the vehicle "through which the Inner Self can speak and guide the personality." She continues, "If you understand your horoscope, you have a mandala that speaks to you, a veritable guide to lead you from the confusions of your life to inner spiritual illumination" (140:4).

Because the power resides within the chart, astrologers often wait upon the chart for guidance, as Sylvia DeLong states, "Again, the chart would have to 'lead me' for the answer to a certain question" (95:213).

But once again, information and guidance of this type is reminiscent of the descriptions of a wide variety of otherwise normal objects through which spiritistic powers can work—from pagan idols to charms and amulets, to the Ouija board and Tarot cards, to divining rods and a dozen other systems of divination (see section 4 below).

3. *The importance and/or necessity of psychic/spiritistic inspiration for chart interpretation. The importance and/or necessity of psychic interpretation arises from the chart itself.* Most astrologers believe proper interpretation of the chart requires intuition and/or psychic ability. Doris Chase Doane confesses, "Knowingly or unknowingly, it is almost impossible to read a birthchart or to give an opinion on what a progressed aspect is likely to bring into the life [of the client] without exercising in some degree, Extra-sensory Perception" (159:3).

The reason for this need of psychic ability is simple: Astrological chart interpretation is entirely subjective, is almost impossibly complex, and deals with a large number of contradictory "indicators." As a result, some type of additional "help" from an allegedly higher mind, or more or less infallible "higher self," is simply a necessity (59:170-79).

For example, DeLong admits, "Each sign, house and aspect has myriad possibilities, and sometimes a trend shown has many possibilities. In reading the finer nuances of a chart, intuitive or psychic gifts can be of great help" (82:2).

But here astrologers make a crucial miscalculation. Because the source of information is intuitive or psychic, they presume that such a source makes the astrologer's chart interpretation accurate or "divine" (140:57-58). Most astrologers believe they are inwardly one with God and that through psychic meditation they may contact their allegedly divine higher Self. They therefore assume any chart interpretation deriving from such a meditative source must be pure, divinely authoritative, and accurate. As explained in chapters 9 and 10, however, God simply does not work through astrology, astrologers, or horoscope charts. This means that any inspiration the astrologer experiences is either a purely fallible human inspiration or, worse, spiritistic inspiration—or a combination of both.

Astrologers claim there are only three basic methods for interpreting the chart: the psychic method, the intuitive method, and the cookbook method—considered useless (59:171).

The cookbook method is the standard interpretation derived by searching the appropriate manuals for the interpretation of a given set of symbols and indicators. But cookbook methods of interpretation are unreliable, of course, because they are written by astrologers with many different viewpoints.

The only recourse for the astrologer desiring some degree of accuracy is entrance into the intuitive or psychic realm. Indeed, even the more scientifically-minded astrologers, such as Richard Nolle, also must admit that the problems inherent in the chart demand an intuitive/psychic method be undertaken: "It is the faculty of intuition, not some immutable, empirically-defined law, that permits the individual astrologer to select, from among a myriad possibilities, the one that fits a particular case" (84:93).

As the astrologer examines the hundreds of bits of data in a chart, without some way to pick out the "relevant" factors he will become lost "in the tangle of hundreds of interrelated variables" (86:7). But if he is faced with far too many variable and contradictory indicators, how can he rationally pick out what is "relevant"? He cannot.

Therefore, he turns inward to his so-called "Higher Self," "Christ Self," "divine mind," his spirit guide, his psychic ability, or whatever he chooses to name it.

Psychic chart interpretation arises from the practice of meditation and the development of psychic powers. Usually it is achieved by Eastern or occult forms of meditation (33:101; 143:120; 62:XIII). These forms of meditation typically lead to altered states of consciousness. For example, Harvard psychologist Daniel Goleman discloses, "Every school of meditation acknowledges them [psychic powers] as by-products of advanced stages of mastery..." (285:218). Astrologers openly acknowledge the importance of meditation practice for astrology.

Astrologer John Jocelyn admits, in *Meditation on the Signs of the Zodiac*, "...the fruit of such [meditative study on the Zodiac] lies in its esotericism, in [its] occult forces..." (284:114). One astrologer teaches that astrology can be properly "comprehended only by thorough study and deep meditation, allowing the abstract principles to become a part of one's consciousness" (23:15).

Professional astrologer Gloria Star, president of the Oklahoma chapter of the National Council for Geocosmic Research (an astrology organization), states:

> I suggest that students learn astrology using both intellect and intuition, since both are required to fully delineate a chart.... To activate the intuitive understanding, try meditating on the astrological symbols.... Certain thoughts may come into your mind. You may also notice particular colors or special energies (45:10-11).

Jane Evans emphasizes that "the individual horoscope must be plumbed with the aid of the higher intuitive mind...[such] intuition can be developed through meditation, constant use and openness to whatever comes 'through'..." (140:4-5). She observes that some astrologers rely entirely upon psychic methods and "use the horoscope more as a point of focus, like a crystal ball" which means their astrology "is only as good as their psychic powers" (140:193).

Many astrologers (up to 80 percent according to our AFA questionnaire results) acknowledge that even "rational" chart interpretation is likely to develop psychic powers. Ronald Davison, editor of *Astrology* magazine and president of the Astrological Lodge of the Theosophical Society in London, observes:

> Whereas few are gifted with sufficient sensitivity to receive true psychic inspiration, most students will find that by concentrating upon a rational approach to the problems of horoscope interpretation, they will gradually enhance their own intuitive [psychic] powers (10:138).

But Eastern and occult forms of meditation are also recognized paths to spirit contact (348). The combination of meditation and altered states of consciousness developed by the astrologer, with the help of the chart, leads to development of psychic powers and spiritistic contacts.

The fact of spiritistic chart interpretation: astrologers' admissions. We have said that the virtual impossibility of an objective chart interpretation forces the astrologer to seek a more "reliable" form of guidance in psychic or intuitive methods believed to originate from a higher or divine source, within or without the astrologer. Because it is often believed the chart is in some sense a divine communicator (138:11), the astrologer turns to what he considers spiritual inspiration. But the real source of such inspiration is often spiritistic.

Marc Edmund Jones provides an example of the logical connection between psychic or intuitive chart interpretation and spiritism:

> After some eight years of largely experimental but rigid professional practice...using conventional procedures he gradually became convinced that the commonly successful or reliable results in the performance of the astrologers he had come to know so well were largely dependent on intuitive or psychic capacity. ...Thus he decided to investigate the whole movement of spiritualism [spiritism]...(59:VI).

Cheryl Martin, who emphasizes the use of astrology for "further exploration of the self," notes the connection of chart interpretation to channeling (a New Age term for spirit possession) when she states, "Much of the [astrological] information is related to the ideas of channeling. I know there's a reason I pick up certain areas for discussion when the details are not seen objectively in the chart" (138:134).

Pamela Crane, founder of the Pamela Crane College of Horoscopy, and assistant editor of England's *Astrological Association Journal,* observes that an ancient muse (a spirit or god) named *Urania* was one of the nine Muses said to preside over astrology. She observes, "...the Muse...may at one extreme be given all the credit for the efforts of the astrologer" (63:191,200).

In one spiritistically inspired astrology text, the astrologer is told that the reading of books is not very helpful for astrology. To really learn astrology, one must develop intuition to contact the spirits on the spiritual plane and receive occult knowledge. Thus, the astrologer must put himself "in a receptive position, state, frame of body, mind and feeling to receive a message"— presumably because "all human beings in the natural state are mediumistic..." (142:XI,175,200-01).

Charles Strohmer knows it is impossible for astrology to work on the basis of its stated principles because they are comprised only of myths, but astrology still works and thus has power to draw people:

A seasoned astrologer, however... will tell you that self-disclosures do occur. Experienced numerologists or fortune-tellers will concur regarding their crafts; their clients will tell you the same. In this way, a large amount of trust develops on the part of the client, trust in the craft and in the spokesperson, as a few quarters of the client's life are laid open and recognized by someone who knows only the client's time, place, and date of birth.

So it is that self-disclosures become large dividends, justifying one's continued investment in the craft. Thus, the greater the precision and regularity of the dividends, the more excited one becomes about investing. Thus the phenomenon of self-disclosures helps to explain why many clients are unafraid to venture the next astrological step: trusting the craft to govern their futures (81:40-41).

Strohmer notes two personal experiences that confirm the power of astrology:

> I knew little about Phyllis. After discussing some generalizations with her, I began to "notice" (in a progression of her birth chart) that she currently faced severe adversity on her job, and that this ordeal was being perpetrated by a fellow employee.... I could not shake off this impression that was coming to me... I spoke to Phyllis about it, suddenly adding that the ordeal had begun about a year and a half earlier. Phyllis confirmed my discovery.
>
> ...When Phyllis confirmed the self-disclosure, I, for some reason, forecasted that within one year the ordeal would end. I did not

know it, but this forecast fit Phyllis' desire. ...In this way astrology [began] to govern Phyllis....

I also remember Tom. Tom taught occult mind development classes.... I wanted to know the astrological *whys* of Tom's supposed powers of astral projection. Eventually, I erected Tom's chart and we discussed it. What sticks out in my mind about this discussion is Tom saying he was uninterested in astrology *before* I delineated his chart.... In Tom's chart I saw strong indicators (influences) specifically for the supposed capability of astral travel as opposed to other forms of psychic manifestations. And I told him so.... If astrology can know one unknown thing about me, people think, perhaps it knows other things—things I don't even know about myself. Perhaps it *can* interpret human nature, and spiritual things as well. And thus, through astrological confirmations, the convinced clients transform a hobby into a way of life (81:41-42).

In discussing these detailed and specific astrological self-disclosures, Strohmer believes that only the influence of the spirit world can logically explain them. After discussing how astrologers seem directed to certain elements in a chart, he states:

It is the spirit that is somehow doing the "focusing." The focusing is influenced not by a planet or a mythological relativism but by a deceptive and invisible being who knows both the spokesperson and the client.... while I was studying the charts the spirits made the psychic connection and tied it all together (81:53-54).

Strohmer is not alone in his convictions that spiritism is the real source of power behind astrology. From the ancient past until modern times, many astrologers have claimed spiritistic guidance in chart interpretation. For example, the ancient Egyptian god "Thoth" had, as one of his purposes, the revealing of "the wisdom of the astrologers" (99:54, cf. 86:147). Claudius Ptolemy, considered the "father" of ancient astrology and the "Prince of Astrologers," confessed that it was totally impossible for people on their own power to predict the future. Thus he admitted, "They only who are inspired by the deity can predict particulars" (286:153).

In the 1600s the famous astrologer William Lilly and others accepted that the spirits gave astrological knowledge: .

> Lilly himself conceded the possibility of knowledge by direct angelic revelation; "many now living" had been so helped, he thought; alchemy indeed could be learned no other way. According to Reginald Scot some held that even knowledge of astrology could be thus acquired: there was a spirit named Bifrons who could make men "wonderfully cunning" in the subject (46:634).

In the late nineteenth century, astrologer, medium, and Mason Thomas Burgoyne claimed that a certain class of spirits worked directly with astrologers. He said this group of spirits (whom he believed too intelligent "to be guilty of fraud") work closely with all astrologers:

> They are the attendant familiars [spirits] of certain classes of mystical students, especially those devoted to alchemy and astrology. It is these beings that usually produce the visions. ... They are indeed planetary in nature.... They

> . . . can give much information regarding the
> orb under whose dominion they act (141:84).

Twentieth-century astrologer Dane Rudhyar teaches that the astrologer's task is to become a vehicle for personal occult powers. He believes the practice of astrology can call down spirit forces and powers which will help transform both astrologer and client (117: 40-47,76; cf. 63:57).

Astrologer Joan Hodgson is also a spiritist, referring to the releasing of tremendous but subtle creative forces in astrology. She believes "powers of true mediumship or seership are unfolded" (94:102).

It is evident that many astrologers openly admit spirits can work through astrology. But is it also possible for spirits to work without the astrologer's knowledge? It is to this question we now turn.

Spirit influence may be inconspicuous in the practice of astrology. The tradition of the occult leaves no doubt that spirits do not need to be felt in order to be present. For example, as occurs in hypnosis, they can even implant an entire sequence of events into the mind, events that never really happened at all. These are not perceived as dream-like but as real as any waking reality.

Consider the experiences of scientist and parapsychologist Dr. Andrija Puharich and medium Uri Geller, who discuss their contact with alleged UFO entities—invisible beings that act in a manner quite similar to the spirit guides of mediums (349:167-223). Dr. Puharich describes the personal impact such power to manipulate the mind made upon him. He refers to a series of events over two days, totally controlled and directed by the spirits—what he calls intelligences from space, or "IS" as he names them:

> These two days' events numbed me. Sara
> and Uri experienced one sequence and Ila and

I experienced another, in the same time frame. I had discovered the truth about Uri's deepest secret, had had a gun in my hand that felt real, and had had a phone call experience that is real in my mind to this day. But most of all I realized that the four of us had had an experience imprinted on our minds by what could only be the agency of IS. I finally learned that, given the existence of IS, I could never again know which of my experiences were directly imposed upon me by IS and which were not. I have never been so deeply shaken in my life as when I realized the full implication of this power... (287:112).

But if invisible spirits can implant whole experiences in the mind, surely then they can implant and direct simple thoughts—as in an astrologer's interpretation of the chart. In the world of mediumism and spiritism, such "spirit-feeding" is widely acknowledged. Here a person's spirit guides can inconspicuously affect thought processes to help direct his life, which after all, is the *purpose* of a spirit *guide*.

But the spirits are under no obligation to announce their presence or influence. This is why both astrologers and spiritists share similar experiences. For example, Robert Leightman, a spiritist and physician, acknowledges the spirits had been giving him important ideas for some time, yet he was completely unaware of the fact. He had believed the ideas were originating in his own mind:

What they did was to give me a whole bunch of ideas. And of course I thought, well, my mind has suddenly become brilliant. It was already great before, but now it is absolutely brilliant. I was getting all kinds of ideas from

time to time and of course, the spooks [spirits]
said they were giving them to me [but at first I
didn't believe it] (288:40).

What is significant is that the astrologer often has no
idea where such information comes from or that such
information could be derived from the spirit world.
Strohmer states:

The knowledgeable, familiar spirit infil-
trates the thinking activity in such a covert
way that the astrologer assimilates the data
and has no inkling that anything other than
his own thoughtlife is responsible for the self-
disclosures. I cannot say how this cover-up
works, but it is possible to discover *when* it
occurs (81:53).

Many astrologers deliberately hide their spiritism.
Others are unaware of it. Still other astrologers only
seem to avoid occultic methods. For example, Marc
Edmund Jones "felt intuition should never be used in
delineating astrological charts" (58:1). From this, one
could assume he avoided subjective or psychic methods
of chart interpretation, but as seen earlier, most of his
astrological information was derived from the spirit
world (58:11; 60:83-87).

Astrologer Philip Sedgwick confesses that information can be received from the spirit world by the astrologer, yet the astrologer may never know the true source
of such information:

However, this type of channeling does not require losing consciousness, trancing or altering
one's state of mind; it just happens. The beauty
of this method is that it remains completely
inconspicuous (144:176).

4. *If all divination is accomplished by psychic/spiritistic inspiration, chart divination is also.* Astrology is only one of scores of various forms of divination. If examination reveals all other forms of divination depend on psychic and spiritistic influence and guidance, then it is logical to expect astrology courts a similar influence. (In fact, in addition to astrology, most astrologers appear to practice at least one of the following forms of divination.)

All divinatory methods utilize some principal object that becomes the focus and/or vehicle through which spirits work to serve the client and produce the needed answer to questions, character analysis, future prognostication, etc. The object becomes the contact material for spirits to work through. Following is a list of contact materials for a number of common forms of divination:

Astrology: the horoscope chart.

Tarot: a deck of cards with symbols.

I Ching: sticks, printed hexagrams.

Runes: dice.

Ouija Board: an alphabet planchette.

Radionics/psychometry: the divining rod, pendulum, "black box," etc.

Palmistry: the hand.

Crystal-gazing: the crystal ball or crystal rock.

Metoscopy/physiognomy/phrenology: the forehead/face/skull.

Geomancy: combinations of dots or points.

Water-dowsing: the forked stick or other object.

Is it logical to expect mere pieces of paper bearing symbols (horoscopes), simple forked sticks, cards, hands, dice, letters of the alphabet, rocks, facial lines, or dots, could ever supply miraculous information about a person? Even the practitioners of these arts refer to "supernatural influences"—to gods and spirits who operate through these methods, as in geomancy (199:87).

Space does not permit documenting the spiritistic nature of all the above, but we can cite sufficient illustrations to document that even practitioners acknowledge or suspect spirit influence in these methods. Typically, these various practices do two things: 1) they develop a person psychically, and 2) they lead to spirit contact, which, as in astrology, is not always discernible.

For example, that Ouija boards lead to spirit contact and spirit possession is well-documented in Gruss' *The Ouija Board: Doorway to the Occult* (355).

Common water-dowsing is also spiritistic, even though this is less well-known. Our own confirming research comprises over 100 pages. The research of Ben Hester, in his *Dowsing: An Exposé of Hidden Occult Forces,* provides further documentation (323).

Tarot cards, the I Ching, runes, and related methods can also work by spiritistic power. Below we cite illustrations for these three methods.

Tarot cards (Middle East divination): It is believed by some traditions that the Tarot deck originated with the ancient Egyptian god Thoth. As in astrology, Tarot cards are known for their ability to produce divination of "uncanny accuracy," and it is admitted that the cards work through intuitive and psychic means. But the Tarot cards can also be used as astral doorways for contacting the spirit world (289:44; 290:213-17; 291:7-8; 292:9).

Runes (Viking divination/European magic): As with astrology and Tarot cards, runes are extolled for their "uncanny ability" to provide accurate information of a supernatural nature. The invention of the runes is credited to the Nordic god Odin, and "the elemental spirits associated with the runes were regarded as the major source of their mysterious power" (293:8,37).

I Ching (Chinese divination): This technique is also lauded for its "amazing precision," but John Blofeld, a scholar and translator of the oracle, writes that his first use of it brought absolute fright—"so strong was the impression of having received an answer to my question from a living, breathing person" (294:25-27).

> The feeling that [the] question had been dealt with *exactly as by a living being* in full possession of even the unspoken facts involved in both the question and answer. At first this sensation comes near to being terrifying... (294:25-27).

Blofeld cautions that the I Ching be treated with due respect, lest it become angered. As astrologers do of their own craft, he admits utter bafflement as to how it works. If the solution were to state it works by "a god or the gods," he would be "inclined to agree." In fact, he admits, "If I were asked to assert that the printed pages do not form the dwelling of a spiritual being or at least bring us into contact with one by some mysterious process, I think I should be about as hesitant as I am to assert the contrary" (294:25-27).

If the several systems of divination listed above are admitted to work by supernatural agency or the power of the spirits, is there any reason to believe divination by astrology works by a different method?

Additional ways in which astrologers may be led into spiritism

To show there are other means by which astrologers may encounter the spirit world, we have listed several below and occasionally we have provided comments.

1. Indications or predictions of death may lead to contacting the spirits of the dead for advice, counsel, or comfort (140:14).

2. Some astrological literature contains clear directives to work with the spirits (143:117-21). Some astrologers are mediums or spiritists who lead other astrologers or clients into spirit contact. They do this because spirit guides have told them it is important for these people to have the assistance of the spirit world.

Other astrologers encourage utilizing the assistance of various spirit beings such as alleged angels and spirit teachers. For example:

> Hosts of stellar-resident angels administer the universal influx of energy.... There are angels to awaken us into various levels of consciousness, and angels to guide us along an often misunderstood path (151:3).
>
> There are guides from other places who are our teachers and who will work with us if we call upon them ... (130:21).

3. Astrologers may encounter "Nature" or "planetary" spirits who control "planet energies," or who work "through the signs of the Zodiac" (94:28; 151:20).

4. Some mediums' spirit guides (though the mediums are not astrologers) desire to teach astrologers.

> Carl [the spirit] decided to get down to business by advising me on a number of family/personal matters. I was stunned by the information he was channeling through my [mediumistic] friend; it was so accurate (144:105).

5. Some astrologers have spirit guides who inspire or direct their writings or help prepare the charts of their clients (144:105,127,170).

6. Some astrologers encounter spirits under another name, and describe their possession by various "energy forces." But these descriptions are often indistinguishable from descriptions given by people spiritually possessed (130:168-69; 151:55).

Any number of impressive names are given for what is really spirit contact (or even spirit possession). Among these are kundalini arousal (130:XVII-XXI,11-12), attainment of super-consciousness (151:7), or metaphysical attunement with the higher self (140:11).

Barbara Clow emphasizes the astrologer's "shamanistic duty" to place a client in contact with powerful forces such as kundalini and similar occult energies— e.g., an "alignment with their brother animal's spirit" (130:13-14). She describes her own transformation by alleged planet energies and fusion with her higher self, as follows:

I experienced a transfiguration...where I ascended to the higher planes and fused with my higher self....Then at my Chiron opposition...I became obsessively involved with esoteric and mystical reading and rituals, and became a recluse. At the third opposition...I experienced more stress and disorientation as I integrated the chirotic force into my being. ...However, there is a price to pay if you say yes to an experience or energy given to you. ...you cannot say "no" when your higher self, or master, asks you to bring in something really difficult and important.... Transmutation and transfiguration...occur when we get out of the physical body and experience the non-physical realms (such as masters and guides)....This chirotic form of transmutation is so systemic, the change so complete, the experience so intense....often it can only be recognized by its effects, such as a sudden new vision, a complete path alteration in life, a feeling of being reborn (130:28-30,42-43; cf. 11-12,35-37,46,168-70,298).

In addition, the spirits may use astrological concepts (e.g., the invisible planets or the invisible energies of visible planets) to foster the occult transformation of the astrologer or even mask their own activities, including the spiritual possession of the astrologer. Thus, the astrologer may become possessed by a "planet's" energies. Or, he may be told that the way to avoid the evil energies or effects of a planet is to commit himself to occult development (129:5-6).

7. *Energy astrology seems to be the most common mask for spirit contact.* Many forms of energy astrology exist, but the key to nearly all of them is the contacting of these energies (whether planetary, mental, super-conscious or whatever), assimilating them into the consciousness and/or body, and using them for occult power (143:90-91,114).

In the quote below, substituting the word "god" or "spirit" for the word "star" will show the possibility of the incorporation of a spirit into one's being:

Since we are not dealing with the physical planets, but rather with conscious beings who are focused in the planets, we can communicate with them in consciousness and relate the planets' kind of energy to the corresponding system in ourselves. The alchemist Agrippa wrote of this process: "for through a certain mental faculty our spirit can thus by imitation be made like some star so that it is suddenly filled with the functions of a star" (38:130).

The concept of "energy" use in astrology is similar to the concept of energy manipulation common to the holistic health and other New Age, occultic disciplines (356). The Hermetic concept of "as above, so below" can result in astrologers seeking to manipulate the alleged planetary energies within themselves. For example, "Humankind has always known intuitively that we were connected to the cosmos by invisible energies.... As above, so below. We are microcosms of the macrocosm; what we find in ourselves, we find in the Universe. And we are intimately linked to the subtle yet pervasive influences of terrestrial and celestial energies..." (93:35). These energies are to be "uncovered," "realized," "invoked," or "directed." They can be manipulated for occult power, higher or altered states of consciousness, for kundalini arousal and a dozen other occult purposes—purposes which typically involve spirit associations and/or possession (348).

Astrologer Mae Wilson-Ludlam observes, "The ancient teachings describe a primordial energy pervading all of the universe. It is the spiritual essence permeating all matter and often is referred to as spirit energy" (151:2). She then proceeds to discuss spirit contact as a manifestation of this energy.

Award-winning astrologer Stephen Arroyo states, "...most astrologers have overlooked the basic foundation upon which astrology is based: *energy*" (116:71). He says the planetary (occult) energies must be permitted entrance into our being:

> The planets characterize the mode of energy exchange between the individual human being and the universal storehouse [of energy]. ...In ancient terms, the planets symbolized the gods which must be worshipped.... They must be recognized, [paid] due attention, and accepted; then the energy inherent in them can be [incorporated inwardly and] consciously directed. If we are not aware of these forces in

our lives, then we are at the mercy of them (116:76-77).

Arroyo thus teaches, "... we must approach astrology itself on the level where it operates; and that is the level of energy patterns, energy flow, and energy transmutation" (116:88). Arroyo identifies the energy of astrology as equivalent to the energy found in the occult and used by spirits (116:28-33,50,71,78,177-87).

Louise Huber, basing her astrology on the spiritistically inspired astrology of Alice Bailey (136:31,65,83), stresses the importance of accepting "the flowing in of spiritual energies" and the inspirations and revelations they bring (136:IX-X). She believes ancient contacts with the gods point the way for the modern astrologer (136:12). She also reveals:

> Many people wish to come into contact with spiritual energies [spirits] so as to derive guidance and help from them.... Astrology has always concerned itself with Man and his relationship to cosmic energies.... According to ancient [witchcraft] tradition a special transmission of energy takes place every month at the time of the full moon. In the Zodiac meditations we can tune in directly to this transmission ... (136:20-24).

Elsewhere she identifies spirit beings as the ones who "control and regulate those energies during the days of the Full Moon. One is Buddha, one is Christ, and one is 'the lord of the world' " (136:56).

She also stresses visualization, but the process described here is reminiscent of the descriptions given by occultists of their spirit possession (e.g., Swami Muktananda's possession by a spirit being described in his autobiography *Play of Consciousness*, 1978, pp. 64-197 [136:76,107,124,176]).

To help define its nature, below we present some typical characteristics of this energy.

This energy is often illustrated by reference to possessed persons. For example, mediums and spiritists, psychic healers and psychic surgeons, shamans and gurus all use the same energies and give similar descriptions (93:36-40; 116:72; cf. 348).

The energy is defined as being equivalent to the traditional (often pantheistic) occult energies of many ancient cultures and their modern equivalents—"kundalini," "prana," "mana," "od," "chi," "orgone," etc. (93:40: 116:177-87; 126:120).

The energy is considered "living" and allegedly divine (116:28). Stephen Arroyo discusses an astrological teaching that at birth a child receives a personal god or spirit-guide to direct his life. The god is the deity of the ruling planet of the ascendant. (Remember that in astrology the planets rule the signs—thus the ruling planet of Capricorn rising is Saturn.) As the planet is the lord of the rising sign, the god is the lord of the child born under that god's particular sign. Arroyo describes how a child born with Capricorn rising experienced a "Saturnian" birth:

> As the child was born, the room became filled with a powerful and almost tangible presence. The intensity of pressure felt in that room at that moment could only be described as a Saturnian energy and vibration, and I remarked to one of the others present that the atmosphere was charged with this powerful force . . . (135:217).

Then energy is amoral; it can be used for good or evil. As one astrology text confesses, "There is white and black astrology . . . (55:638).

The energy is the same energy explored in parapsychology, the scientific study of the occult (116:71).

These energies are transformative. They produce dramatic and fundamental changes in the consciousness and world view of the person who is open to them (116:78). For example, they can produce the traditional spiritual "enlightenment" of Eastern cults which itself is reminiscent of spirit possession (98–208; 350:39-73).

These energies may be "channeled" for various purposes to receive or give information, develop psychically, etc. (62:34; 83:4-5; 126:120; 135:13,24).

> The basis of the astrological sciences is the emanation, transmission and reception of energies.... The capacity to receive and profit by the planetary energies...[which] constitutes an unalterable law and accounts for the power of certain planets.... They will ...only become potent...when a man has reached a certain point of development and is becoming sensitive to higher influences ...(55:266-67).

Man is intimately linked to this energy which pervades the entire universe (116:32).

The energies are related to the spirit world (116:76-77; 126:120; 55:9,266-69; 62:72-74). For example:

> High ceremonial astrology...depends upon the knowledge of the Initiate of those immaterial Forces and spiritual Entities that affect matter and guide it.... That which is the *surviving* Entity *in us* is partly the direct emanation from and partly those celestial Entities themselves (55:636-37).

The spirits stress the importance of making use of these energies (55:9-12).

The energies may enter and possess the person. Former astrologer Strohmer reminds us, "The horoscope chart is contact material for mediumship" (81:59). Thus, we should not be surprised to discover the spirits themselves entering the astrologer. Alice Bailey writes: "The forces of these Hierarchies...then sweep into and through the Initiate and awaken those major group responses which eventually give him systemic ["enlightened"] consciousness..." (55:268).

In Hindu astrology, for example, Rahu and Ketu are not planets but calculated points in the sky that are accepted because they "generate recognizable effects in a horoscope" (62:33). We are told they are "masses of energy" that behave "like two parts of a demon" (62:33).

Not surprisingly, their "indications" sound like the results of demonization: "Occultism...compulsive and unconscious behavior...mental derangement...dirt, filth, parasites...spasms...undiagnosable and incurable ailments, theft, murder...witchcraft, magic..." (62:36).

If the indications of a planet are indistinguishable from demon possession, how does the astrologer, Hindu or American, know the client is not demon-possessed?

16

The Dangers of Astrology

The basic argument of the astrologer is that it "works," but we have seen that this rationale is not valid. Many things in life "work" that are either false (such as false religion) or dangerous (such as cancer). In fact, many things work extremely well, but are nevertheless dangerous; for example, dynamite, guns, and car bombs.

There are dangers in astrology as well. Science writer and engineer Lawrence E. Jerome observes, "How much physical and psychological damage such false astrological practices and advice cause cannot even be estimated" (102:212). Bart Bok, a former president of the American Astronomical Society, has commented, "The study and ready availability of astrological predictions can exert an insidious influence on a person's personal judgment" (310:1). But most people continue to believe that astrology is just a harmless pastime.

Most astrologers believe their practices help people. This is one reason why astrology has sought to strengthen its association with one of the most powerful helping professions in today's society—psychotherapy (116–127). But can astrology really help people?

To *help* is to engage in an act for the benefit of someone in need. The problem for astrology is that the "help" is based upon the premises of astrology. If astrology reinforces falsehoods about self, morality, God, and the universe, then decisions based upon those falsehoods will be anything but helpful.

If helping means aiding people to live better lives—personally, morally, ethically, spiritually; if it means aiding them to become good parents, children, and members of society, to instill in themselves and their children the good values of love for neighbor and God—then astrology fails. It fails because even when it attempts these, it has no logical basis to sustain them.

The fact is that counsel based upon astrology often leads the client to accept myths and falsehoods as truths, place self above all else, reject reason and common sense, reject absolute moral values and standards, and accept occult philosophy and practices.

The counsel offered by astrology is based on a number of false premises, including monism/pantheism (we are all part of God), religious humanism (as gods we may do whatever we wish), amoralism (absolute morality is a myth), reincarnation (one of the more consequential religious ideas in human history [307]), and occult philosophy (which has traditionally been opposed to conventional social values). How can counseling based upon such things, logically applied according to the astrological world view, ever be "helpful"? In this chapter, therefore, we shall discuss some of the dangers and problems of astrology.

Three principal dangers of astrology

Astrology is dangerous because it is a lie. If astrology is not true in any sense (chapters 3-8), then it cannot give either accurate or useful information, for a system founded upon falsehood can never generate truths. But if it gives false or inaccurate information on vital matters in life, then those who act upon such advice open themselves to the consequences. Living a lie is unhealthy.

Astrology is dangerous because it is an occult system that leads people to accept the assistance and advice of demons. If astrology functions in collaboration with demons, then it is dangerous by definition. To help introduce people to sociopathic personalities hardly reflects an innocent pastime. That the spirits are sociopathic is more than abundantly proven by their actions in 1) the New Testament (possessing, mauling, and attempting to murder people) [192–197]; 2) their deceptions and lies about God and salvation while at the same time claiming to "deeply love" their contacts (309); 3) the entire history of spiritism, parapsychology, and occultism that is littered with case histories of tragedies induced by spirit contact (300).

Astrology is dangerous because it insulates people against salvation in Christ. Astrology is an anti-Christian system of philosophy and practice, leading people away from God and Christ through false religious beliefs and activity. It thereby increases their chances of leaving this life without their sins forgiven. Any system that leads people to face God in judgment is not "harmless."

Profiles of people who become astrologers and of people who become their clients

The astrologer can command great power over his client because most people who consult an astrologer believe he is a kind of "cosmic priest," an infallible interpreter of the universe. Thus, even astrologers admit, "Behind the astrologer's statements, as far as the client is able to perceive, lies the power and the authority of the cosmos" (116:53).

But what kind of person becomes an astrologer? Should we assume that it is only the moral and ethical person? Or by its very nature does astrology tend to lure the power-hungry, the occultist, the manipulator, the insecure, and the nonconformist? Even astrologers have admitted, "Astrologers are not ordinary people—mostly we're mavericks—so we may react differently to many run-of-the-mill circumstances in life" (126:II). But even among the moral and ethical, how might the influences of astrology mold and conform such persons into its own image so that there occurs an occultic transformation in their lives and a rejection of moral values? Astrology seeks to affect key areas in life—spiritual life, health, family, children, spouse, finances, etc. Who should counsel people on the issues of life?

Leading astrologer Tracy Marks identifies several potential problems between the astrologer and the client: The astrologer may perceive himself as superior to the client; the astrologer may encourage client dependency; the astrologer may give what the client appears to want rather than really needs; the astrologer may present personal values and ideas under the cloak of astrological authority; the astrologer's "own sense of powerlessness" may lead him to "disempower [his] clients, imparting deterministic [fatalistic] attitudes"; the astrologer's fears concerning certain planets and signs may influence the interpretation and "result in [his] imparting pronouncements which could become destructively self-fulfilling prophecies"; the astrologer may use mystical language authoritatively to create "the illusion that you are imparting high truths, when indeed you may be saying little of significance"; and astrologers may "speak in vague, ungrounded generalities" (86: 151-53).

Marks observes that "most professional astrologers are guilty on occasion of at least several of the above inadequacies..." (86:151-53). In addition, she admits astrologers may react more to the chart than to the client; may become egotistical; may devalue the client; and may draw hasty conclusions (86:155-61).

Given the right circumstances, a particular chart interpretation and its powerful influence upon a person might lead even to criminal acts in order to help fulfill or forestall what the client believes is the cosmic influence or destiny upon himself or another. For example, if a chart reveals that a company may fail, then the president might embezzle funds for his own security; a child may be born mentally retarded, so there is an abortion; an enemy may seek to destroy the client, so someone is killed. The possibilities are endless. In one instance, a woman murdered her son because an astrologer predicted he would suffer a life of mental illness. The shattered mother went to jail, but the astrologer remained free (190:11-12). Dr. Kurt Koch observes, "Astrology has been responsible for a number of suicides and murders" (308:20).

Is it wise, therefore, to permit unqualified and often unethical people to direct our lives? Remember that an astrologer is usually unlicensed and unregulated; is not required to have any education; may become a "professional" astrologer overnight; is likely an occultist who rejects absolute moral values; and, as admitted by astrologers, is likely to use his power over others in a manipulative and authoritarian manner. If such a person is an astrologer and if his practices steer him into demonic collaboration, what kind of answers are people getting in astrological counseling?

But we may also ask, what kind of person seeks out an astrologer? At least some of them are extremely susceptible to astrology's destructive potential. Even according to astrologers, many of their clients have some of the following characteristics.

They lack values. Stephen Arroyo observes, "Many

people who request astrological assistance are suffering from a lack of values..." (135:246).

They are easily duped or deceived. Astrologer Jane Evans observes, "I have known too many people to whom self-deception was second nature" (140:200).

They are looking for the astrologer to make their decisions for them. This problem is almost universally admitted among astrologers. Astrologers vary in their response, some attempting to help such clients become more independent, but others willingly becoming their "gurus" and enjoying their client's dependence. Dr. Robert A. Morey concludes that many astrologers, if they had their way, would regulate our lives:

> Astrology would ultimately make us the slaves of the astrologers. They would control our marriages, careers, even war. Modern medicine and psychology would be destroyed. Astrologers would tell us when and where to operate, and would blame all mental illness on the stars, particularly the moon. Business would collapse because workers would stay at home whenever the astrologers predicted a bad day. Astrologers would even tell us when to make love with our mate. Famine and starvation would spread as farmers waited for the astrologers to tell them if and when to plant.
>
> Astrology is an all consuming world view which can potentially dictate every aspect of our daily lives. Astrology would ultimately bring about the destruction of reason, hope, meaning, significance, and love (70:47).

They wish to justify their own behavior. Marcus Allen observes:

> I studied "conventional" astrology for several years, and then let it go...gave it up

...because I was not at all satisfied with the
results of conventional astrology...people
used it so often as an excuse, a justification for
their weaknesses and shortcomings, and a
way of blaming other people for their least
evolved characteristics (137:56).

Psychological astrologers Liz Greene and Howard
Sasportas observe:

There are still many people who go to an
astrologer for these reasons—predictions and
a pat on the back about one's apparently fixed
and unalterable behavior—and there are still
many astrologers who will happily oblige such
clients by providing the information requested
(124:XI).

Stephen Arroyo asserts that all "advice given clients
should be in accord with the clients' ideals, with what
they are trying to be and become" (135:247). Thus the
astrologer seeks to "empower the client" (86:145), to
reenforce his own views in accordance with astrological
precepts, whatever they are. Astrology thus does not
advocate what is moral or true according to God.

This ability of astrologers to justify a person's selfish
tendencies caused Dr. John Warwick Montgomery to
give the following warning:

The very elasticity of astrological interpretation is its most dangerous characteristic.
Where people desperately desire a shortcut to
self knowledge and solutions to their problems, and where the answers are ambiguous,
they inevitably choose according to self-inter-
est. Thus the floodgates are opened to the
reinforcement of evil tendencies...it should

not be regarded as strange that astrology has
so frequently been used to guide evil farther
along the path it has already taken (72:118).

Because astrologers reject any absolute standard of
morality, they prefer a "situation ethics" approach
where moral decisions are determined largely by the
whim and preference of the astrologer or client. Astrologer Alan Oken observes, "No Path is the Truth Path, for
in the Absolute there is not Truthfulness or Falsehood,
no right and no wrong, no yes and no no" (2:85).

And Edward Doane states, "Throughout The Religion
of The Stars there is not one single 'thou shalt not.' On
the contrary, positive thinking, feeling and action is
taught..." (143:25). Another astrologer testifies, "The
preoccupation with self is really in the interest of evolution.... In modern astrology we seek confirmation of our
personal importance" (151:5-6).

In addition, many astrologers deliberately reject
moral values. For example, astrologer Dr. John Manolesco observes, "Religious and moral values are declin-
ing, the fiction of free will, moral obligation, [of] immutable, eternal values has been exposed for what it is—
myth" (6:33). Thus, astrologers choose not to influence
the public morally. Jeff Mayo, founder of the Mayo
School of Astrology, emphasizes astrology sets no moral
guidelines, that "the birth-chart indicates weakness or
strength [only] in this respect: Choice of action is the
individual's" (3:4).

Admissions that astrology may logically be used for evil

It is impossible for Christians logically to use their
beliefs to justify evil acts, because God is holy. But this is
not so for astrologers who can, if they choose, use their
practices for evil. Sydney Omarr admits, "Astrology is

there, to be used for the good—or the evil (Hitler!)" (26:23). An astrology text refers to the making of "the powers of a magic spell for good or evil..." (142:211). Leading astrologer Nicholas deVore confesses that "astrology has often been used to unworthy ends" (42:VIII). Ptolemy himself confessed, "Many of its practitioners are in it for gain rather than truth or wisdom, and pretend to know more than the facts permit" (97:85).

Adolph Hitler, the ancient Aztecs, the modern Zodiac killer, modern witches, and Satanists all have used astrology for evil purposes, realizing astrology's power may be used just as effectively for evil as (allegedly) for good. They decided to choose evil, and this is the point: The astrologer is free to choose (53; 139; 149–150; 152).

One leading astrologer confesses the practice "can be used detrimentally—to coerce as well as to misguide others, to worship as some kind of an occult power. A few practitioners tie it to witchcraft. It is easy to see why, in the past, and still unfortunately sometimes in the present, astrology has gained a rather tarnished reputation" (144:1).

In his *Person Centered Astrology,* Dane Rudhyar discusses Christian morality as constituting a belief in right versus wrong actions. He then says that the "new morality" of astrology involves "a change of attitude toward the concept of morality itself." He explains:

> If we are to speak significantly of a "new" morality we have to refer to an attitude to life according to which the *moral value* of any action depends almost exclusively on the conscious meaning this action has for the individual performing it. According to such an attitude morality refers to consciousness, rather than to action (301:111-12).

In this view, morality is determined by a subjective or "higher" state of consciousness, not by beliefs or actions. Obedience to God would be (perhaps) moral for one person and immoral for another.

But most astrologers are not very concerned with morality in the first place. In fact, many of them believe that it is moral judgments themselves which are the real evil (144:53,70). As one guru who endorses astrology states, "I would like to say to you: obedience [to God] is the greatest sin" and "I teach you disobedience.... The devil did a tremendous service to humanity" (351:368, 372,376).

An astrologer's job is simply to validate the client's own views, whatever they are. Astrologer Jeff Green observes:

> As Carl Jung pointed out, the prime role of the counselor is to validate objectively the subjective reality of the client. As counselors, or just as friends, we will do our best if we can simply identify reality as it exists for those with whom we interact, and to give them what they need according to their own reality—not ours.... As we attempt to answer the questions "Why am I here?" "What are my lessons?" We must attempt to understand the "reality" implied in the birth chart (131:3).

Astrologer Tracy Marks declares the following under, "The aims of the astrologer":

> We wish to confirm and therefore support our client's sense of self and sense of reality, particularly insofar as astrological interpretation confirms these perceptions.... We wish to help our client develop a more viable philosophy of life, or a belief system which makes

sense to her.... Developing such a belief system, along with the overall perspective which astrology can provide, may provide challenging false, outdated or destructive assumptions and beliefs transmitted by parents and society (86:145).

Astrology's denial of human responsibility

One reason for astrology's popularity is that it permits us to blame our own failures and evils, or whatever we do not like in ourselves, not on ourselves, but on the "stars." It provides an attractive escape from personal responsibility. Astrologers may say of their own evil actions that "Saturn did it" or that "the stars weren't auspicious." Consider the following statements that show virtually anything can be rationalized, any sin or evil attributed to the stars instead of to the person's choice.

What happens to us is what needs to happen to us (7:99).

With no special effort, *Ketu* [an invisible "planet"] can produce some of the most intense, compulsive, and unconscious behavior. ...Both [Ketu and Rahu] are responsible for all sorts of evils, such as incurable diseases, murder, theft, poison, snakes, fears, phobias, undiagnosable illnesses, imprisonment, and on and on and on! (62:33-34).

There really was no such thing as *chance* in nature, declared the astrologer John Butler. Astrological hypothesis explained everything, from the compatibility of two persons in love to the unexpected failure of a surgical operation (46:330).

Statements such as the above raise concern among many of astrology's critics. Eisler comments:

Countless defects and diseases, spiritual and moral gifts or weaknesses are sent down, suicides are predetermined, as well as accidental death by water, fire, earthquakes, thunderstorms, at the hand of the executioner, by royal decree, or through wild animals, poisonous snakes, epidemics, brigands, rebels. Children of one [astrological] degree die young, those of another reach a horary old age, those of still another are strangled, hanged on gallows, drowned or submerged in swamps. Just imagine what it means for a credulous person to be born under the fifth degree of *Aquarius* and to read in this book no better forecast than that he will hang himself by the neck in a noose! (98:127).

The astrological penchant for explaining personal failures is why Keith Thomas observes:

Many of the clients who entered an astrologer's consulting room were seeking an explanation for the sundry misfortunes which had beset them—illness, sterility, miscarriage, political failure, bankruptcy. No doubt it was more comforting to learn that one had been crossed at birth than to be told that one had no one to blame for one's misfortunes but oneself. John Aubrey was able to console himself for his sundry worldly failures with Henry Coley's opinion that he had since birth been "laboring under a cloud of ill directions."... Such instances give point to Edmund's sardonic reflections in King Leer: "This is the excellent foppery of the world, that when we are sick in fortune—often the surfeit of our own behavior—we make guilty of our disasters the sun, the moon, and the stars: as if we were villains by necessity, fools by heavenly compulsion, knaves, thieves and treachers by spherical predominance; drunkards, liars and adulterers by an enforced obedience of planetary influence; and all that we are evil in, by a divine thrusting on: an admirable evasion of whoremaster man, to lay his goatish disposition to the charge of star!" Astrology could thus appeal as a means of evading responsibility, removing guilt from both sufferer and society at large (46:329-30).

Astrology's promotion of sexual immorality

If there is any place astrology appears to justify sin, it is the area of sexual behavior (140:170). For example, astrologer William Chaney, father of novelist Jack London and a philanderer who married six times, would not acknowledge London as his son. He did, however, affirm that his astrological chart justified his sexual immorality: "...he admitted that he was overly fond of the ladies, but said it was plainly indicated in his nativity" (160:29).

Jeff Green illustrates how this can work in a person who desires astrology to provide "divine" justification for a sexual preference:

> A client of mine... compulsively sought out one sexual partner after another and in her own words, was seeking "to extract the power of my partners into myself so that I could have more power myself." [Through astrological counseling she learned] how to use her sexual energy in a spiritual [Tantric] way. Through masturbation and sexual union with another she learned how to bring her sexual energy up

the spine to promote a conscious unity with the Source.... She learned how to unite with the Source, and her own Soul, through meditation and through sexuality (131:146-47).

This woman, obsessed and troubled by her sexual behavior, discovered through astrological counseling (coupled with Tantric theory) that she could enjoy sexual affairs without guilt by making them "spiritual," a divine activity, simply because she "had Pluto in the Eighth House in Leo conjunct the South Node in the Seventh House, and in opposition to Mars in Pisces in the Second House!" (131:146).

In *The Astrology of Sexuality* we are taught a similar belief, that sex "in all its forms" can be "the avenue that leads to true harmony and understanding" (157:2). "Sex is neither good nor evil. It just is" (157:15).

Sexual acts such as fornication are said to be a *divine* process, the "most natural part of existence," the merging of two people into cosmic oneness (157:26). Sex "is a force, an energy, a part of the Divine Inspiration that we are here to experience" (157:5).

Another astrologer observes indicators for bisexuality, homosexuality, lesbianism, sexual sadism, and transsexualism in the chart (2:64-75). Since such activities are "indicated," perhaps the person who desires to pursue them will thus justify them in his own mind. And the one who does not desire to pursue them may live in worry or fear over the possibility—perhaps until he gives in to his astrological "destiny."

In *Astrology and Homosexuality* we also learn there are specific astrological indicators of homosexuality. For example, most astrologers believe Uranus and Neptune "are particularly liable to cause homosexual behavior... when involved in an opposition in Taurus/Scorpio ... [etc.]" (156:16). Thus, "A badly aspected Uranus in the horoscope is liable to make the native a homosexual"

(156:16). Or, if there are "several planets in the twelfth house" (156:17), this is also an indication of homosexuality. Other astrologers say there is "a clear trend" for homosexuality involving "the interaction of the Moon, Saturn, and houses six and twelve" (156:70).

But what would an impressionable teenager, confused about his own sexuality in this age of so-called sexual enlightenment, think if he went to an astrologer and discovered such "indicators" in his chart?

Consider the advice to a client by Maxine Bell, a famous astrologer to Hollywood's homosexual community:

> He didn't come to me for help, he came to me to find out when his next affair was due. He was just finishing up one [affair] and after two nights of being alone he was desperate, so he wondered what his prospects were for a new affair. I gave him the rundown on when the next affair would be likely. Whenever transiting Mars goes over the fifth house that starts things going (154:213-14).

One homosexual had several serious lovers, but an endless number of casual affairs that so hurt his "serious" lovers that they would seek out Bell for her advice. They discovered their lover was fickle and promiscuous because of the Moon in Cancer, Uranus in the eighth house and Saturn in the fifth (154:212).

Many astrologers believe homosexuality is as much a part of a person's "destiny pattern" as birth or death. " 'I have no wish to change, only to help,' insisted Edith Randall, celebrated Hollywood astrologer, whose 60,000 astrological readings over the years included a sizable slice of the homosexual community" (154:215). As Maxine Bell states, "If they were homosexuals as they closed their last life and had no desire to quit or reform, then they come back as a homosexual and they have their own karma they bring with them" (154:210).

Astrology and fear and bondage

One astrologer emphasizes that "an astrological chart is not something to be feared" (144:3), but thousands of clients of astrologers will disagree. For many people, astrology produces a fear of the future (172:174).

Although the goal of astrology is allegedly to give the client power over the future, it doesn't work this way because it teaches people to acknowledge the impersonal whim of the power that stars and planets exert over them. The stars and planets are not persons; they cannot be reasoned with, nor can their influence easily be escaped. Compared to the alleged power and influence of the planets, men are as insects. What can one person do in the face of the power of the universe?

Acknowledging the practice of astrology can bring ruin to people by the fear it produces (42:310), astrologers complain that their colleagues who predict personal disaster, illness, or death are being insensitive or callous. But the complainers are powerless to do anything about it because astrologers who make such predictions are, after all, only engaging in astrology.

Astrologer-psychiatrist Bernard Rosenblum confesses:

> The bad reputation astrology must contend with is partly due to those astrologers who make definite predictions about people's death, divorce, or illness, and other statements that suggest the client must suffer the rest of his life with a difficult psychological problem in order to correct a karmic imbalance. Such astrologers are exhibiting arrogance and insensitivity in the extreme (118:121).

But other astrologers respond that, after all, such events are "seen" in the chart, and it is a moral duty to warn the client, so that he might possibly escape his fate. Therefore, this is not being "insensitive" to the client.

Alice O. Howell also complains, "I am appalled sometimes at the damage that can be done by astrologers who have no understanding of psychology and who are free with 'predictions' and sow seeds of doubt and fear in their clients" (120:7; cf. 6:27; 117:12).

But again, other astrologers respond, "Why be appalled at astrology?" The very *purpose* of the chart is to make predictions, so if such predictions sow seeds of doubt and fear that damage people, this is not the fault of astrology.

And why should astrologers be expected to become Ph.D.'s in psychology? So what if some admit it is far too easy for astrology students to set themselves up as experts and "make devastating prognostications which can seriously undermine the hope and confidence" of the client (94:7)? It is an astrologer's duty to read the chart; it is a divine responsibility. After all, it is God who speaks through the chart (138:111), and the astrologer must speak God's truth.

Thus, even if the chart reveals "illness, death, or disaster" most astrologers will reply in the following manner:

> I feel that I do not have the right to block information. Since I believe that all comes from a Master Intelligence, that would be like saying, "Hey, God, you're wrong! You shouldn't be telling me this now!" So it's all a matter of how I say it (138:128).

> Yet the astrologer has the responsibility to give his client as much information as possible so that he can, with full awareness, deal constructively with the results of his actions (95:1).

If a severely afflicted Mercury and/or moon denote the client may or will experience insanity, who can blame the astrologer for expressing this to the client (159:154)? Perhaps lifelong psychotherapy will prevent it! And what if the birth chart with "Mars afflicted and Saturn and Neptune prominent, usually afflicted" denote the child will have leukemia (159:155)? Clearly the stars have revealed it! If the parents are concerned and worried, therefore, at least they have been warned. Ironically, many astrologers complain about astrologers who make such predictions but do the very same themselves.

Dane Rudhyar describes a common occurrence:

> The person came disturbed, confused and sensing difficulties ahead; he leaves the astrologer's office with a crystallized expectation of tragedy. "Saturn" is about to hurt him; his wife *may* die, or his kidney *may* need an operation. Saturn. What is there one can do about Saturn, or to Saturn? Nothing apparently. Fear has taken shape and name. The anticipation of disaster torments the mind.... It will not help the situation to say the "influence" of Saturn is of the nature of electromagnetic waves; or that it can be expressed in a statistical average. It may be much worse to know one's husband has seventy-five percent chances of dying or becoming insane, than to know he *will* die or become insane. Uncertainty breeds devastating fear far more than the confrontation with the inevitable. And let us not say "forewarned, forearmed!" It does *not* apply where Mars, Saturn, squares, oppositions are present as objective, *evil entities* which are actually and concretely doing something to men. It does not apply where there is fear (7:24).

To predict crippling illness, disease, and insanity is bad enough, but when astrologers "see" death in a chart and predict it, one wonders how they can justify the possible consequences in people's lives. Unfortunately, the questions of "When will I die?" or "When will my spouse die?" are among the most common questions asked of astrologers (6:127).

And if, as even astrologers admit, up to 90 percent of astrologers are frauds (173:265), we should not think that astrologers will never use a person's greatest fears against him for their own profit:

> As often as not these star-mongers will resort to the criminal expedient of frightening their credulous client by threatening him or her or their next relatives with death or serious disease in a certain year of life, suggesting at the same time that a more thorough-going and, of course, more expensive analysis of the position of the planets, etc., on that day and at the particular hour and minutes might enable them to rectify or "correct" his terrifying prophecy (98:111).

Nor should we think that predictions of death can never be self-fulfilling. There are many cases of people apparently "willing" themselves to death. These people lose virtually all interest in life and expect to die—and they do, whether they believe in black magic (a "death hex") or the fate of the stars (352).

The Roman emperor Titus so believed in the astrological predictions of his death that he died in apparent good health (102:32). The poet Horace died in 8 B.C. because he believed his "star" had fated his death (102:104).

When astrology captures the political life of a nation, there are always some only too happy to help "fulfill" astrological predictions, whether past or present:

Finally, it was Emperor Domitian's belief in his predicted death during the fifth hour of September 18th, 96 A.D. that inspired the conspirators to choose that "fated" moment to assassinate him as he prepared for his bath without having taken any precautions to protect himself. In his rise to power, Domitian had murdered his own mother, just as his birth horoscope had predicted! ... The [modern] example of Argentina's Colonel Rega should serve as warning: the type of person who turns to astrology and the occult is likely to be devoid of conscience and responsibility. When the "stars" say, "torture, bribe, and conspire," astrologers themselves are likely to be the first to follow their own advice (102:32,212).

If, for example, "astrology enables true patriotism to be detected" (122:140), then it must also enable true loyalty to the state to be detected. And if the stars "prove" a man is a traitor to the state, or a criminal, or guilty in some other sense, then those in power who believe it may be expected to act.

In discussions with professional astrologers, we were surprised to discover how many of them accepted the legitimacy of predicting death. Below are representative death predictions from the literature:

- The client will die at age 32 (98:255).

- "An afflicted eighth house is likely to indicate death through illness or accident..." (10:155).

- "An individual frequently dies when there are both harmonious and discordant progressed aspects operative in his chart; but in each case there was always a discordant aspect present at the time of death. ... In all 608 charts, at the time of death of individual and relatives, there was a progressed aspect to the ruler of the eighth" (159: 22-23).

• The deaths of an astrologer's brother, father, two uncles, and a cousin are attributed to the power of the "planet" Chiron in their charts (130:29).

• Four predictions: "... you may safely judge that the querant will not be long-lived or else subject to many calamities; and this I know by many verified examples. . . . All the significators promised death. . . . If anyone asks concerning the probable length of his life, or when he may probably die, observe the ascendant and its lord . . . and you may determine the death of the querant, according to the number of degrees between the significator and the aspect of the afflicting planet. . . . This student will perceive that his death was plainly foreshewn . . ." (48:85,178,250,288).

• In a scant five pages of one text, death is predicted no less than *28 times* for varying astrological indicators: "Death is likely to happen"; "Death may be expected"; Death is to be predicted"; "The native will die"; "The native's brother will die"; "The native's son will die"; "The native will die"; "Death is certain"; "Death is likely"; "Death will take place"; "Death will happen"; etc. (61:105-09).

• In discussing sudden death: "I find Jupiter almost always centrally involved when people leave their bodies [die]. Whether we think of death as going home to God, or as a trip to another sphere, Jupiter patterns are appropriate at such times" (146:340).

In their own defense, many astrologers today claim that it is no longer "proper" for astrologers to predict death (42:224-25)! But this is obviously not unanimous—all but one of the above death predictions are recent. In fact, some astrologers seem *less* reluctant to predict death today because their philosophy teaches that death is inconsequential—"There is NO finality associated with death. It is simply a moving into another state of being . . ." (56:57). After all, "Death is a fulfillment—one step closer to perfection" (151:18). In the end, death destroys nothing because "there is no death." Those who think death is significant are deceived (55:596).

Regardless—this does not excuse the injustice of having done such things for 4,000 years in the past:

> Astrologers of the past had one striking characteristic in common—the cock sure way they predicted the exact time of such vital events as fatal accidents and death. . . . In either case, there is no evidence to show that their record of accuracy was something to be envied (109:165).

Given the fact that such astrological predictions promote fear and, as a logical result, an irrational outlook, what kinds of tragedies might astrology cause? All kinds. For example, what of a baby born under an evil sign or planet? Dr. Sherman Kanagy, a professor at Purdue University observes, "In ancient times women whose babies were born under the sign of Scorpio would often kill their babies by drowning because of the evil significance" (97:108). But this did not only happen in ancient times.

In our debate with two AFA astrologers on "The John Ankerberg Show," both insisted their charts did not reveal such things. However, one of them privately admitted at the AFA Convention that he had stopped doing charts of a child because he found he could predict the outcome of a potentially fatal disease.

The fact is that a chart can reveal such things because charts can be made to reveal anything an astrologer wants to see or thinks he sees. But if a baby is to be born crippled, such knowledge could lead the prospective parent to abort the child—which poses no problem from an astrological world view. As one astrology text promises, in harmony with occult philosophy:

> They [individual souls] DO NOT enter the body at the time of conception, but only when the body has reached completion of development which is just prior to birth. Therefore, abortion that may occur at any time prior [to birth] does not kill a human being (16:6).

Astrology's self-fulfilling prophecies

People seek out astrologers because they have problems or because they need information on a subject of importance to them. But when an astrologer tells people certain things about themselves, many clients accept the information as they would diagnoses by their personal physicians.

Accepting an astrologer's evaluation or prediction carries several liabilities: Odds are that sooner or later the chart itself will spell out ruin or disaster; the astrologer may have a spirit guide directing his interpretation (and spirit guides are not known for their love of humanity); the prophecies are often self-fulfilling.

Dane Rudhyar observes the problems associated with specific predictions or "definite forecasts" based on progressions and transits:

> The individual has no recourse against the impact of such revelations. He is almost totally unprotected against their possible negative effect. Even if he reasons himself out of being

280 / *The Dangers of Astrology*

consciously affected by the forecast, his sub-
conscious memory does not let go. This is
worse obviously if the event or trend proph-
esied is unfortunate and if fear of its results is
aroused—which is the case in nine cases out of
ten!—but it can even have psychologically dis-
integrating effects *when the thing expected is
very fortunate,* for it may lead to a self-satis-
fied expectancy blurring the edges of the
individual's efforts (7:95-96, emphasis added).

In other words, whether the prediction is good or bad,
the client loses. And in some people's cases, the outlook
is tremendously dark. Leading astrological consultant
Doris Hebel correctly observes:

When I started studying astrology many
years ago, I read all the available books on the
subject. Unfortunately, most of these older
texts are filled with what I call "wrist slitters"
statements. Based on these interpretations
alone, if you have mostly "hard" aspects, you
are worthless and nothing good will ever happen to you. For instance, sun Square Mars
denotes a person with a violent temper who is
capable of murder or who will be murdered;
physical violence is endemic to the aspect [i.e.,
the subject] (126:2-3).

Hebel implies that such things are true only for
"older" astrological texts, but this is not the case. Such
statements are just as prevalent in modern astrology.
Another astrologer confesses:

As a teacher of astrology, I have had the
opportunity to watch hundreds of students go
through the process of reacting to the negative

treatment given . . . *in the majority of the books on the subject*. They read the descriptions and come into class aghast at the wretched fate— to have twelfth house planets, or Venus retrograde, or a void-of-course moon at birth. They want to have the South Node removed and woe be the one with Saturn Aspects. Cancer, Scorpio or Pisces placements guarantee a weakness of character which will no doubt result in some kind of institutionalization, or at least misery, suffering and antisocial behavior (144:55, emphasis added).

Culver and Ianna observe:

Perhaps the extreme example of astrological determinism came in 1576 when astrologer Girolimo Cardan felt obliged to commit suicide for the sake of fulfilling his prediction of the day of his own death! Interestingly, this underlying fatalism places astrology on a direct collision course with the bulk of the religious sector, most of which holds that as human beings are accountable for our actions on the face of the planet (96:205).

Even today, the seeds for suicide are occasionally implied as a possible solution to personal problems in both spiritistic and astrological literature (16:5; 309:37). Thus, as one astrologer warns, "Should both [astrological] indications show up, they [the clients] are definitely inclined to suicide" (154:210).

In *A Time For Astrology*, psychic researcher Jess Stearn observes:

I have seen astrologers prepare their subjects for good events and bad—even to the

deaths of loved ones—by not only foreseeing
the future, but encouraging people's acceptance of it through this demonstration of the
inevitability of human affairs (154:14-15).

If "an afflicted eighth house is likely to indicate death
through illness or accident..." (10:155), then astrologers feel it is better the person be prepared. If the chart
says he will die, he probably will die, so it is better to
have time to set his affairs in order.

The magazine *Astrology Now* interviewed Lore Wal-
lace who, at age 17, consulted a famous astrologer and
received predictions of a difficult birth and the death of a
child. Although these never occurred, the predictions,
she claims, "Have damaged me probably for the rest of
my life" (172:184).

Charles Strohmer reveals, "Major sorrows came my
way due to my involvement with astrology. I did not
understand that I would have been spared some major
life disasters if I had not listened to the occult" (81:55).

Astrology and marriage

Astrologer Henry Weingarten claims, "In marriage
counseling, astrology plays a potentially valuable role.
First, one determines whether the difficulties are
simply transitory, or whether they are a permanent
part of the relationship.... Should the two people have
married in the first place.... Is it evidence of the need
for a breakup?" (5:40).

In other word, astrology, not the spouse, determines if
a marriage is good or bad, whether it will succeed or fail,
and whether the couple should stay married or divorce.

Irresponsibly, millions of persons are lumped together
in predictions of their chance of divorce according to
only their sign or their spouse's sign:

Astrologically speaking, certain birth signs
possess a greater chance of achieving success

within marriage than others.... There are some characteristics which are not compatible with lengthy relationships and these characteristics can usually be located under a particular Zodiac sign.... Geminians can be a sore trial to their partners and many of them bring infidelity and financial problems into their marriages.... They [Aries] rarely learn from past mistakes. Many born under this sign pass through several marriages before they begin to realize that they must be doing something wrong.... Marriage and Sagittarius could be like unto sausages and custard —incompatible.... Infidelity is a common cause for divorce—their undeniable charm means it is easy for them to get away with murder (155:223,227-28).

Consider the following true stories that further illustrate the problem of astrology and marriage counseling. A young man consults an astrologer who informs him the stars reveal he will marry young but that his first wife will not be the one destined for him. Only the second wife will bring him true happiness. The man deliberately marries young in order to get his first wife, that is to fulfill the prophecy, so that he will not miss finding his second wife who alone will make him happy. His first wife is a very good and devoted wife and bears him three children. But after the third child is born, the husband abandons his wife and family and later obtains a divorce on the grounds of his own complicity. He marries the second wife whom he believes is the one the stars have destined to make him happy. Yet within a few months, she joins a cult and makes his life utterly miserable, so he divorces her (189:17-18).

Thus a single astrologer with a single prediction brings pain and tragedy into the lives of six people—

three adults and three children. Now multiply this destructive power by millions of astrological predictions and advice given every year and you can see the potential for disaster. Far too many tragedies are "arranged" by astrological predictions. The pattern is clear: Clients are amazed by accurate self-disclosures; these self-disclosures generate trust; trust leads to deception; deception produces unwise or immoral decisions and actions; bad actions bring ruin or destruction (81:47).

In the second story a woman, engaged to be married, felt that seeking the advice of an astrologer might be useful. After drawing the horoscope, the astrologer predicted, "Your engagement will break up. This man will not marry you. You will not marry at all, but remain single." The woman was devastated. She was so much in love with her fiancé she could not bear the thought of losing him, so she became paralyzed with fear. She continually worried that the engagement would break up, that she would never marry, and she finally resolved to end her life. On the day she intended to kill herself, however, a friend of her fiancé was able to stop her. Upon the advice of that friend, she sought pastoral counseling, revealed her plight, repented, and gave her life to Christ. Soon after, her fiancé also gave his life to Christ. Today they are married with several children and are quite happy. Nevertheless had it not been for Christ, the disaster initiated by the astrologer would have occurred (308:20-21).

Far from being a harmless pastime, astrology is fraught with danger.

17

Astrology and the Christian

Arthur M. Hale, D.D., was a minister who became disillusioned and decided to leave his church. In searching for answers to his questions, he "tried many answers, and was finally directed to astrology more out of a last ditch curiosity than anything else" (272:3).

He decided to test the validity of astrology by having a horoscope cast for his brother-in-law, yet "was unprepared for the startling accuracy of the horoscope, but intrigued . . . studied further . . . and am now a convinced student of astrology" (272:3). He now claims, "I have yet to meet anyone who has studied astrology without becoming at least partially convinced of its validity" (272:3). Hale calls "this science . . . a marvelous thing," a tool that is "vastly beneficial" to both the clergyman and the psychologist, even though "the astrologer as counselor is not forced to deal in terms of a preconceived code of ethics" (272:4).

Hale concludes his article by stating:

> God *has* provided a road map [for life], and
> has written it in the very heavens above where
> all can see it. It is the most concrete evidence
> we have of His concern and His essential good-
> ness. . . . I would like to close this article with a
> few words addressed to those within the Church
> I have left. . . . Don't let the prevailing mood stop
> you from investigating astrology!. . . Learn to
> cast and read the horoscope and it will speak
> for itself; I believe you will be convinced. . . .
> You will have found a gift God intended us to
> have and to use. For Heaven's sake, use what
> has been given! (272:5).

Since this article was written by a minister, many
would conclude that there is no disharmony between
Christianity and astrology. We have already seen, however, that the Bible rejects astrology. In addition, a study
of Christian history presents a strong testimony against
astrology, despite astrologers' claims to the contrary
(69:77-89). Yet there have always been some Christians
who, in ignorance or rebellion, have practiced astrology.
We have divided them into three categories.

1. *Astrologers who claim to be Christian, yet are hostile to Christianity:* Dr. Robert Morey has observed,
"even though the majority of astrologers claim to be
Christian, they are generally hostile to the teachings of
historic and biblical Christianity" (70:48-49). These
people who claim to be Christian would probably admit
themselves that they have a preference for occultism
(however they define it) and that they are not *biblically*
Christian.

2. *Astrologers with moderate-to-strong church affil-
iation who say they are Christians but nevertheless reject
the Bible as the final authority in matters of astrology:*

Their faith is usually in God in a general sense. They do not admit to knowing God personally and show little interest in being born again (John 3:3-8). Since these people practice astrology and reject God's instruction on this topic, the following verses may apply to them: "They claim to know God, but by their actions they deny Him" (Titus 1:16); "If we claim to have fellowship with Him yet walk in the darkness, we lie and do not live by the truth" (1 John 1:6); "The man who says, 'I know Him,' but does not do what he [God] commands is a liar, and the truth is not in him. But if anyone obeys his word, God's love is truly made complete in him. This is how we know we are in him: Whoever claims to live in him must walk as Jesus did" (1 John 2:4-6).

Sadly, many Americans believe psychic Jeane Dixon is a good Christian, yet in *Yesterday, Today and Forever* she claims to have been guided by the "Holy Spirit" in integrating Christianity and astrology (64:6):

> Some of my friends consider this a strange practice for a Roman Catholic. As I understand it, however, the Catholic church and many other religious bodies as well—has never condemned the study of astrology.... I have never experienced any conflict between my faith and the guidance I receive from my church on the one hand and the knowledge I find in the stars on the other.... actually, much of what I know about astrology I learned from a Jesuit priest, who was one of the best-informed scholars I have ever met (64:7-9).

She relates that through a series of visions she was led to adopt astrology. From these visions she discovered:

> ... the answer which could pull together the facts of Scripture and the data of astrology.

> ...now I understand why, in my vision, each
> apostle was associated with a different Zodiac
> sign; for each was being revealed to me as to
> the archetype of that sign. Each [apostle]
> embodied all the mental and emotional char-
> acteristics of his own segment of the Zodiac.
> ...that simple yet profound truth was the mes-
> sage I received both through my meditations
> and in subsequent visions during the follow-
> ing weeks (64:12).

She concludes:

> Astrology fits into God's plan for mankind by
> helping us understand both our talents and our
> shortcomings. Being better informed about our-
> selves, appreciating our strengths and aware
> of our weaknesses, we will be much better
> equipped to turn everything we are to the ser-
> vice of the Lord (64:502).

To understand why Jeane Dixon is mistaken concerning astrology, consider the comments in the next category.

3. *In spite of all the Bible says against astrology, there
have been a few true Christians who have embraced
astrological views.* Dr. John Warwick Montgomery refers to Lutheran scientists Tycho Brahe and Johann
Kepler as Christian men who "were convinced that
astrology was not incompatible with divine revelation"
(72:110).

A man wrote to John Ankerberg, claiming to be a
"Christian professional astrologer" and insisting he
finds "no clear and specific injunction against astrology
in the Bible." In presenting his defense, he said, "True,
astrologers are called to task for...misuse of their

skills—as are prophets, priests and kings—but are not called to deny or shun the practice of those skills."

This individual made three major points in his lengthy letter: 1) Christian astrologers do not worship the stars so the biblical prohibitions do not apply to them; 2) astrology that is *not* divinatory is permissible (e.g., psychological counseling based on astrological truth); 3) the scriptural prohibition against divination was directed only against *pagan* divination—the use of astrology for godly "divination" (discerning God's will in matters, etc.) is permitted as long as one relies only upon *Christian* astrologers and not pagan, unbelieving astrologers.

We will now briefly respond to each of these three arguments.

Do Christian astrologers worship the stars?

Those who call themselves Christian astrologers claim they do not worship the stars, and so, therefore, the biblical prohibitions are not directed to them. But when a Christian astrologer claims he is not engaging in worship of the stars, this is at best a half-truth. Worship involves an *acknowledgement of providential power* and an attitude of praise or thankfulness to that power. Modern astrologers, Christian or non-Christian, often do have such an attitude toward the sun, moon, planets, and stars.

Worship includes the idea of religious devotion and reverence for an object, whether a living "god" or an inanimate object (i.e., a planet or star). For astrologers, the alleged power of the stars does evoke feelings of religious awe and devotion, particularly when they are believed to be divine objects. Through the chart and their obedience to the power of the stars, astrologers serve these objects in the sky. To serve means to wait upon and to perform duties for, to give reverent honor and obedience to something. All astrologers serve the heavens in this manner.

The second commandment states, however, that the Christian is not to "serve" false gods. When Christian astrologers dutifully record the positions of the stars, carefully "wait" upon their advice, and religiously obey the information they receive from the stars, are they not "serving" them? Do they not honor the power the heavens have over their lives? However, since the heavens do not actually exert any power, is this not idolatrous, is it not "exchanging the truth of God for a lie," worshiping and serving the creation rather than the Creator (Romans 1:25)?

In Romans 12:1,2, worship is defined as a *lifestyle*—of submitting and conforming one's life and standards to that acknowledged source of absolute power. Astrologers, Christian or non-Christian, do conform their lives to the philosophy and powerful influences of the "religion of the stars."

For most astrologers the heavens are living and divine. Manly P. Hall asserts:

> The astrologer is a priest in the temple of the cosmos; he speaks for the old gods who reside in the farthermost and in the innermost. It is his duty to teach as well as to delineate.... The astrologer ... must realize his responsibility not only to his client but to the great assembly of the stars to which he has dedicated himself as a servant in their house (86:147).

Perhaps Christian astrologers do not understand how astrology conditions their views on God, life, the church, the gospel, evangelism, etc. The very nature of worship teaches that whether or not Christian astrologers worship God, they do, in some sense, worship the stars.

Is psychological counseling based solely on astrological "truth" valid?

Christian astrologers believe they are acceptable to God because they engage only in astrological counseling—not in divination. However, if astrology itself is false, then any counseling based upon it will give flawed advice. Astrological counseling may or may not avoid divination, but if the advice it gives is false, it is dangerous nonetheless. Therefore, if legitimate astrological "truth" cannot improve psychological counseling, why support a false and occultic practice? Even some astrological counselors admit the benefit their clients derive from astrological counseling comes not from astrology but from those elements that make any counseling successful—caring and listening, commonsense advice, etc.

Thus, psychological counseling based on astrological advice is invalid because the data of astrology is false. Christians who engage in this form of astrological counseling are doing a great disservice to the body of Christ.

Do Christian astrologers escape the charge of divination?

Christian astrologers claim Christian astrology is a form of godly divination. It is true that in the Old Testament the Urim and Thummin were accepted by God as a means to discern His will, but this was only because God had promised to work through these instruments. This prevented spiritistic or human deception and made the oracle a trustworthy means to decide God's will on matters of importance. It was not to be used for trivial concerns. God has nowhere promised to work through astrology, however, nor to safeguard it from demonic or human deception. In addition, the Urim and Thummin were to be used only by the high priest, not the laity—so one cannot justify the universal Christian use of astrology by appealing to these items.

Tragically, divination is still used in Christian astrology. The Christian astrologer gives the same kind of advice as a non-Christian astrologer because the basic premises of astrology are retained—the signs and planets affect people's lives and so they must pay heed to them. *All* astrology charts reveal false information about the future—and this is the essence of divination. Christian astrologers *do* engage in pagan divination and therefore fall under the biblical prohibition (202).

The argument of the Christian astrologer is similar to the argument used by "Christian parapsychologists" to justify their studies. These parapsychologists scientifically study the occult and, among other things, apply it to the church. Like Christian astrologers, they claim the Old Testament condemnation of mediumistic and spiritistic practices (Deuteronomy 18:9-12) was intended only for those who misuse these practices, but were not meant to condemn those who use such practices "ethically," "wisely," with good motives, and for God's glory (195: 331-440). They ignore the fact that God unconditionally called these practices evil.

If Christian astrology or Christian spiritism were important, we should expect that God would have made such a distinction. After all, God has done so in many other cases. For example, sex is glorified within marriage but condemned outside of marriage or among persons of the same sex; and certain foods and drink are permissible in one situation, but not in another (Romans 1:26,27; 14:20; 1 Corinthians 6:18).

The basic argument of the Christian astrologer that astrology can be beneficial if it avoids *worshiping* the stars or engaging in *divination* is a conclusion based largely upon pragmatism. They say astrology "works" and is "helpful or useful," therefore, it should not be condemned.

But the arguments of Christian astrologers never address six important issues: 1) Can astrology really be separated from its occult connections? 2) Are the basic premises and principles of astrology scientifically accurate? 3) Can it be said that astrology is in any sense concerned with moral principles? 4) Does Scripture really justify the practice of astrology for any purpose? 5) What are the unforeseen risks or consequences of practicing astrology? 6) Why would God forbid astrology if it were truly helpful?

The Consequences of Christian Astrology

Because "Christian" astrology accepts the basic premises of astrology, Christians who practice it may not necessarily protest other forms of astrology or related forms of the occult. New Christians, untaught Christians, and secular friends may be encouraged to practice astrology because someone they respect uses it, but this will only lead them away from Christ, not closer to Him.

This point is well illustrated by Karen Winterburn, who wonders just how the Christian astrologer reads the Christian's chart:

> Where does the astrologer see Jesus Christ in my chart—or the Father? Where does he see my sin, my need to repent? My forgiveness? How does he read my walk with the Lord? Does he see history culminating in Jesus Christ? Where are the categories of the saved and the lost? Where are my moral decisions? . . . Such knowledge can only come to me by the Holy Spirit and the conviction of the Word of God (202).

When people are ignorant of the subtlety of the devil, they are more easily his victims; when confronted with supernatural manifestations, they conclude such power comes from God. Even the desire to disprove astrology may result in a conversion to it because a person discovers it "works." Even Christian ministers may be deceived:

> A minister who saw his mission as fighting superstition had a horoscope cast for the sake of study. He wanted to prove that horoscope casting was just superstition and deceit.... But he was amazed to see that the prophecies were fulfilled. For eight years he observed that all the predictions came true, even to the smallest details. He grew uneasy at this and reflected on the problem.... He knew that as a Christian he had not been the victim of suggestion. Finally he saw no other way of escape than to repent and to ask God for his protection. The thought came to him that he had sinned through this experiment, and had placed himself under the influence of the powers of darkness. After his repentance he discovered to his surprise that his horoscope was now no longer correct. Through this experience the minister clearly understood that demonic powers can be active in astrology (190:17-18).

Some Christians are converted to astrology through their interest in psychology. Dr. Atlas Laster had been a Christian for 30 years. But for 13 of those years, he had also been an astrologer. His Ph.D. dissertation at the University at Pittsburgh was titled, "On the Psychology of Astrology: The Use of Genethliacal Astrology in Psychological Counseling." Laster explained how he became involved in astrology:

> While a graduate student at the University of Pittsburgh, I was introduced to the work of C. G. Jung as a part of the graduate training

curriculum.... Jung's [collected works] were filled with references to astrological symbolism. [I decided to have my natal chart interpreted by an astrologer.] It was after the chart interpretation that I became convinced of the efficacy of using an astrological chart as a personality assessment tool. From that point, I enrolled in an astrological course, and began to make plans for the integration of astrology into my graduate studies, including the writing of a dissertation on the psychology of astrology. I was actively involved with astrology from 1972 until 1985, a total of 13 years (205:1-2).

But after more than a decade of involvement with astrology, he eventually concluded:

It must be made clear that this writer has confessed and asked the Lord for forgiveness, and repented of all philosophical or mundane involvement with astrology.... Any attempt to divine the future is not of faith and is an abomination.... God's people do not deal in the realm of astrology and idolatry.... Consult with the elders of the church, not with an astrologer (204:1,4,5).

Dr. Laster described some of the consequences of astrology in his own life:

Every day for 10 years I would rise and calculate my chart, my wife's and my children's. Instead of devoting time each day to prayer and Bible study, I was driven to involve myself in complicated astrological computations and interpretations. All the while, I sincerely felt that I was living my life according to God's will. In order to fully justify myself, I would tell anyone concerned that I was a consulting psychologist, and not an astrologer, because I felt that most astrologers were charlatans. On one occasion, I was referred to a Tarot reader in order to verify the special calling to promulgate astrology theory. I experimented with the I Ching for a short while. . . . I did not feel that astrology was an occult art (205:4).

Our final illustration of the consequences of Christian flirtation with astrology is seen in evangelical missionary David Womack's *12 Signs 12 Suns: Astrology in the Bible*. Womack is known for his books on world evangelism and church growth, however astrology bothered him (77:IX,3). He did not like the idea of an occult system of divination growing in popularity and yet being unchallenged by the church. He determined to "uncover the truth" about astrology. To his amazement, he discovered that astrology "worked" and could allegedly "identify" basic personality types (77:IX). He proceeded to cast hundreds of horoscopes (77:3). The end result was the adoption of a unique (nontraditional) form of astrology. This interprets horoscope charts in light of his "revolutionary" discovery of the secret "Hebrew personality science" which will help us develop our psychic abilities to grow spiritually and commune with God (77:91,118,136). Unfortunately this approach only helps to justify a "Christian" form of astrology, emphasizing personality diagnosis and psychic development.

By accepting that the stars do exert power to influence or control character and destiny, a person, by definition, abandons belief in God's sovereignty and replaces it with the power of the creation. No sound evidence, however, exists for such influence. The Bible teaches that God is the one who shapes our character and destiny, not the stars. If a Christian confuses or replaces the work of God with the work of His creation, he confuses matters and provides justification for other Christians to seek out occultists.

If we have been blessed "with every spiritual blessing in Christ" (Ephesians 1:3) "in whom are hidden all the treasures of wisdom and knowledge" and in whom we "are complete" (Colossians 2:3,10), what can astrology possibly give to the church that God has not or cannot give?

Astrology and Christianity are incompatible. Christian astrologers ignore what God says in the Bible and instead practice a pagan art and nature religion that claims to give men wisdom. Nevertheless, in spite of its claimed origins, "such 'wisdom' does not come down from heaven but is earthly, unspiritual, of the devil" (James 3:15).

Below we present just a few of the contrasts between Christianity and astrology.

Topic	Astrology	Christianity
1. God	Impersonal—nature	Personal—triune
2. Jesus	Astrologer, psychic	Savior and God
3. Means of personal salvation	By personal merit through self-perfection	By grace through faith
4. Source of redemption	Inevitable evolutionary process	Propitiatory atonement
5. Death	Reincarnation	Glorification
6. The final state	Cosmic absorption	Personal immortality
7. Source of authority	Astrological doctrine and practice	Bible
8. Mediator	Professional astrologer	Jesus Christ

Topic	Astrology	Christianity
9. Sin	Ignorance or karma	Disobedience to a personal God
10. Philosophy	Pantheism, gnosticism, polytheism	Theism
11. Nature of faith	Subjective, mystical, blind	Objective, historic, factual
12. Morality	Relative, amoral	Absolute
13. Man	One in nature with the divine cosmos	Created (in God's image)
14. Relation to the occult	Accepts	Rejects
15. Source of information	Horoscope chart	Bible
16. Object of consultation	The star's influence	God
17. Emphasis	Divination	Sanctification
18. Object of faith	Self	Christ
19. Object of worship and trust	Creation	Creator
20. Interpreter and revealer of ultimate reality	Chart	Holy Spirit/ Scriptures
21. Object of accountability	Stars	God

Christian astrologers are offering the Church a false god. If the Church is concerned about the spiritual safety of its people, she must respond with appropriate inquiry and discipline:

> Test everything. Hold on to the good. Avoid every kind of evil (1 Thessalonians 5:21,22).

> If your brother sins against you, go and show him his fault, just between the two of you. If he listens to you, you have won your brother over. But if he will not listen, take one or two others along, so that "every matter may

be established by the testimony of two or three
witnesses." If he refuses to listen to them, tell
it to the church; and if he refuses to listen even
to the church, treat him as you would a pagan
or a tax collector (Matthew 18:15-17).

18

Astrology and Government

"We are on the threshold of the Aquarian Age.... in this age, astrology will regain its lost respectability. It will be taught in the schools and colleges and will be considered a profession on a par with medicine and law" (260:3).

—Joan Quigley
Astrologer to
Nancy Reagan

At almost any time in history, at least for the last 3,000 years, politicians at some point on the globe have trusted astrology to help them govern their nations. Politicians in India depend on it daily. And whether the Shah of Iran, the Prince of Sikkhim, Winston Churchill, Franklin D. Roosevelt, or many other heads of state, astrologers and/or psychics have been consulted (22: 347-48; 6:92).

In response to the disclosure that astrology has influenced even the White House,* researcher Brooks Alexander emphasizes:

> . . . [a] disturbing reoccurrence of an ancient temptation: resorting to occultism and the exercise of political power. Astrology and politics have gone hand in hand throughout history. . . . Power is what astrology promises, and absolute power is its highest reward (297:1).

Though people were shocked to hear of President Reagan's interest in astrology, it should have surprised no one that astrology commands the attention of heads of state, given its claim to power and future knowledge.

Some modern heads of state maintain their own astrologers, as did the ancient Roman emperors. For example, in ancient Rome:

> For over 150 years the family of the astrologer Thrasyllus used astrological "predictions" to manipulate the political decisions and unending intrigues during the reigns of nearly every emperor from Tiberius to Domitian. . . . In Rome, astrology became such a political and psychological weapon that astrologers decided the fate of several emperors simply by convincing their opponents that the "stars were with them" and that their conspiracies were "fated" to succeed (102:30-31).

---

*In interviews, Nancy Reagan has maintained the issue of astrology at the White House was blown out of proportion. She claims Donald T. Regan's book did not tell the truth and that a forthcoming book by her would set the record straight. Regan has affirmed on television interviews, however (*Larry King Live*), that his book records the situation accurately.

In our own Christian history, the influence of astrology in politics has not been small. Consider these examples from sixteenth- and seventeenth-century England:

Most Tudor monarchs and their advisors encouraged astrologers and drew upon their advice. Both Henry VII and those engaged in plotting against him maintained relations with the Italian astrologer William Parron. ...The secretary of state, Sir William Paget, ...[had] the Basle edition of the Italian astrologer, Guido Bonatus, dedicated [to him] in 1550....For Sir Thomas Smith, the ambassador and future secretary of state, the practice of astrology was no casual interest, but so consuming a passion that he could "scarcely sleep at night from thinking of it." Similar enthusiasm was displayed by the courtiers of Elizabeth I. The Earl of Leicester employed Richard Forster as his astrological physician and commissioned Thomas Allen to set horoscopes....[Occultist and astrologer] John Dee chose an astrologically propitious day for the coronation of Elizabeth I. Dee maintained relations with many of the leading nobility of his day....Small wonder that the Puritan Laurence Humphrey complained in 1563 that among the nobility the science of astrology was "ravened, embraced, and devoured of many." It was customary for aristocratic families to have horoscopes cast at the birth of their children, and more or less unavoidable for them to have recourse to doctors who used semi-astrological methods.

During the seventeenth century this situation changed only slowly. Many of the leading nobility and politicians retained astrological leanings.... Charles II himself took astrological advice upon occasions.... Louis XIV thought it worth appointing a French astrologer...as a special diplomatic agent to England.... Even after the Revolution of 1688 astrological interests were to be found in high places. Sir John Trenchard, secretary of state to William III, had his horoscope cast, and confessed on his death-bed that everything the astrologer had predicted for him had come true.... It is certain that until the mid-seventeenth century astrology was no private fad but a form of divination to which many educated people had recourse (46:289-92).

Astrology in the White House has had similar influence today. Significantly, there are historical indications that the common acceptance of astrology is a sign of the downfall of a culture:

A scan of human history reveals that when a society begins to embrace such irrational and fatalistic views, the end is close at hand. ... The rise of astrology in a culture does not *cause* that culture's undoing, but rather is a sign or a symptom of the conditions in a culture which betrays its inner weaknesses at that moment in history. So it was with classical Greece, imperial Rome, and medieval Christianity (96:207).

Franz Cumont, one of the foremost authorities on classical religion, explained, "Does not astrology formulate a principle destructive of all morality and all religion, the principle of fatalism? Fatalism indeed is the capital principle which astrology imposed on the world" (47:84).

Because it is irrational, occultic, amoral, and fatalistic, in 4,000 years astrology has never contributed to the advancing of human welfare, only to its destruction.

Leading astrologer de Vore asserts that in "mundane" astrology (predictions for states and nations), whether the prediction is "right or wrong," there is no harm done (42:310). Such a statement is incredible, for whether the prediction is right or wrong, a politician who makes a decision on the basis of astrology could start a war! In fact, such fatalism and rejection of absolute morality has historically married the idea of cosmic destiny to militarism. Human freedom becomes an illusion, thus "totalitarian government and a belief in cosmic destiny based on astrological ideas have always gone hand in hand in history" (71:21). The effects of astrology in the life and political influence of Adolph Hitler are a prime example.

Adolph Hitler and Astrology

Perhaps the most infamous blending of the occult and government occurred in the Third Reich. Astrological determinism and occultism in general pillared the horrors of Nazi Germany, whose real goal was the achieving of its cosmic "astrological destiny" (71:22-23). Pre-Nazi Germany was fascinated and consumed by astrology, Theosophy, hypnosis, and Eastern mysticism (152:107-20).

> From the late nineteenth century on, the Germans were eager to use astrology in their daily lives. They had been particularly impressed with Franz Anton Mesmer's attempts to place astrology on a scientific footing. ...Mesmerism [hypnotism] was studied in German universities. Court physicians and medical professors wrote learned treatises on it....The German astrologer Wilhelm Wulff

reports in his book, *Zodiac and Swastika:* ". . . by the November revolution of 1918, inflation was making headway, well established businesses were crashing, and suicides were a daily event. In this period of tremendous economic and political uncertainty, hypnosis, mesmerism, clairvoyance, and every form of occultism flourished. Such interests are promoted by catastrophic situations. In post-war Germany, hypnosis, clairvoyance and mind readers were suddenly able to fill huge concert halls. There was scarcely a single large music hall or cabaret that did not stage a telepathic act" (152:117-19).

Psychic researcher Allen Spragget talked personally with Wilhelm Wulff, the personal astrologer of S.S. chief Heinrich Himmler. In the *Arizona Republic* (November 11, 1973), Spragget observes:

Wilhelm Wulff first was conscripted to work for the Nazis at an Institute for Occult Warfare in Berlin. There under government sponsorship, various occult practitioners, from transmediums to pendulum swingers, were paid to come up with something, anything, which would help Germany win the war. . . . Wulff had to prepare regular horoscopes indicating what Himmler should and shouldn't do. . . . He quotes Himmler as saying: "It's strange, isn't it, that you warned me about a possible accident on December 9th [which came true]. . . . The accuracy of your horoscopes, Herr Wulff, is phenomenal."

According to *Gods and Beasts: The Nazis and the Occult,* Himmler was totally *committed* to a belief in astrology and the occult. According to Wulff, "German astrology was supreme in the 1930's" and it engaged the attention of other important Nazis, like Walter Shellenburg and Rudolph Hess. It was largely thanks to Hess that the so called "witchcraft act" of 1934 against astrologers and occultists was circumvented (152:123-24).

As early as 1921, Hitler exhibited an interest in astrology. A friend of Hitler stated, "When I first knew Adolph Hitler in Munich in '21 and '22, he was in touch with a circle that believed firmly in the portents of the stars" (152:120). Hitler saw in the doctrines of astrology not only a means to divine the future but also a cosmic justification for his racism and militarism. Thus, in *The Occult and the Third Reich,* two French historians state:

> For Hitler and his disciples...astrology
> and its rebirth as a "sacred art" were laying
> the groundwork for the white man's rebirth.
> For them, astrology added a third dimension,
> as well as a confirmation of the soundness of
> their cause.... All the historical sources allude
> to horoscopes carefully kept up to date by the
> regime's official astrologist (150:190-91).

Hitler's political plans were enmeshed with his belief in a magical astrological relationship between man and the cosmos ("as above, so below"). The Third Reich would succeed because the heavens had destined it.

> Thus the destiny of the nation or race
> becomes the tyrant which rules the masses.
> Acting in accordance with the cosmic pattern,
> and led by a divine despot who rules by right of
> birth, the nation will achieve the realization of
> its destiny. All those nations who are unaware
> of this Order or those who actively oppose it by

opposing the Divine Right of the Chosen People will be destroyed. This type of thinking was current in Nazi Germany (71:20; cf. 306: 228-49).

For Hitler, politics were only a temporary if necessary outward and fragmentary aspect of this cosmic destiny. Any seeming injustice could be rationalized as the necessary outworking of cosmic evolution toward its final goal. All injustice was thus true mercy. All events, good or bad, could be explained by recourse to the "wisdom" of a cosmic order in the process of evolving to a "higher" level. Indeed, today many astrologers are predicting the birth of a new world leader, a "savior," a great Avatar who will literally incarnate the principles of the New Age (71:35). But if he does appear, it will be astrology and related occultism that have helped pave the way for what will perhaps turn out to be one more round of "cosmic destiny."

The White House and Astrology

The most significant recent example of astrology's influence on government is seen in Donald Regan's *For the Record: From Wall Street to Washington*. Regan was for four years the Secretary of the Treasury and for two years the President's Chief of Staff. The book reveals that Mrs. Reagan's life (at least as it related to her husband's safety) was strongly guided by astrology— actually by the astrologer she trusted.

Regan emphasizes, "Except where press reports are quoted, this book is free of hearsay. In all but a very few cases I have reported only what I observed with my own eyes or heard with my own ears" (198:XIV). He thus reveals:

> Virtually every major move and decision
> the Reagans made during my time as White

House Chief of Staff was cleared in advance with a woman in San Francisco who drew up horoscopes to make certain that the planets were in a favorable alignment for the enterprise.... [e.g.] when it was propitious to move the President of the United States from one place to another, or schedule him to speak in public, or commence negotiations with a foreign power (198:3-4; 367).

Regan observes, "Few in the White House ever suspected that Mrs. Reagan was even part of the problem—much less that an astrologer in San Francisco was approving the details of the Presidential schedule" (198:290).

The astrologer who commanded the attention of the First Lady was later identified as Joan Quigley. Consider below a few instances of her influence over the most powerful man on earth. (In the quotes below the astrologer is referred to as "Mrs. Reagan's Friend"):

Mrs. Reagan's Friend had provided a list of good, bad, and iffy days for 1988 that eliminated many key events (198:68).

Mrs. Reagan's Friend had told her that January was a bad month for the President—any activity might produce unhappy results. This prognostication had the effect of immobilizing the President. His schedule was in a state of chaos. Mrs. Reagan had cancelled or refused to approve a number of important appearances.... She disapproved two other important appearances in February—the National Prayer Breakfast on the fifth and the Executive Forum on the sixth.... These decisions would isolate the President from the American people during the most crucial period of his presidency (198:70-72).

The President's trip to Bitburg was plagued by inexplicable changes in scheduling that arose, as I subsequently learned, from the astrologer's warnings to Mrs. Reagan concerning possible threats to the President's safety (198:73).

Astrology even influenced the meeting of the president with the Russian leader Gorbachev. Consider how misinformation at this point could have produced a disaster:

As usual, Mrs. Reagan insisted on being consulted on the timing of every Presidential appearance and action so that she could consult her Friend in San Francisco about the astrological factor. The large number of details involved must have placed a heavy burden on the poor woman, who was called upon not only to choose auspicious moments for meetings between the two most powerful men on our planet, but also to draw up horoscopes that presumably provided clues to the character and probable behavior of Gorbachev (198:300-01).

Donald Regan discusses the problems resulting from a lone San Francisco occultist's control over the schedule of the president of the United States:

The frustration of dealing with a situation in which the schedule of the President of the United States was determined by occult prognostications was very great—far greater than any other I had known in nearly 45 years of working life (198:359).

...the President's schedule is the single most potent tool in the White House, because it determines what the most powerful man in the world is going to do and when he is going to do it. By humoring Mrs. Reagan we gave her this tool—or, more accurately, gave it to an unknown woman in San Francisco who believed that the Zodiac controls events and human behavior and that she could read the secrets of the future in the movements of the planets (198:74).

Bernard Gittelson, a psychic investigator and former public relations consultant for several governments, states that several astrologers "claim that Ronald Reagan has long been [astrologer Carroll] Righter's client. Sidney Omarr told me, 'I would say one of the world's worst kept secrets is Ronald Reagan's interest in astrology' " (22: 348).

One source at the AFA Conference confirmed this and said Reagan had been interested in astrology and/or had an astrologer since his acting days. Allegedly, his previous astrologer was Ralph Kraum, a recognized authority on older horoscope methods. When Kraum died, Righter apparently took over. *Time* magazine (May 16, 1988, p. 41) reported prominent astrologer Joan Quigley had admitted being the astrologer who, based on the president's horoscope, helped Mrs. Reagan to formulate and regulate the president's schedule. She claims the president did accept her advice through Mrs. Reagan. The president himself has denied that astrology influences his decisions, yet has also admitted to an interest in astrology and a fascination with horoscopes (296).

Why did the Reagans seek astrological counsel? Apparently their trust in astrology was solidified because an astrologer had predicted the Hinkley assassination attempt "nearly to the day" (198:359). Thus one correct prediction (never mind all the false ones) led to a single astrologer's wielding influence over important decisions at the White House. In her desire to safeguard her husband, the First Lady became committed to an occult art.

How much damage the influence of astrology inflicted at the White House will never be known (317: 129). Yet, as conservative columnist George Will commented on *This Week* (May 8, 1988), "It's not funny to have it [astrology] intruded among people who have nuclear weapons" (203:11). And Daniel S. Greenburg, the editor of *Science and Government Report*, stated in *Newsday* (May 5, 1988):

> The spectacle of astrology in the White House—the governing center of the world's greatest scientific and military power—is so appalling that it defies understanding and provides grounds for great fright.... It's plain scary (203:12).

Good Lord, deliver us.

Bibliography/Key to Footnotes

G   =   General astrology
GC =   General (critical) astrology
R   =   Reference work
H   =   History
T   =   Types of astrology
CA =   Christian analysis (critical)
I   =   Interpretation (astrological)
O   =   Occult/Occult connections (true for most books)
S   =   Secular analysis (critical)
GA =   Gauquelin
M   =   Medical astrology
P   =   Psychology and astrology
C   =   Children and astrology
A   =   American Federation of Astrologers
PL =   Planetary bodies (imaginary)
GS =   Gospel in the stars theory
OC =   Occult (Christian critique)
NA =   Non-astrological cosmic effects
MP =   Miscellaneous; or particular or specialized treatment
        of astrology

M   1. Marian Futterman. *Your Dog and Astrology*. Lakewood, Calif.:
           Jay Publishing, 1976.

G   2. Alan Oken. *Astrology, Evolution and Revolution: a Path to Higher
           Consciousness Through Astrology*. New York: Bantam, 1976.

G   3. Jeff Mayo. *Astrology*. London: Hodder & Stoughton Ltd., 1978.

M   4. Lyall Watson. *Super Nature: A Natural History of the Super-
           natural*. New York: Bantam, 1974.

G   5. Henry Weingarten. *A Modern Introduction to Astrology*. New
           York: ASI Publishers, 1974.

G   6. Sir John Manolesco. *Scientific Astrology*. New York: Pinnacle
           Books, 1973.

313

314

G   7. Dane Rudhyar. *The Practice of Astrology as a Technique in Human Understanding*. New York: Penguin Books, 1975.

G   8. Anthony Norvell. *Astrology, Your Wheel of Fortune: How to Discover and Use the Powers and Influences of the Zodiac*. New York: Harper & Row, 1975.

G   9. Ronald Davison. *Synastry: Understanding Human Relations Through Astrology*. New York: ASI Publishers, Inc., 1978.

G   10. Ronald Davison. *Astrology*. New York: ARC Books, 1970.

G   11. Robin MacNaughton. *Robin MacNaughton's Sun Sign Personality Guide*. New York: Bantam, 1978.

G   12. John Anthony West and Jan Gerhard Toonder. *The Case for Astrology*. Baltimore: Penguin Books, 1973.

G   13. Isidore Kozminsky. *Zodiacal Symbology and Its Planetary Power*. Washington, D.C.: American Federation of Astrologers, n.d.

G   14. Joseph F. Goodavage. *Astrology: The Space Age Science*. New York: Signet, 1967.

GC   15. Owen S. Rachleff. *Sky Diamonds: The New Astrology*. New York: Popular Library, 1973.

O   16. Cynthia Bohannon. *The North and South Nodes: The Guideposts of the Spirit: A Comprehensive Interpretation of the Nodel Placements*. Jacksonville, Fla.: Arthur Publications, 1987.

G   17. Eleonora Kimmel. *Patterns of Destiny: Suddenly Interrupted Lives*. Tempe, Ariz.: America Federation of Astrologers, 1985.

G   18. Cyril Fagan. *The Solunars Handbook*. Tucson: Clancy Publications, 1976.

MP   19. Evelyn M. Nagle. *Winning With Astrology*. Tempe, Ariz.: American Federation of Astrologers, n.d.

MP   20. Doris Chase Doane. *How to Prepare and Pass an Astrologers Certificate Exam*. Tempe, Ariz. American Federation of Astrologers, 1985.

MP   21. Doris Chase Doane. *How to Read Cosmodynes: An Astrological Guide to the Use of Personal Power*. Tempe, Ariz.: American Federation of Astrologers, 1974.

O   22. Bernard Gittelson. *Intangible Evidence*. New York: Simon & Shuster, 1987.

T   23. June Wakefield. *Cosmic Astrology: The Religion of the Stars*. Lakemont, Ga.: CSA Press, 1968.

MP   24. Tiffany Holmes. *Woman's Astrology*. New York: E. P. Dutton, 1977.

G   25. Jeanne Avery. *The Rising Sign: Your Astrological Mask*. Garden City, N.Y.: Doubleday, 1982.

G   26. Sydney Omarr. *My World of Astrology*. Hollywood: Wilshire Book Company, 1968.

T   27. Eric Russell. *Astrology and Prediction*. Secaucus, N.J.: Citadel Press, 1975.

G   28. Charles E. O. Carter. *The Principles of Astrology*. Wheaton, Ill.: Quest/Theosophical Publishing House, 1977.

G   29. Jeannette Yvonne Glenn. *How to Prove Astrology*. Tempe, Ariz.: American Federation of Astrologers, 1987.

G   30. Dorothy Beech Hughes. *The Basic Elements of Astrology*. Tempe, Ariz.: American Federation of Astrologers, 1970.

H   31. Manly P. Hall. *The Story of Astrology*. Los Angeles: Philosophical Research Society, 1975.

G   32. Theodore Laurence. *The Foundation Book of Astrology*. Secaucus, N.J.: University Books, 1973.

G   33. Henry Weingarten. *The Study of Astrology: Book I*. New York: ASI Publishers, 1977.

G   34. Frances Sakoian and Louis S. Acker. *The Astrologers Handbook*. New York: Harper & Row, 1973.

G   35. Frances Sakoian and Louis S. Acker. *The Astrology of Human Relationships*. New York: Harper & Row, 1978.

G   36. Isabel M. Hickey. *Astrology: A Cosmic Science*. Watertown, Mass.: Isabel M. Hickey, 1974 (privately published).

MP   37. Mark Urban-Lurain. *Astrology as Science: A Statistical Approach*. Tempe, Ariz.: American Federation of Astrologers, 1984.

O   38. Ralph Metzner, *Maps of Consciousness*. New York: Collier Books, 1976.

G   39. Derek and Julia Parker. *The Compleat Astrologer*. New York: Bantam, 1978.

R   40. Allen Leo. *The Complete Dictionary of Astrology*. New York: Astrologers Library, 1978.

R   41. James Jason Francis. *The New English Astrological Thesaurus*. Lakemont, Ga.: CSA Press, 1977.

R   42. Nicholas de Vore. *Encyclopedia of Astrology*. Totowa, N.J.: Littlefield Adams & Co., 1976.

CA   43. John Ankerberg and John Weldon. *The Facts on Astrology*. Eugene, Ore.: Harvest House, 1988.

C   44. Max Heindel. *Your Child's Horoscope Volume II*. Oceanside, Calif.: The Rosicrucian Fellowship, 1973.

C   45. Gloria Star. *Optimum Child: Developing Your Child's Fullest Potential Through Astrology*. St. Paul, Minn.: Llewellyn Publications, 1987.

H   46. Keith Thomas. *Religion and the Decline of Magic*. New York: Charles Scribner's Sons, 1971.

316

H   47. Franz Cumont. *Astrology and Religion Among the Greeks and Romans*. New York: Dover, 1960.

H   48. William Lilly. *An Introduction to Astrology [Original title: Christian Astrology, 1647]*. Hollywood: New Castle Publishing Co., 1972.

H   49. Christopher McIntosh. *The Astrologers and Their Creed: An Historical Outline*. New York: Frederick A. Prager, 1969.

H   50. Firmicus Maternus. *Ancient Astrology Theory and Practice [Original title: Matheseos Livri VIII, 334 A.D.]*. Translated by Jean Rhys Bram. Parkridge, N.J.: Noyes Press, 1975.

T   51. Margaret H. Gammon. *Astrology and the Edgar Cayce Readings*. Virginia Beach, Va.: ARE Press, 1987.

T   52. Gouri Shankar Kapoor. *Remedial Measures in Astrology*. New Delhi, India: Ranjan Publications, 1985.

T   53. K. C. Tunnicliffe. *Aztec Astrology*. Essex, Great Britain: L. N. Fowler & Co., Ltd., 1979.

T   54. Udo Rudolph. *The Hamburg School of Astrology: An Explanation of its Methods*. England: The Astrological Association, 1973.

T   55. Alice A. Bailey. *Esoteric Astrology*. New York: Lucius Publishing, 1975.

T   56. Edward K. Wilson, Jr. *The Astrology of Theosophy*. Tempe, Ariz.: American Federation of Astrologers, 1987.

T   57. Derek Walters. *Chinese Astrology*. Wellingborough, North Ampton-shire, England: The Aquarian Press, 1987.

MP   58. Sabian Publishing Society. *Astrology Books by Marc Edmund Jones: A Commentary*. Stanwood, Wash.: Sabian Publishing Society, 1987.

T   59. Marc Edmund Jones. *The Counseling Manual in Astrology*. Tempe, Ariz.: American Federation of Astrologers, 1982.

O   60. Marc Edmund Jones. *The Sabian Manual: A Ritual for Living*. Boulder, Colo.: Sabian/Shambhala Publications, Rev. 1976.

T   61. Sage Mantreswara. *Jataka Phaladeepika or Hindu Astrology's Light on the Fruits of Action*. Translated by K. N. Saraswathy. Madras, South India: Kadalangudi Publications, 1983.

T   62. James T. Braha. *Ancient Hindu Astrology for the Modern Western Astrologer*. North Miami, Fla.: Hermetician Press, 1986.

T   63. Pamela A. F. Crane. *Draconic Astrology: An Introduction to the Use of Draconic Charts in Astrological Interpretation*. Wellingborough, North Amptonshire, England: Aquarian Press, 1987.

G   64. Jeane Dixon. *Yesterday, Today and Forever: How Astrology Can Help You Find Your Place in God's Plan*. New York: Bantam, 1977.

CA   65. Ben Adam. *Astrology: The Ancient Conspiracy.* Minneapolis, Minn.: Bethany Fellowship, 1963.

CA   66. J. H. Pember. *Earth's Earliest Ages.* Grand Rapids, Mich.: Kregel, 1975.

CA   67. William J. Petersen, ed. *Astrology and the Bible.* Wheaton, Ill.: Victor Books, 1972.

CA   68. Joseph Bayly. *What About Horoscopes?* Elgin, Ill.: David C. Cook, 1970.

CA   69. James Bjornstad and Shildes Johnson. *Stars, Signs and Salvation in the Age of Aquarius.* Minneapolis, Minn.: Bethany Fellowship, 1971.

CA   70. Robert A. Morey. *Horoscopes and the Christian.* Minneapolis, Minn.: Bethany House, 1981.

CA   71. Jerry Exel. *Jesus and the Spirit of Astrology.* Berkeley: Christian Information Committee, 1971.

OC   72. John Warwick Montgomery. *Principalities and Powers: The World of the Occult.* Minneapolis, Minn.: Bethany Fellowship, 1973.

MP   73. Emmet Fox. *The Zodiac and the Bible.* New York: Harper & Row, 1961.

MP   74. Irene Diamond. *Astrology and the Holy Bible.* Privately published, 1983.

MP   75. Helen Adams Garrett. *Astrology in the Bible.* Privately published, 1987.

GS   76. Joseph A. Seiss. *The Gospel in the Stars.* Grand Rapids, Mich.: Kregel, 1978.

GS   77. David A. Womack. *12 Signs, 12 Suns: Astrology in the Bible.* New York: Harper & Row, 1978.

GS   78. Kenneth C. Fleming. *God's Voice in the Stars: Zodiac Signs and Bible Truth.* Neptune, N.J. Loizeaux Brothers, 1987.

GS   79. D. James Kennedy. *The Gospel and the Stars: Booklet One.* Fort Lauderdale, Fla.: Coral Ridge Ministries, n.d. (part of a series of 13 booklets).

GS   80. E.W. Bullinger. *The Witness of the Stars.* Grand Rapids, Mich.: Kregel, 1967.

CA   81. Charles Strohmer. *What Your Horoscope Doesn't Tell You.* Wheaton, Ill.: Tyndale, 1988.

O   82. Sylvia De Long. *Guideposts to Mystical and Mundane Interpretations.* Tempe, Ariz.: American Federation of Astrologers, 1985.

G   83. David and Gina Cochrane. *New Foundations for Astrology.* Alachua, Fla.: Astrological Counseling and Research, 1977.

318

I 84. Richard Nolle. *Interpreting Astrology: New Techniques & Perspectives*. Tempe, Ariz.: American Federation of Astrologers, 1986.

GC 85. Richard Nolle. *Critical Astrology: Investigating the Cosmic Connection*. Tempe, Ariz.: American Federation of Astrologers, 1980.

I 86. Tracy Marks. *The Art of Chart Interpretation*. Sebastopol, Calif.: CRCS Publications, 1986.

T 87. Charles E. O. Carter. *An Introduction to Political Astrology*. London: L. N. Fowler, 1973.

MP 88. J. K. Karmakar. *Earology: A Study on the Language of Ear Volume I*. Calcutta, India: Research Institute of Earology, 1981.

MP 89. W. A. Sherrill, ed. *The Astrology of I Ching*. Translated by W. K. Chu from the "Ho Map Lo Map Rational Number." New York: Samuel Weiser, 1976.

MP 90. Eden Gray. *A Complete Guide to the Tarot*. New York: Bantam, 1980.

MP 91. Martin Freeman. *Forecasting by Astrology: A Comprehensive Manual of Interpretation and Technique*. Wellingborough, North Amptonshire, England: Aquarian Press, 1982.

O 92. Mary Devlin. *Astrology and Past Lives*. West Chester, Pa.: Para Research, Inc., 1987.

O 93. Dusty Bunker. *Numerology, Astrology and Dreams*. West Chester, Pa.: Whiteford Press, 1987.

O 94. Joan Hodgson. *Reincarnation Through the Zodiac*. Reno, Nev.: CRCS Publications, 1978.

T 95. Sylvia DeLong. *The Art of Horary Astrology and Practice*. Tempe, Ariz.: American Federation of Astrologers, 1988.

S 96. R. B. Culver and P. A. Ianna. *The Gemini Syndrome: A Scientific Evaluation of Astrology,* rev. ed. Buffalo, N.Y.: Prometheus Books, 1984.

CA 97. Sherman P. Kanagy II and Kenneth D. Boa. "Astrology—Scientific, Philosophical and Religious Issues." Mss., 1986.

S 98. Robert Eisler. *The Royal Art of Astrology*. London: Herbert Joseph Ltd., 1946.

S 99. Roy A. Gallant. *Astrology, Sense or Nonsense?* Garden City, N.Y.: Doubleday, 1974.

S 100. Paul Kurtz, ed. *A Skeptics Handbook of Parapsychology*. Buffalo, N.Y.: Prometheus Books, 1985.

S 101. Bart J. Bok and Lawrence E. Jerome. *Objections to Astrology*. Buffalo, N.Y.: Prometheus Books, 1975.

S 102. Lawrence E. Jerome. *Astrology Disproved*. Buffalo, N.Y.: Prometheus Books, 1975.

319

S/GA 103. Michel Gauquelin. *The Scientific Basis of Astrology: Myth or Reality.* New York: Stein and Day, 1973.

S/GA 104. Michel Gauquelin. *Dreams and Illusions of Astrology.* Buffalo, N.Y.: Prometheus Books, 1979.

S/GA 105. Michel Gauquelin. *The Cosmic Clocks: From Astrology to a Modern Science.* London: Peter Owen, 1969.

S/GA 106. Michel Gauquelin. *Birth Times: A Scientific Investigation of the Secrets of Astrology.* New York: Hill & Wang, 1983.

S/GA 107. Michel Gauquelin. *The Cosmic Clocks: From Astrology to a Modern Science.*, rev. ed. San Diego: Astro Computing Services, 1982.

S/GA 108. Francoise Gauquelin. *Psychology of the Planets.* San Diego: Astro Computing Services, 1987.

M 109. Omar V. Garrison. *Medical Astrology: How the Stars Influence Your Health.* New York: Paperback Library, 1973.

M 110. C. Norman Shealy. *Occult Medicine Can Save Your Life.* New York: Bantam, 1977.

M 111. Peter Damian. *The Twelve Healers of the Zodiac: The Astrology Handbook of the Bach Flower Remedies.* York Beach, Maine: Samuel Weiser, 1986.

M 112. Marcia Stark. *Astrology: Key to Holistic Health.* Birmingham, Mich.: Seek It Publications, 1987.

M 113. Kathryn Davis Henry. *Medical Astrology: Physiognomy and Astrological Quotations.* Privately published, 1978.

M 114. Robert C. Jansky. *Modern Medical Astrology.* Van Nuys, Calif.: Astro-Analytics Publication, 1978 (2nd Rev.).

M 115. Harry F. Darling. *Essentials of Medical Astrology.* Tempe, Ariz.: American Federation of Astrologers, 1981.

OP 116. Stephen Arroyo. *Astrology, Psychology and the Four Elements: An Energy Approach to Astrology and Its Use in the Counseling Arts.* Davis, Calif.: CRCS Publications, 1978.

P 117. Dane Rudhyar. *From Humanistic to Transpersonal Astrology.* Palo Alto, Calif.: The Seed Center, 1975.

P 118. Bernard Rosenblum. *The Astrologer's Guide to Counseling.* Reno, Nev.: CRCS Publications, 1983.

P 119. Dane Rudhyar. *Astrology and the Modern Psyche: An Astrologer Looks at Depth Psychology.* Davis, Calif.: CRCS Publications, 1976.

OP 120. Alice O. Howell. *Jungian Symbolism in Astrology.* Wheaton, Ill.: Quest/Theosophical, 1987.

P 121. Dr. Karen Hamaker-Zondag. *Planetary Symbolism in the Horoscope (The Jungian Symbolism and Astrology Series Volume II).* York Beach, Maine: Samuel Weiser, 1985.

320

R   122. C.E.O. Carter. *An Encyclopedia of Psychological Astrology*. London: Theosophical Publishing House, 1977.

P   123. David Goodman. *Psychological Astrology*. Tempe, Ariz.: American Federation of Astrologers, 1983.

P   124. Liz Greene and Howard Sasportas. *The Development of the Personality (Seminars in Psychological Astrology Volume I)*. York Beach, Maine: Samuel Weiser, 1988.

P   125. Arthur Dione. *Jungian Birth Charts: How to Interpret the Horoscope Using Jungian Psychology*. Wellingborough, North Amptonshire, England: The Aquarian Press, 1988.

P   126. Doris Hebel. *Celestial Psychology: An Astrological Guide to Growth and Transformation*. Sante Fe, N. Mex.: Aurora Press, 1985.

R   127. Henry Niemann and Judith Cooper. *Astrology of Psychology: The Reference Book for Astrologers*. Tempe, Ariz.: American Federation of Astrologers, 1986.

MP   128. Demetra George. *Asteroid Goddesses*. San Diego: Astro Computing Services Publications, 1987.

PL   129. Ted George and Barbara Parker. *Sinister Ladies of Mystery: The Dark Asteroids of Earth*. Jacksonville, Fla.: Arthur Publications, 1987.

O   130. Barbara Hand Clow. *Chiron: Rainbow Bridge Between the Inner and Outer Planets*. St. Paul, Minn.: Llewellyn Publications, 1988.

O   131. Jeff Green. *Pluto: The Evolutionary Journey of the Soul Volume I*. St. Paul, Minn.: Llewellyn Publications, 1988.

PL   132. John Robert Hawkins. *Transpluto or Should We Call Him Bacchus the Ruler of Taurus?* Dallas: Hawkins Enterprising Publications, 1978.

O/S   133. Edward J. Moody. "Magical Therapy: An Anthropological Investigation of Contemporary Satanism," In Irving I. Zaretsky and Mark P. Leone, *Religious Movements in Contemporary America*. Princeton, N.J.: Princeton University Press, 1974.

OC   134. John Weldon, Zola Levitt. *Psychic Healing*. Chicago: Moody Press, 1984.

OP   135. Stephen Arroyo. *Astrology Karma and Transformation: The Inner Dimensions of the Birth Chart*. Davis, Calif.: CRCS Publications, 1978.

O   136. Louise Huber. *Reflections and Meditations on the Signs of the Zodiac*. Tempe, Ariz.: American Federation of Astrologers, 1984.

O   137. Marcus Allen. *Astrology for the New Age: An Intuitive Approach*. Sebastopol, Calif.: CRCS Publications, 1979.

O   138. Carol Cocciardi, ed. *The Psychic Yellow Pages*. Saratoga, Calif.: Out of the Sky, 1977.

MP   139. Robert Graysmith. *Zodiac.* New York: Berkley Books, 1987.

O   140. Jane A. Evans. *Twelve Doors to the Soul: Astrology of the Inner Self.* Wheaton, Ill.: Quest/Theosophical, 1983.

O   141. Thomas H. Burgoyne. *The Light of Egypt or the Science of the Soul and the Stars,* Volume I. Albuquerque: Sun Publishing, 1982.

O   142. Thomas H. Burgoyne. *The Light of Egypt or the Science of the Soul and the Stars,* Volume II. Albuquerque: Sun Publishing, 1982.

O   143. Edward Doane. *Aquarian Age Philosophy.* Tempe, Ariz.: American Federation of Astrologers, 1979.

O   144. Joan McEvers, ed. *Spiritual, Metaphysical and New Trends in Modern Astrology.* St. Paul, Minn.: Llewellyn Publications, 1988.

O   145. Richard Cavendish. *The Black Arts.* New York: G. P. Putnam's Sons, 1967.

O   146. Zipporah Dobyns and William Wrobel. *Seven Paths to Understanding.* San Diego: Astro Computing Services Publications, 1985.

O   147. Doreen Valiente. *An ABC of Witchcraft Past and Present.* New York: St. Martins Press, 1973.

O   148. Colin Wilson. *The Occult: A History.* New York: Vintage Books, 1973.

O   149. Sybil Leek. *My Life in Astrology.* Englewood Cliffs, N.J.: Prentice Hall, 1972.

O   150. Jean-Michael Angebert. *The Occult and the Third Reich: The Mystical Origins of Nazism and the Search for the Holy Grail.* New York: MacGraw Hill, 1975.

O   151. Mae R. Wilson-Ludlam. *Interpret Your Rays Using Astrology.* Tempe, Ariz.: American Federation of Astrologers, 1986.

O   152. Dusty Skylar. *Gods and Beasts: The Nazis and the Occult.* New York: Thomas Y. Crowell, 1977.

G   153. E. Howe. "Astrology" in Richard Cavendish, ed., *Man, Myth and Magic: An Illustrated Encyclopedia of the Supernatural, Volume I.* New York: Marshall Cavendish Corp., 1970.

G   154. Jess Stearn. *A Time for Astrology.* New York: Signet, 1972.

MP   155. Teri King. *Marriage, Divorce and Astrology.* New York: Harper & Row, 1988.

MP   156. Wim Van Dam. *Astrology and and Homosexuality.* York Beach, Maine: Samuel Weiser, 1985.

MP   157. Martin Schulman. *The Astrology of Sexuality.* York Beach, Maine: Samuel Weiser, 1986.

MP   158. T. Patrick Davis, *Sexual Assaults: Pre-identifying Those Vulnerable (A Research Report on the Cosmic Patterns in the Horoscopes of the Sexually Assaulted).* Windermere, Fla.: Davis Research Reports, 1978.

G   159. Doris Chase Doane. *Astrology: Thirty Years Research.* Tempe, Ariz.: American Federation of Astrologers, 1985.

H   160. James H. Holden and Robert A. Hughes. *Astrological Pioneers of America.* Tempe, Ariz.: American Federation of Astrologers, 1988.

G   161. American Federation of Astrologers. *50th Anniversary AFA 1988 Convention Program.* Tempe, Ariz.: American Federation of Astrologers, 1988.

MP   162. Irene Diamond. "Let's Talk About God." (Seminar at the AFA Convention, Las Vegas, Nev., July 1988.)

MP   163. Randall Leonard. "The Crystal and Astrology." (Seminar at the AFA Convention, Las Vegas, Nev., July 1988.)

MP   164. Capel McCutcheon. "Esoteric Astrology." (Seminar at the AFA Convention, Las Vegas, Nev., July 1988.)

MP   165. Sue Lovett. "Make Lemonade Out of Those Lemons." (Seminar at the AFA Convention, Las Vegas, Nev., July 1988.)

MP   166. Doris Chase Doane. "The Art of Transmutation." (Seminar at the AFA Convention, Las Vegas, Nev., July 1988.)

MP   167. Maxine Taylor. "Can I Rise Above My Chart?" (Seminar at the AFA Convention, Las Vegas, Nev., July 1988.)

MP   168. Terry Warneke. "The Archetype of Planets." (Seminar at the AFA Convention, Las Vegas, Nev., July 1988.)

MP   169. Karen Hamaker-Zondag. "Elements & Crosses." (Seminar at the AFA Convention, Las Vegas, Nev., July 1988.)

S/GA   170. Michel Gauquelin. "Zodiac and Personality: An Empirical Study." *The Skeptical Inquirer* 6, no. 3: 57-65.

S   171. Philip Ianna and Charles Tolbert. "A Re-test of Astrologer John McCall." *The Skeptical Inquirer* 9, no. 2: 167-70.

S   172. Geoffrey Dean. "Does Astrology Need to be True? Part 1: A Look at the Real Thing." *The Skeptical Inquirer* 9, no. 2: 166-85.

S   173. Geoffrey Dean. "Does Astrology Need to Be True? Part 2: The Answer is No." *The Skeptical Inquirer* 11, no. 3: 257-73.

S   174. Ron Westrum. "Scientists as Experts: Observations on 'Objections to Astrology,' " with response by Paul Kurtz and Lee Nesbet, *The Zetetic [The Skeptical Inquirer]* 1, no. 1: 34-52.

S   175. Ralph W. Bastedo. "An Empirical Test of Popular Astrology." *The Skeptical Inquirer* 3, no. 1: 17-38.

S   176. *The Skeptical Inquirer* 7, no. 2.

S   177. H. J. Eysenck and D. K. B. Nias. "Astrology: Science or Superstition," book review. *The Skeptical Inquirer* 7, no. 3: 65-67.

S   178. (1) Geoffrey A. Dean, I. W. Kelly, James Rotton, and D. H. Saklofske. "The Guardian Astrology Study: A Critique and Reanalysis." *The Skeptical Inquirer* 9, no. 4: 327-38.
(2) James Rotton. "Astrological Forecasts and the Commodity Market: Random Walks as a Source of Illusory Correlation." Ibid.: 339-47.

S   179. Ivan W. Kelly and Don H. Saklofske. "Alternative Explanations in Science: The Extroversion-Introversion Astrological Effect." *The Skeptical Inquirer* 5, no. 4: 33-39.

S   180. Gary Mechler, Cyndi McDaniel and Stephen Mulloy. "Response to the National Enquirer Astrology Study." *The Skeptical Inquirer* 5, no. 2: 34-41.

S   180a. I. W. Kelly, James Rotton and Roger Culver. "The Moon Was Full and Nothing Happened." *The Skeptical Inquirer* 10, no. 2: 129-43.

S   181. Paul Kurtz and Andrew Fraknoi. "Tests of Astrology Do Not Support Its Claims." *The Skeptical Inquirer* 9, no. 3: 210-12.

S   182. Douglas P. Lackey. "Controlled Test of Perceived Horoscope Accuracy." *The Skeptical Inquirer* 6, no. 1: 29-31.

S   183. George O. Abell and Bennett Greenspan. "The Moon and the Maternity Ward." *The Skeptical Inquirer* 3, no. 4: 17-25.

S   184. *The Skeptical Inquirer* 4: 4.

S/NA 185. (1) Paul Kurtz, Marvin Zelen and George Abell. "Results of the U.S. Test of the 'Mars Effect' are Negative." *The Skeptical Inquirer* 6, no. 2: 19-25).
(2) Dennis Rawlins. "Report on the U.S. Test of the Gauquelins 'Mars Effect.' " Ibid.: 26-30.
(3) Michael and Francoise Gauquelin. "Star U.S. Sportsmen Display the Mars Effect." Ibid.: 31-43.
(4) Paul Kurtz, Marvin Zelen and George Abell. "Response to the Gauquelin's." Ibid.: 44-63.

S   186. David Pingree. "Astrology." In *The New Encyclopedia Britiannica, Macropaedia, Vol. 2,* Chicago: University of Chicago, 1978, pp. 219-23.

S   187. John D. McGervey. "A Statistical Test of Sun-sign Astrology." *The Zetetic [The Skeptical Inquirer]* 1, no. 2: 49-54.

S   188. Dennis Rawlins. "Follow-up" [on the "Mars Effect"]. *The Skeptical Inquirer* 6, no. 2: 58-68.

OC   189. Kurt Koch. *The Devil's Alphabet.* Grand Rapids, Mich.: Kregel, 1969.

OC   190. Kurt Koch. *Between Christ and Satan.* Grand Rapids, Mich.: Kregel, 1962.

OC   191. Kurt Koch. *Christian Counseling and Occultism.* Grand Rapids, Mich.: Kregel, 1978.

324

OC   192. Merrill Unger. *Biblical Demonology*. Wheaton, Ill.: Scripture Press, 1971.

OC   193. Merrill Unger. *Demons in the World Today*. Wheaton Ill. Tyndale, 1972.

OC   194. C. Fred Dickason. *Angels: Elect and Evil*. Chicago: Moody, 1975.

OC   195. Clifford Wilson and John Weldon. *Psychic Forces*. Greenville, N.C.: Global, 1988.

OC   196. John W. Montgomery, ed. *Demon Possession*. Minneapolis, Minn.: Bethany Fellowship, 1976.

OC   197. John L. Nevius. *Demon Possession*. Grand Rapids, Mich.: Kregel, 1970.

MP   198. Donald T. Regan. *For the Record: From Wall Street to Washington*. New York: Harcourt Brace Jovanovich, 1988.

O   199. Charles W. Roback. *The Mysteries of Astrology and the Wonders of Magic: Including a History of the Rise and Progress of Astrology and the Various Branches of Necromancy; Together With Valuable Directions and Suggestions Relative to the Casting of Nativities and Predictions by Geomancy, Chiromancy, Physiognomy, etc.: Also Highly Interesting Narratives, Anecdotes, etc. Illustrative of the Marvels of Witchcraft, Spiritual Phenomena and the Results of Supernatural Influence*. Charles W. Roback, 1854.

O   200. The Church of Light. *The Church of Light: Its History and Principles/Declaration of Principles*. Los Angeles: The Church of Light, n.d., pp. 1-8.

O   201. The Church of Light. *Brotherhood of Light Lessons, Students Supplies and Other Publications Catalog*. Los Angeles: The Church of Light, n.d.

MP   202. Karen Winterburn. Personal phone conversation. August 1988.

MP   203. Various authors. "Special Report: Astrology and the Presidency." *The Skeptical Inquirer* 13, no. 1: 3-16.

MP   204. Dr. Atlas Laster, Jr. Letter. September 12, 1988.

MP   205. Letter from Dr. Atlas Laster, Jr., September 23, 1988, containing a copy of a letter by astrologer Harry Darling M.D., approving his Ph.D dissertation on astrology submitted to the University of Pittsburgh ("On the Psychology of Astrology: The Use of Genethliacal Astrology in Psychological Counseling," 1976).

S   206. Roger B. Culver and Philip A. Ianna. *Astrology: True or False—A Scientific Evaluation* [update of their *The Gemini Syndrome*]. Buffalo, N.Y.: Prometheus Books, 1988.

S   207. Geoffrey Dean. "Forecasting Radio Quality by the Planets." *The Skeptical Inquirer* 8, no. 1: 48-56.

T   208. Susan White. *The New Astrology*. New York: St. Martins Press, 1986.

P   209. Joanne Sanders. "Connecting Therapy to the Heavens." *The Common Boundary*, Jan.-Feb. 1987.

MP   210. One-page promotional brochure for the American Federation of Astrologers Golden Anniversary Convention (included with product price list, Winter 1987-1988).

S   211. Kenneth J. Delano. *Astrology: Fact or Fiction?* 1973.

S   212. Anthony Standen. *Forget Your Sun-sign.* 1977.

S   213. Geoffrey Dean. *Recent Advances in Natal Astrology: A Critical Review, 1900 to 1976.* 1977.

S   214. Research reports in the following journals: *Psychological Reports*, 1979; *Journal of Psychology*, 1973, 1977, 1980, 1982; *Nature*, 1985; *Journal of Clinical Psychology*, 1977.

S   215. H. J. Eysenck and D. K. B. Nias. *Astrology: Science or Superstition?* New York: St. Martins Press, 1982.

NA   216. Guy Playfair and Scott Hill. *The Cycles of Heaven: Cosmic Forces and What They Are Doing to You.* New York: St. Martins Press, 1978.

R   217. Walter A. Elwell, ed. *Evangelical Dictionary of Theology.* Grand Rapids, Mich.: Baker, 1984.

OC   218. Gary North. *None Dare Call it Witchcraft.* New Rochelle, N.Y.: Arlington House, 1976.

MP   219. Seminars attended at the July 1988 American Federation of Astrologers Convention in Las Vegas, Nevada. Statements are by the instructors: Irene Diamond ("Let's Talk About God"); Randall Leonard ("The Crystals & Astrology"); Capel McCutcheon ("Esoteric Astrology"); Sue Lovett ("Make Lemonade Out of Those Lemons"); Doris Chase Doane ("The Art of Transmutation"); Maxine Taylor ("Can I Rise Above My Chart?"); Terry Warneke ("The Archetype of Planets"); Karen Hamaker-Zondag ("Elements and Crosses").

G   220. "The Astrologers Reply." *The Humanist*, Nov./Dec. 1975.

MP   221. Nigel Pennick. *The Ancient Science of Geomancy.* Sebastopol, Calif.: CRCS, 1988.

T   222. Joan Negus. *Astro-Alchemy.* n.d.

G   223. C. Stickels and K. McCuistion. *Astrology in a Nutshell.* Privately published, 1984.

MP   224. Laurie Efrein. *How to Rectify a Birth Chart.* England: Aquarian Press, 1987.

G   225. Clara A. Weiss. *Astrological Keys to Self-actualization and Self-realization.* New York: Samuel Weiser, 1980.

G   226. Liz Greene. *The Astrology of Fate.* New York: Samuel Weiser, 1986.

G   227. Kathleen Burt. *Archetypes of the Zodiac*. St. Paul, Minn.: Llewellyn, 1988.

MP   228. Allen Epstein. *Psycho Dynamics of Inconjunctions*. New York: Samuel Weiser, 1984.

P   229. Liz Greene. *Relating*. New York: Samuel Weiser, 1978.

T   230. Khma Andres Takra. *The Wisdom of Sidereal Astrology*. Sunbooks, 1983.

P   231. Hi Halevi and Zahava Halevi. *Astrology and Psycho-Analysis: A Transformation Towards Synthesis*. Jerusalem: S.Y.S. Publishers, 1987.

MP   232. Ebertin/Hoffman. *Fixed Stars and Their Interpretation*. Tempe, Ariz.: American Federation of Astrologers, 1988.

PL   233. L. H. Weston. *The Planet Vulcan: History, Nature, Tables*. Tempe, Ariz.: American Federation of Astrologers, n.d.

MP   234. Fritz Brunhubner. *Pluto*. Tempe, Ariz.: American Federation of Astrologers, 1971.

G   235. Donna Cunningham. *Being a Lunar Type in a Solar World*. New York: Samuel Weiser, 1985.

MP   236. Ginger Chalford. *Pluto: Planet of Magic and Power*. Tempe, Ariz.: American Federation of Astrologers, 1984.

G   237. Miss Dee. *Health, Astrology and Spirituality*. Tempe, Ariz.: American Federation of Astrologers, 1988.

T   238. Robert Powell. *Hermetic Astrology*, Volume I. West Germany: Hermetica Publishers, 1987.

T   239. Robert Powell. *Christian Hermetic Astrology Volume III*. West Germany: Hermetica Publishers, n.d.

G   240. Ed Perrone. *Astrology: A New Age Guide*. Wheston, Ill.: Quest/Theosophical Publishers, 1983.

T   241. Ry Reed. *Toward a New Astrology: The Approach of Edgar Cayce*. Virginia Beach, Va.: Association of Research and Enlightenment, 1985.

G   242. Ronald Harvey. *Mind and Body in Astrology*. L. N. Fowler & Co., 1983.

PL   243. Charles Jayne. *The Unknown Planets*. Astrological Bureau, 1974.

G   244. Enrique Linares. *A Scientific Approach to the Metaphysics of Astrology*. Seek It Publishers, 1982.

P   245. Dane Rudhyar. *Person Centered Astrology*. New York: Aurora Press, 1980.

G   246. Patricia Crossley. *Let's Learn Astrology*, rev. ed. Tempe, Ariz.: American Federation of Astrologers, 1987.

MP 247. John Sandbach. *Degree Analysis: Dwadashamsas and Deeper Meanings*. Seek It Publishers, 1983.

T   248. Faith Javane and Dusty Bunker. *Numerology and the Divine Triangle*. Rockport, Mass.: Para Research Publishers, 1980.

MP 249. Alda Meriam Jangl. *The Astrological Prayer Book*. New York: Samuel Weiser, 1985.

MP 250. Donald Bradley. *Picking Winners*. Tempe, Ariz.: American Federation of Astrologers.

MP 251. Emily Faigno. *Astro-Power at the Race Track*. Tempe, Ariz.: American Federation of Astrologers, 1984.

MP 252. Evelyn M. Nagle. *Lady Luck Calendar [The Best Days to Gamble]*. Tempe, Ariz.: American Federation of Astrologers, n.d.

MP 253. Evelyn M. Nagle. *Astrologers Handbook to Gambling*. Tempe, Ariz.: American Federation of Astrologers, 1987.

MP 254. Evelyn M. Nagle. *Winning With Astrology*. Tempe, Ariz.: American Federation of Astrologers, 1987.

G   255. *The Los Angeles Times*. Jan. 15, 1975.

O   256. Daniel Logan. *The Reluctant Prophet*. 1980.

O   257. Sepharial. *A Manual of Occultism*. New York: Samuel Weiser, 1978.

NA 258. Arnold Lieber. *The Lunar Effect: Biological Tides and Human Emotions*. Garden City, N.Y.: Anchor Press, 1978.

T   259. Geraldine Davis. *Horary Astrology With Authentic Charts and Predictions*. North Hollywood, Calif.: Symbols and Signs, 1970.

G   260. Joan Quigley. *Astrology for Adults*. New York: Holt, Rinehart and Winston, 1969.

G   261. Sydney Omarr. *My World of Astrology*. North Hollywood, Calif.: Wilshire Books, 1965.

G   262. Grant Lewi. *Heaven Knows What*. New York: Bantam, 1978.

G   263. Linda Goodman. *Linda Goodman's Sun-signs*. New York: Taplinger, 1968.

G   264. *Llewellyn's 1977 Moon-sign Book and Daily Planetary Guide*. St. Paul, Minn.: Llewellyn, 1976.

G   265. S. R. Parchment. *Astrology: Mundane and Spiritual*. Washington, D.C.: American Federation of Astrologers, 1933.

NA 266. Michel Gauquelin. *Cosmic Influences on Human Behavior*. New York: ASI Publishers, 1978.

MP 267. Charles E. O. Carter. *The Astrological Aspects*. London: L. N. Fowler, 1971.

MP 268. Leigh Hope Milburn. *The Progressed Horoscope Simplified*. Washington, D.C.: American Federation of Astrologers, 1936.

G   269. Zolar. *It's All in the Stars*. Greenwich, Conn.: Fawcett, 1962.

G   270. Sydney Omarr. *Sydney Omarr's Astrological Guide for You in 1980*. New York: Signet, 1969.

MP   271. C. E Forsythe. "Neptune's Role in Parapsychology." *Del Horoscope*, Dec. 1972.

MP   272. Arthur M. Hale. "Christianity and Astrology: A Minister's Viewpoint." *American Astrology*, Dec. 1971.

G   273. Ruth Hale Oliver and M. G. Harter. *The Basic Principles of Astrology: A Modern View of an Ancient Science*. Washington, D.C.: American Federation of Astrologers, 1962.

O   274. C. C. Zain, *The Laws of Occultism: Astral-Vibrations*. Los Angeles: The Church of Light, 1964.

MP   275. Marc Robertson, *The Transits of Saturn*. Seattle: The Astrology Center of the Northwest, 1973.

MP   276. Kuno Foelsch. *Transits in Astrological Prognosis*. Privately published, n.d.

G   277. Paul Grell. *Key Words*. Tempe, Ariz.: American Federation of Astrologers, 1970.

G   278. Robert Pelletier. *Planets in Aspect: Understanding Your Inner Dynamics*. Rockport, Mass.: Para Research, 1974.

G   279. John Townley. *Planets in Love: Exploring Your Emotional and Sexual Needs*. Rockport, Mass.: Para Research, 1978.

G   280. Robert Hand. *Planets in Transit: Life Cycles for Living*. Rockport, Mass.: Para Research, 1976.

MP   281. Robert Carl Jansky. *Astrology, Nutrition and Health*. Rockport, Mass.: Para Research, 1975.

MP   282. Letter on file, dated June 2, 1986.

S   283. I. W. Kelly and R. W. Krutzen. "Humanistic Astrology: A Critique." *The Skeptical Inquirer* 8, no. 1: 62-73.

O   284. John Jocelyn. *Meditation on the Signs of the Zodiac*. Blauvelt, N.Y.: Steiner Books, 1970.

R   285. Charles Tart, ed. *Transpersonal Psychologies*. New York: Harper Colophon, 1977.

H   286. J. M. Ashmand, trans. *Ptolemy's Tetrabiblios*. Hollywood: Symbols and Signs, 1976.

O   287. Andrija Puharich. *Uri*. New York: Bantam, 1975.

O   288. Robert Leichtman. "Clairvoyant Diagnosis." In the *Journal of Holistic Health*. San Diego: Association for Holistic Health/Mandala Society, 1977.

O   289. J.H. Brennan. *Astral Doorways*. New York: Samuel Weiser, 1972.

O   290. Alfred Douglas. *The Tarot*. New York: Penguin, 1977.

O   291. Juliet Sharman-Burke. *The Complete Book of Tarot.* New York: St. Martins, 1985.

O   292. Sasha Fenton. *Tarot in Action.* Wellingborough, England: Aquarian Press, 1987.

O   293. Michael Howard. *The Magic of the Runes.* Wellingborough, England: Aquarian Press.

O   294. John Blofeld. *I Ching.* New York: Dutton, 1968.

G   295. "Good Heavens!" *Time,* May 16, 1988.

G   296. "The Presidents' Astrologers." *People's Weekly,* May 23, 1988, and *Moody Monthly,* July-August, 1988: 10.

CA   297. Brooks Alexander, "My Stars!: Astrology in the White House." Berkeley: Spiritual Counterfeits Project, 1988.

CA   298. John Weldon. "Astrology: An Inside Look" (Part I). *News & Views,* August 1988.

CA   299. John Weldon. "Astrology: An Inside Look" (Part II). *News & Views,* October 1988.

OC   300. John Weldon. *The Hazards of Psychic Involvement: A Look at Some Consequences,* mss., 1986.

P   301. Dane Rudhyar. *Person Centered Astrology.* New York: Aurora Press, 1980.

G   302. "Astro/Carto/Graphy Explained." Brochure from Astro/Carto/Graphy, Box 959, El Cerrito, CA.

O   303. Jeffrey Mishlove. *The Roots of Consciousness.* New York: Random House, 1975.

MP   304. The Gallup Poll of October 19, 1975.

MP   305. The Gallup Poll of mid-May 1988. Cited in *National and International Religion Report,* July 4, 1988: 1.

O   306. Louis Pauwels and Jacques Bergier. *The Morning of the Magicians.* New York: Avon, 1968.

CA   307. John Weldon. *Reincarnation: An Examination of the Spiritual and Social Consequences in Human Society,* mss., 1987. For analyses see John Snyder, *Reincarnation vs. Resurrection.* Chicago: Moody, 1984; and Mark Albrecht, *Reincarnation: A Christian Appraisal.* Downers Grove, Ill.: InterVarsity, 1982.

OC   308. Kurt Koch. *Satan's Devices.* Grand Rapids, Mich.: Kregel, 1978.

OC   309. John Ankerberg and John Weldon. *The Facts on Spirit Guides.* Eugene, Oreg.: Harvest House, 1988, cf. *The Facts on the New Age.*

MP   310. *Los Angeles Times.* September 14, 1975.

MP   311. *Los Angeles Times.* July 5, 1985.

MP   312. See American Federation of Astrologers tape list.

330

O   313. John Symonds and K. Grant. *Alister Crowley: The Complete Astrological Writings*. Dallas: Duckworth, 1979.

MP   314. Alexander Solzhenitsyn. *Warning to the West*. New York: Farrar, Straus and Giroux, 1977.

CA   315. Norman Geisler. *Christian Apologetics*. Grand Rapids, Mich.: Baker, 1976.

S   316. Guy Chatillon. "Acceptance of Paranormal Among Two Special Groups." *The Skeptical Inquirer* 13, no. 2: 216-17.

S   317. Robert Sheaffer. "Psychic Vibrations." *The Skeptical Inquirer* 13, no. 2: 129-30.

O   318. Note 186: *Micropaedia*, Vol. 1, "Augury" article and references.

S   319. *Mercury,* March–April, 1976.

O   320. See, e.g., White Eagle, *The Gentle Brother*. Hamphshire, England: The White Eagle Publishing Trust, 1978. (Cf. Grace Cooke. *Wisdom from White Eagle*. 1978, pp. 7-8.)

O   321. See, e.g., Sri Chinmoy. *Astrology: The Supernatural and Beyond*. Jamaica, N.Y.: Agni Press, 1973.
Elman Bacher. *Studies in Astrology,* 9 vols. Oceanside, Calif.: The Rosicrucian Fellowship, 1968.
Bibliography numbers 28, 42, 120, 240.

CA   322. John Weldon and Zola Levitt. *Is There Life After Death?* Irvine, Calif.: Harvest House, 1977.
Tal Brooke. *The Other Side of Death*. Chattanooga, Tenn.: The John Ankerberg Show, 1988.

CA   323. Ben G. Hester. *Dowsing: An Exposé of Hidden Occult Forces,* rev. 1984. Copies from the author at 4883 Hedrick Avenue, Arlington, Calif. 92505.

MP   323a. *National and International Religion Report*. July 4, 1988.

MP   324. *Ambassador*, Vol. 12, 1979.

CA   325. In Kurt Goedelman. "Seeking Guidance from the Stars of Heaven." *Personal Freedom Outreach*. July–September 1988. (The figure is probably exaggerated though it is widely agreed a significant number of major corporations use astrology in some fashion.)

MP   326. Fred Schwarz. *You Can Trust the Communists (To Be Communists)*. Long Beach, Calif.: Chantico, 1966. (Cf. Bernard-Henri Levy. *Barbarism With a Human Face*. New York: Harper & Row, 1979; Andre Gide et al. *The god That Failed*. New York: Bantam, 1965.)

MP   327. See, e.g., the January 1989 issues.

CA   328. William Lane Craig. *The Son Rises*. Chicago: Moody Press, 1982.

MP   329. Article C, "Astrology." Sections 14-5091–14-5096 of Licensing and Regulation Code.

R   330. Norman L. Geisler and William E. Nix. *A General Introduction to the Bible,* rev. ed. Chicago: Moody Press, 1986.

CA   331. John Ankerberg, John Weldon, Walter Kaiser, Jr. *The Case for Jesus the Messiah: Incredible Prophecies That Prove God Exists.* Chattanooga, Tenn.: John Ankerberg Evangelistic Association, 1989.

O   332. Rudolf Steiner. *Christianity and Occult Mysteries of Antiquity.* Blauvelt, N.Y.: Steinerbooks, 1977. (Cf. Rudolf Steiner, *An Outline of Occult Science.* Spring Valley, N.Y.: Anthroposophic Press, 1979, pp. 100-254.)

OC   333. Raphael Gasson. *The Challenging Counterfeit.* Plainfield, N.J.: Logos, 1970.

OC   334. Victor Ernest. *I Talked With Spirits.* Wheaton, Ill.: Tyndale, 1971.

OC   335. Merrill Unger. *The Haunting of Bishop Pike.* Wheaton, Ill.: Tyndale, 1971.

OC   336. Ben Alexander. *Out From Darkness: The True Story of a Medium Who Escapes the Occult.* Joplin, Mo.: College Press, 1986.

OC   337. Doreen Irvine. *Freed From Witchcraft.* Nashville: Thomas Nelson, 1973.

OC   338. Johanna Michaelsen. *The Beautiful Side of Evil.* Eugene, Oreg.: Harvest House, 1982.

OC   339. Mike Warneke. *The Satan Seller.* Plainfield, N.J.: Logos, 1972.

OC   340. Gary North. *Unholy Spirits: Occultism and New Age Humanism.* Ft. Worth, Tex.: Dominion Press, 1986.

OC   341. Malachi Martin. *Hostage to the Devil: The Possession and Exorcism of Five Living Americans.* New York: Bantam, 1977.

OC   342. William Menzies Alexander. *Demonic Possession in the New Testament: Its Historical, Medical and Theological Aspects.* Grand Rapids, Mich.: Baker, 1980.

MP   343. See, e.g., P. Thomas. *Hindu Religion Customs and Manners.* Bombay, India: D. B. Taraporevala Sons & Co., 1960.

Alain Danielou. *Hindu Polytheism.* New York: Bollingen/Random House, 1964.

Nigel Davies. *Human Sacrifice in History and Today.* New York: William Morrow & Co., 1981.

T. K. Oesterreich. *Possession: Demoniacal and Other Among Primitive Races, in Antiquity, the Middle Ages, and Modern Times.* Secaucus, N.J.: Citadel Press, 1974.

Felicitas D. Goodman, et al. *Trance Healing and Hallucination: Three Field Studies in Religious Experience.* New York: John

Wiley & Sons, 1974.

Paul Hawken. *The Magic of Findhorn*. New York: Bantam, 1976.

O   344. Paul Hawken. *The Magic of Findhorn*. New York: Bantam, 1976.

O   345. Kenneth Ring. *Heading Toward Omega: In Search of the Meaning of the Near Death Experience*. New York: Quill, 1985.

O   346. Shakti Gawain. *Living in the Light: A Guide to Personal and Planetary Transformation*. Mill Valley, Calif.: Whatever Publishing, 1986.

Shakti Gawain. *Creative Visualization: Using the Power of Your Imagination to Create What You Want in Your Life*. Mill Valley, Calif.: Whatever Publishing, 1983.

Frances E. Vaughan. *Awakening Intuition*. Garden City, N.Y.: Anchor Press/Doubleday, 1979.

Philip Goldberg. *The Intuitive Edge: Understanding Intuition and Applying It in Everyday Life*. Los Angeles: Jeremy P. Tarcher, 1983.

O   347. Jon Klimo. *Channeling: Investigations on Receiving Information from Paranormal Sources*. Los Angeles: Jeremy P. Tarcher, 1981.

OC   348. "Spiritism and Altered States of Consciousness," in John Weldon. *Deceit of the Gods: New Age Spiritism in an Era of Higher Consciousness, Its Influence in American Society and the Church*, mss., 1988.

OC   349. Clifford Wilson and John Weldon. *Close Encounters: A Better Explanation*. San Diego: Master Books, 1978.

MP   350. Tal Brooke. *Riders of the Cosmic Circuit: Rajneesh, Sai Baba, Muktananda ... Gods of the New Age*. Batavia, Ill.: Lion, 1986.

MP   351. Bhagwan Shree Rajneesh. *The Rajneesh Bible, Vol. 1*. Rajneeshpuram, Oreg.: Rajneesh Foundation International, 1985.

MP   352. Joan Halifax-Grof. "Hex Death." *Parapsychology Review*, September–October, 1974.

OC   353. Sondra A. O'Neale. "The Ultimate Hazard of Pagan Religion—Child Sacrifice and Societal Collapse: The Atlanta Child Murders." (An introduction prepared by Dr. O'Neale for John Weldon's *Deceit of the Gods*.)

MP   354. Nigel Davies. *Human Sacrifice in History and Today*. New York: William Morrow, 1981.

OC   355. Edmund C. Gruss, *The Ouija Board: Doorway to the Occult*. Chicago: Moody Press, 1985; cf. Stokes Hunt, *Ouija: The Most Dangerous Game*. New York: Perrennial, 1985.

OC   356. Paul Reisser, Teri Reisser, John Weldon. *New Age Medicine*. Downers Grove, Ill.: InterVarsity, 1988.

Appendix

Due to space considerations, a number of chapters in this text were deleted. Briefly, those chapters document 1) that fatalism plays a greater role in astrology than astrologers are willing to admit; 2) that astrologers accept and practice divination and call it such more than they are willing to realize; 3) the influence of astrology in modern medicine, education, psychology, and "holistic health"; 4) how astrology is used to influence children through astrological child rearing; 5) the false and/or irrelevant nature of claims concerning the influence of astrology in Christian history; 6) the historic relationship between astrology and human sacrifice, including modern illustrations and implications; 7) how astrologers use newspaper columns to cunningly promote astrology in society, and the consequences; 8) how astrologers' "intuition" is often a euphemism for psychic powers; 9) the pros and cons of the "Gospel in the Stars" theory and why even if it is true, it does not support astrology; 10) how astrological readings promote additional occult involvement in the life of clients through scores of different astrological indicators encouraging a wide variety of occult pursuits; 11) why the newer areas of scientific and astronomical investigation cited by astrologers as evidence for astrology are false; 12) the astrology community's highly negative and critical assessment of itself and why it is justly deserved; 13) how astrological teachings and beliefs evolve and are nurtured by a) astrological speculation, b) false correlations to sociocultural events, c) ties to ancient polytheism, d) interaction with other disciplines and astrologies, e) invented or manufactured chart "effects," and f) spiritistic inspiration; 14) technical documentation for many sections of the book; 15) detailed critical reviews of texts by Christians who accept astrology in one form or another (e.g., David Womack's *12 Signs 12 Suns: Astrology and the Bible* showing the logical consequences of Christian acceptance of astrology in any form); 16) a detailed listing of scores of errors and contradictions in modern astrology; and 17) many additional problems in astrology that are often not considered. For example, there is the problem of the infant "inbreathing" earlier celestial patterns prior to its birth. This would naturally occur by means of the baby "breathing" the mother's air through the placenta but would take place prior to the baby's actual first breath, which is the moment astrologers *claim* that the alleged imprinting of celestial patterns occurs.

Other Good
Harvest House Reading

"THE FACTS ON" SERIES
By *John Ankerberg* and *John Weldon*

"The Facts On" booklet series by award-winning television host,
John Ankerberg, and occult expert and researcher, John
Weldon, addresses current events and controversial issues
confronting our society and the Christian church in the
twentieth century.

The Facts on Astrology
The Facts on Spirit Guides
The Facts on the New Age Movement
The Facts on False Teaching in the Church

AMERICA: THE SORCERER'S NEW APPRENTICE
by *Dave Hunt* and *T.A. McMahon*

Many respected experts predict that America is at the threshold
of a glorious New Age. Other equally notable observers warn
that Eastern mysticism, at the heart of the New Age
movement, will eventually corrupt Western civilization.
Dave Hunt and T.A. McMahon, bestselling authors of *The
Seduction of Christianity*, break down the most brilliant
arguments of the most-respected New Age leaders.

WHEN THE WORLD WILL BE AS ONE
The Coming New World Order in the New Age
by *Tal Brooke*

Today there is an emerging global consciousness that is either
an incredible historical coincidence or is, in fact, part of a
sophisticated plan whose beginnings can be traced to antiquity.
Could this be the global reality predicted 2,000 years ago by a
prophet on the Isle of Patmos?

Tal Brooke spent two decades intently exploring the occult. Tal
is a graduate of the University of Virginia, and Princeton, and
is a frequent speaker at Oxford and Cambridge universities.